Handbook of Urban Landscape

CONSULTANT EDITOR
Cliff Tandy FILA, ARIBA

EDITED BY
**THE ARCHITECTS' JOURNAL
TECHNICAL SECTION**

Crane, Russak & Company, Inc.
New York

Consultant editor

Consultant editor for this handbook is Cliff Tandy FILA, ARIBA; Principal in Land Use Consultants. He also lectures in landscape at the AA Tropical school, was a founder member of the landscape group and is president of the Institute of Landscape Architects.

Authors

Shirley Andrew ARIBA FRAIA Architect and landscape architect in private practice

Michael Brown MLA ARIBA AILA Landscape architect in private practice and author of articles on the landscape of housing

Timothy Cochrane AILA ARIBA MLA (Penn) DipLD (Dunelm) Architect and landscape architect in private practice in London. DOE and lecturer in landscape at Thames Polytechnic.

Allan Hart AILA AIPRA (Dip) Consultant landscape architect

Hal Moggridge AILA ARIBA AADip Landscape architect in private practice, in partnership with Brenda Colvin. Lectures at Brixton School of Building on landscape in relation to planning

A. E. J. Morris DipArch (UCL) DipTP (Lond) ARIBA Senior lecturer at School of Town Planning, Polytechnic of the South Bank; author of a number of books and articles on architecture and allied subjects

Gordon Patterson DipLA AILA Landscape architect in private practice

G. A. Perrin DipTP AMTPI ARIBA Consultant architect to National Playing Fields Association and in private practice

Cliff Tandy FILA ARIBA Principal in Land Use Consultants (see also under Consultant editor)

© Architectural Press 1970, 1971
Published in the United States by
Crane, Russak & Company, Inc.
52 Vanderbilt Avenue, New York, N. Y. 10017
Library of Congress Catalog No. 72-81192
ISBN 0-8448-0021-X
Printed in Great Britain

Introduction

Architectural Press Handbooks are mainly for architects, but much of their content is by experts in related fields. Although landscape architecture is a separate profession, contributing to work such as motorway alignments, shelter-belts for agriculture, treatment of derelict land and landscape planning on a regional scale—matters of little direct interest to architects—landscape architects are as often concerned with the 'built environment' and frequently act as consultants to architects. This handbook therefore deals with aspects most related to architecture while, at the same time, it aims to serve the landscape profession itself.

Scope

Because the field of landscape work is so wide, the handbook is limited to *urban* landscape.

The handbook is intended as a desk-side guide for all designers of urban space, including architects, landscape architects, planners and engineers—and for students of these professions. It should also help to improve understanding of the work and procedures of landscape architects, so that all who use them as consultants will be better equipped to brief them.

Contents

Reviews on current trends in landscape design for urban situations—including housing, parks and open spaces, recreation, children's play and gardens—are followed by a design guide on procedure with references to the later information sheets and other publications used in designing landscape spaces.

Use

The handbook can be used at three levels. Its technical studies and reviews form a general guide to current thought on the design of various kinds of open space; its design guide and information sheets are a daily reference for the landscape design process; and through its sources and references, readers can obtain background information or more specific guidance on particular aspects.

Metric units

Throughout this handbook metric SI units will be used for dimensional and environmental data. Imperial measurements will not normally be given.

Contents

Section 1 **Urban landscape review**

Technical study
Landscape 1

Introduction to landscape design

CLIFF TANDY, *consultant editor for this handbook, explains the relationship of landscape architecture to allied professions, reviews factors currently influencing landscape design and forecasts future trends*

1 Context of landscape design

1.01 Writers on the art of landscape design either equate it with gardening, and—assuming that Adam was a gardener —place it as the earliest art, or believe it to be the youngest. In fact, although it has centuries of history, landscape design comes late to every civilisation, usually not appearing until a period of stable peace has prepared the people for this gentle and somewhat fragile pursuit.

1.02 All the arts are, of course, inter-related to some degree. Landscape design appears to have closest relationship with the 'practical' arts of architecture and civic design. Historically, however, it has close links with painting. Painters have always been visionaries, seeing far ahead of more practical men; consequently painting has often been a pathfinder to landscape design. Sometimes, as in the late seventeenth and early eighteenth centuries, painters have created an 'ideal' landscape which inspired its physical execution fifty or more years later. In this century, painters such as Cezanne, Braque and Mondrian have taken new roads which architecture has followed and which landscape design has only just begun to follow. At first sight it appears that at present the fine arts reflect the dissatisfaction and confusion of society and have rejected their role as leader. Probably a retrospective view will show this to be untrue and will reveal a path leading in a new direction, but certainly from our position in the centre of the melee, such guidance is undiscernible.

2 Role of the landscape architect

2.01 Up to about 1860 the role of landscape architects was clear. Although they had not the same unmistakeable professional status as architects, Repton, Paxton and Loudon were clearly *professionals*. During the eclectic 'seventies and 'eighties Robinson and Jeckyll were not accorded this status, and though in Britain the profession was kept alive by men like Milner and Mawson **1** it became somewhat eclipsed by the rise of 'landscape gardeners', many of whom did excellent work at garden scale, but in a well-worn style that had not progressed since William Robinson. Not surprisingly, the revival caused by the creation of the Institute of Landscape Architects in 1929 met a mental climate which, while not hostile, relegated the profession to the role of 'external decorator'.

2.02 However, other countries escaped this inhibiting restriction and early in the century the profession flourished in the US and in Germany, Switzerland and other European countries. It must be admitted that because professionals on the Continent were allowed to contract and execute work, comparisons between professional landscape designers and landscape contractors did not occur. The ethical separation of the two functions is probably the first change to record. While always in force in Britain and America, only now is this becoming effective on the Continent.

2.03 Unlike artists and sculptors, landscape designers depend wholly upon being commissioned, and their effectiveness is limited by clients' whims and bankbooks. As in architecture, the state has largely replaced the wealthy private landowner as patron, but as the process was rather slower in landscape, the image of garden-designer for the wealthy lingered even into the immediate post-war period. Since then, through opportunities from competitions, public commissions, improved training, and above all through new social problems set by demands for open space and recreation, the scope of landscape architects' work has widened enormously, even to the level of rural planning on a regional scale.

1 *Garden at Broad Oak, Accrington, Lancs, by Thomas H. Mawson (c1880)*

1 VIEW of GARDEN BROAD OAK ACCRINGTON for GEORGE MACALPINE ESQ

3 Relationship with other professions

3.01 This country has one of the strongest systems of planning control in the world, with consequent benefits and disadvantages which have been well argued professionally. One limitation of special concern is the rarity of opportunities for planning commissions to go out to private consultants; consequently there are few chances for balanced comprehensive teams—including a landscape designer—to work on large planning projects. This is unfortunate, as team working is the only way in which 'total environment' projects can be tackled, and the professions should have every opportunity of working together. It would be beneficial—as has been proved in Germany—for the 'land-based professions' to start their training with a common first year.

3.02 At present, co-operation with architects is good: they are often in a quasi-client relationship with the landscape architect. With planners there is slight competition over the role of 'country planners', a title which town planners relinquished soon after the war. Engineers often have landscape architects working with them on large projects. Earlier misunderstandings over the aesthetic component of major works have evaporated and the partnership is now usually very fruitful. Collaboration with members of the Institute of Parks and Recreation Administration is now more common and younger members of that organisation recognise the scope for working together. It is also to be hoped that landscape architects recognise the benefits of working with qualified horticulturalists.

3.03 There is still a considerable shortage of qualified and senior landscape staff in this country, although educational facilities are constantly increasing and about twenty qualified graduates enter the profession annually. There is also a small but continuous 'reverse brain-drain' of staff who have received further training or experience in the US. Whether the shortage continues or not, undoubtedly a large proportion of external space will *not* be designed by landscape architects, just as a lot of buildings are created without architects. As there are few teachers of landscape design and appreciation other than those on wholly landscape courses, the subject is inadequately covered in the training of architects, planners and other professions. This handbook is intended to help to fill this gap.

4 Recent trends

4.01 The post-war period has seen many changes and developments which have stimulated the growth of landscape design and the need for designers. A few of these must be noted as a guide to future trends:
The Town and Country Planning Acts of 1947 and 1962 were the most significant legislation as they controlled, for the first time, any form of development of land. The National Parks and Access to the Countryside Act, 1949, and the Landscape Areas Special Development Order, 1950 were perhaps more directly concerned with landscape. Though the early stages of their implementation consisted mainly of designating existing areas of beauty, work has expanded to take in problems of upkeep, public access and recreation needs.
The Countryside Act of 1968 set up the Countryside Commission and emphasised use of rural land for recreation. It included an interest in commons, coast, and particularly the creation of country parks. Use of inland water for

2

recreation was covered by the Transport Act of the same year.
The amenity clauses in the Hydro-Electric Power Acts and Electricity Acts ensured that existing beauty of the sites mentioned in the Acts was preserved and set a precedent for using professional advice in planning the surroundings of major engineering works. This was followed up in Acts controlling opencast coal and other mineral workings, while the offer of government grants encouraged reclaiming past dereliction, including reshaping and planting of shale and other waste tips.
Other legislation which had repercussions on landscape work includes the Caravan Sites Act, 1960 and subsequent Orders, tree preservation legislation and the Civic Amenities Act, 1967.

4.02 In recent years, local authority housing standards have been progressively upgraded. While most professionals would agree that this has not yet gone far enough, and while external space-treatment standards have not remotely reached those for interiors, there has nevertheless been improvement and a recognition that external layout is

2 *Multi-storey housing blocks set in a mature landscape, Roehampton* (LCC)
3 *Married officers' quarters, Putney, built within a mature landscape (Architects department* MPBW; *landscape architect C.R.V. Tandy)*
4 *Communal landscaped gardens in the private sector. The Hall, Blackheath (Eric Lyons for Span)*
5 *Dense planting in Jacobsen's housing at Bellevue, Denmark*
6 *Extensive communal landscape in a new housing layout at Tapiola, Finland*

3

4

significant **2, 3**. Similarly, provision for children's play is now an integral part of every housing estate, even though problems of siting and detail design are rarely adequately solved.

Formerly, in the private house building sector only large properties had gardens worthy of the name; speculative 'semis' were laid out on land geometrically divided into long narrow plots of little value. Developers of the calibre of Span and Wates have shown that much more imaginative layouts are possible, even for middle incomes, and that landscape treatment of an estate is an important selling factor **4, 5, 6**. Britain has even accepted the concept of communal garden areas and unfenced fronts, though not exactly with nation-wide enthusiasm.

4.03 Experts say that industrial demand for land may reach a peak and then fall off, as industry becomes more efficient, more intensive and less expansive. Meanwhile, demand for industrial land is still increasing, and this has influenced landscape opportunities in two ways. In the first place strategic location of industry—particularly power plants—on the coast, in national parks and other places of natural beauty, has meant a call on services of landscape designers to assist in assimilation of these artefacts by the countryside **7**. At its minimum this can be little more than concealment or camouflage, but at the highest level of work there is team co-operation in which the location, exact siting, design of the industrial plant, and landscape treatment of a large area of adjoining land, all contribute to a successful composition. In rare cases the nobility and scale of large engineering works may even benefit mediocre pieces of country.

The other half of the problem is re-use of derelict land by new industry, and the consequent need to reclaim land,

remove dereliction and find ways to create a new man-made but attractive landscape setting.

4.04 Probably the greatest pressure on land today is the demand for recreational use **8**. As a result, much land is coming out of agriculture or other use and must now often be redesigned for dual or multiple use; weekday grazing being shared with weekend camping, forestry interspersed with picnic sites, water catchment areas crossed with trekking routes and nature trails. Furthermore, public pressures on land for recreation cause much greater wear and tear than before, so that a form of landscape *reinforcement* needs to be planned.

4.05 Agriculturalists rarely feel the need for what they regard as the 'aesthetic' professions, but there are signs of a change, particularly in the design of farm buildings as more acceptable features in the countryside. Opportunities to create new farmland usually only occur when reclaiming land from the sea (eg Dutch polders) or restoring after dereliction. In such work landscape designers can contribute to better shaping, draining, sheltering and planting of land so that it is better economically, as well as more attractive.

4.06 The most recent influential factor is the growth of the conservation movement and the rousing of the public conscience to care for the environment. This has already taken many forms from increased interest in historical gardens to the melting down of old cars. It calls for landscape design and management skills in rejuvenating old town centres; protecting features of natural beauty; restoring derelict canals; removing sources of toxic waste, reclaiming old colliery tips and other industrial waste

5

6

7 *Landscaping around Lee Valley power station*
8 *Polytechnic sports ground, Chiswick. Wet gravel pits forty years ago*

deposits; in restoring land after extractive industries **8**; in the planting component of Civic Trust type facelifts and in many other ways.

5 Progressive techniques

5.01 Professional and technical skills of the trade have not stood still in the face of these demands. Though transplanting large trees had been practised for centuries, it received such impetus through the availability of many large trees in nurserymen's gardens which had grown unsold during the war years as to amount to a new technique **10**. The demand for 'instant landscape' has continued unchecked, but trees have now to be grown-on deliberately to large size, though a more modest middle height with better future prospects is usually chosen.

5.02 Sowing grass by hydroseeding, a new technique from the US, is now well established. Many different emulsions, seed-mixes and mulches can be used. When used intelligently and on suitable surfaces hydroseeding has proved itself, though it suffered somewhat from extravagant publicity.

5.03 Of methods to extend the planting season, one of the most effective is the use of plastic sprays to reduce transpiration through leaves and stems during dry or warm weather following planting. The use of inert materials as substrates in place of soil has also been tried, including plastic foams to encase roots during transplanting and transport. Though in their infancy, these methods surely have a future. Perhaps the greatest development has been in containerisation (transferring plants into plastic or other containers in the nursery—even if not 'pot-grown') enabling

9 *Recreational use: Olympic boat-race course in the Amsterdam Bos*
10 *Michigan tree transplanting machine in operation*

them to be offered for sale at all times of the year and safely planted out. This technique has been related mainly to the growth of retail 'cash and carry' garden centres, but it has also benefited the contracting sector.

5.04 Selection of plants grown by the nursery trade has become somewhat better related to the demand for indigenous species for landscape work, though there is still a long way to go. The trend has been hampered by the opposite demand by the retail public for almost unlimited supplies of the latest fashionable plant mentioned on radio or tv.

5.05 Following an article* complaining that there were no British Standards for landscape work, BSI set up a committee structure to prepare standards for materials, techniques, definitions, maintenance methods and nursery stock. Although at present in abeyance for lack of adequate financial support, many standards have been published and work has now extended into the international field.

6 Future trends

6.01 It is difficult—and often unwise—to predict future trends, but by looking back at progress in the last quarter century and projecting forward, several possible ways for advancement stand out.

6.02 Changes in land use are inevitable as agriculture becomes an intensive industry and consumer countries are obliged to grow more of their own food. Though there will probably be no real shortage of farm land, first-class land will become sacrosanct for food growing only. It will be too valuable even for grazing, and farm animals will be reared in buildings and fed from fodder crops. Marginal and hill land will be in demand for forestry, water catchment and recreation rather than being used for poor farming. A result of this intensification should be that large scale changes in land use—even in agriculture and forestry—will need planning approval in future.

6.03 The rising demand for space for leisure, particularly water recreation, seems likely to continue. Of course many forms of sport do not need a beautiful green setting and could be accommodated on hard urban wastelands or in tattered remnants of 'green belts'—now often a dirty grey.

* AJ 25.10.61 *The lack of technical information for the landscape designer* C. R. V. Tandy.

11

6.04 More rational approaches to open space standards is likely, with hygiene-orientated municipal parks giving way to a logically planned open space *system* throughout a town. Urban pressures will mean that such open space will no longer be able to imitate arcadian values but will have to cater for sophisticated tastes of the 'King's Road' kind.

6.05 Change in housing patterns to cater for population increase is too big a subject to argue here, but whatever the form, a more intensively used—hence hard and more consciously designed—landscape setting will be demanded **11**. This may eventually extend to creation of open spaces— even to well-planted sitting and recreation areas—on decks over buildings, car parks **12** or other land uses. They may reach several storeys, following the Montreal 'Habitat' concept.

11 *Is this the future trend in garden design?* (*The Individualist's garden by Günther Schulze, Hamburg*)
12 *Large tree planting in a public open space created over an underground garage, Chicago*

6.06 As in towns, so in the countryside, public pressures will destroy the very qualities that people seek, unless means are found to cope with them. This should *not* make concrete, asphalt and wire fences in the countryside inevitable. Instead there is scope for considerable experiment into biological methods of withstanding use and controlling wear and tear.

6.07 In technology one can expect attempts to meet the desire for 'instant' landscape through increased container selling at larger sizes, more ideas to prolong the planting season and another crop of inventions to enable horticultural maintenance to be done by amateurs and unskilled labourers. Among ideas to be resisted will be attempts to grow tropical plants in this country through cheap-rate electricity; attempts to turn our diversified soils into a standard growing medium by chemicals and containers; and continued plant-breeding for fashion until every flower is available in every colour and all distinguishing characteristics of form, fragrance and plant-habit have been bred out. In contrast one must commend the new retail garden centres for displaying such an exciting array of species, that the public are even beginning to buy plants other than standard rose trees.

6.08 In three aspects of professional skill, new methods are essential. The first is classification of landscape quality. Though many authorities are experimenting with this problem, there is no recognised technique by which national or international landscape values can be compared. Allied to this is the need for a method of comparing values of different resources. Cost-benefit analysis has proved inadequate to deal with amenity values—some non-monetary method of 'value-analysis' could perhaps be devised. Finally, though the concept of 'grounds maintenance' as a technical skill for upkeep of cultivated landscape has begun to catch on in this country, there is still scope for upgrading staff to positions of seniority—even perhaps for introducing landscape managers in the way that housing managers have evolved to care for buildings.

Technical study
Landscape 2

Urban landscape review: Current and future trends

In the first technical study, CLIFF TANDY *reviewed the work and responsibilities of a landscape architect and briefly outlined discernible trends in landscape design. In this present study* TIMOTHY COCHRANE *examines those trends in greater detail and in a more pictorial form*

1

1 The beginnings of an urban landscape

Urban landscapes of supreme power for King and Church
1.01 The first glimmerings of urban landscape came inevitably with cultures of the 'Fertile Crescent' in the Middle East. Assyrian hunting parks and Persian gardens showed the way, but none of these matched the closely integrated urban infrastructure of the hanging gardens of Babylon **1**. Of apparently enlarged ziggurat form it shows how the trees were fitted into the structure.

1.02 While Kublai Khan's 'Green Hill' in China, one of the first town arboreta known, was but an example of little-known Chinese urban landscape, urban landscape as such was hardly practised by supremos until the Renaissance, apart from the brief interlude of the 'carmen' philosophy of Moorish Spain. Here, there was complete unity as building spaces flowed into one another. Although the Renaissance overshadowed the end of supreme power—its landscape flourished in the Italian squares, piazzas **2** and in the work of Le Notre for Louis XIV **3**, while Nash produced grandiose plans for the Georgian kings **4**.

Democratic urban landscapes
1.03 Some first flowerings of democracy were to be noted

1 *Hanging gardens of Babylon. This reconstruction shows complete fusion of structure and soft landscape*
2 *St Mark's piazza, Venice. Unequalled space articulation*
3 *Gardens at Versailles (Le Notre). Formalised statement of power*
4 *Nash's plans for St James's. Superb essay in new English style, foreshadowing a democratic landscape after previous formalised statements*

2

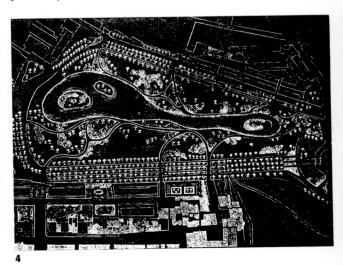

3

4

in the urban open spaces or agora of the Greeks and Romans. In medieval times market places sufficed for the commoners but few urban landscapes for them were created until the collective conscience of the nineteenth century led to the insertion of green spaces into the by-law streets. These designs, green would-be arcadian squares in our urban pattern, are still conditioning our minds as to what we should expect of our public open spaces, still shown in green ink on planning maps.

2 What is happening now?

Low density urban situations
New and expanded towns

2.01 Note how the concept of *rus in urbe* has continued, with the work of Ebenezer Howard's Welwyn and Hampstead Garden Suburbs being crystallised in the post-war New Towns. Harlow's green blandness in the midst of the arable scene **5a** with only clumsy attempts at urbanity in the centre **5b** gives way to the aborted concept of Hook, partially realised in Cumbernauld. Placed, against all logical siting rules for Scotland, on a windswept hilltop it yet showed signs of a new landscape in its closely set housing with children's play integrated into its hard surfaced linear corridors **6**.

2.02 Later work still tends to follow this trend with smoothly rounded grassy sweeps and only the odd urban touches in the centres. Even the latest entrant—Milton Keynes—does not look as if it will break away, rather the reverse.

General development

2.03 Landscape standards are either negligible or appalling, except for a few enlightened developers, Wates, Wren and Span among others. Span in their estates created for middle-class 'Span man' have provided some of the few refreshing glimpses of low-density housing landscapes in this country. In its short life (1955-69) while maintaining a consistently high standard of detail, Spanscapes have ranged from the prettified and eclectic face of Parkleys **7** through the more uncompromising and simple palettes of Field End **8** and some of the Blackheath estates to the more rampant and exuberant use of plant material in their later Weybridge estates of Templemere and Weymede.

New Ash Green **9** points a way for small community developments with its integration of small and larger spaces (see also **15**).

High density urban situations
Housing

2.04 High-density housing generally shows a pathetic disregard for the new open spaces supposedly liberated by tall blocks. Even in well-designed schemes architecturally the external spaces have been left as caged flat green spaces **10**. Two exceptions are Winstanley Road and Lillington Street. Although fussy in detail Winstanley **11** yet shows a pattern

5a

5b

6

7

5 *Harlow new town.* **5a** *Fill up the spaces with grass—it's useless but it's cheap in first cost.* **5b** *Centre—a mess of furniture*
6 *Cumbernauld (Cumbernauld Development Corporation). Fluid flow of pedestrian routes linking spaces with children's play at nodes*
7 *Span at Parkleys, Ham Common, Richmond (Eric Lyons & Partners). First example of new landscape. Variegated and coloured planting matches brashness of coloured glass and bright red Surrey tiles*

8

11a

9

8 *Span at Field End, Waldegrave, Twickenham (Eric Lyons & Partners). Close up birches and limited palette of ground covers, give pleasantly quiet effect*
9 *Churchill Gardens, Pimlico (Powell & Moya). Good architecture of its time with solitary trees in useless caged green spaces*
10 *Span at New Ash Green, Kent (Span Kent Ltd). Note sophisticated advances in detailing from Parkleys* **7** *(and fluid linkage of spaces in shopping street* **15***)*
11a *Anonymous architecture with good landscape of hard surfaces and trees—marred only by some over-fussy detailing (housing at Winstanley Road, Battersea, George, Trew, Dunn; landscape architect: Michael Brown)*

10

11b

12

13

for the future with its design for high intensity, high-density urban use, with an imaginative use of levels, and hard pavings. Lillington Street's access balcony planting provides a further promise **12**, even if the over-rustication of its internal courts and its use of trees are not as successful as they should be.

Precincts, plazas and pedestrian ways
2.05 Current examples of old-fashioned static spaces include Seagram Plaza **13**, the Economist podia **14** with the sophisticated Mellon Square, Pittsburgh, as successors to those squares which were inserted into the urban fabric in previous centuries.
On the other side of the coin the civic spaces at St Paul's, Paternoster Square, is a grim reminder of unachievement in

11b *Sensible, sturdy landscape detailing at Winstanley Road housing, Battersea*
12 *Superb balconies with planting (Housing at Lillington Street, London* sw1, *Darbourne & Darke). Later versions have been severely curtailed by* MHLG *cost yardsticks*
13 *Seagram Plaza, New York (Mies van de Rohe and Philip Johnson). Well articulated static approach to a static building, with fountains and creeping beech*

14

this field. Fluid linkage of spaces in the urban fabric appears a forgotten art—apart from some small-scale attempts **15**.

Shopping malls
2.06 Little progress appears to have been made from the US developments of a decade back (Detroit and Santa Ana **16**) though half-hearted attempts have been made in Coventry and in Rotterdam **17** while the most dreadful warning is

14 *Economist building, London. Good example of a simply detailed hard space (A. & P. Smithson)*
15 *Fluid linkage of urban spaces. Model of shopping centre, New Ash Green (Span Kent Ltd)*
16 *Sophisticated and smooth shopping mall surrounded by acres of cars (Santa Ana, California. Architects: Pereira & Luckman. Landscape architect: Ruth Shellhorn)*

15

16

17

19

17 *Well-known, long established Dutch shopping centre (Lijnbaan, Rotterdam, Van den Broek & Bakema)*
18 *Norr Malarstrand, Stockholm (Holger Blom). Still about the best example of linear waterside park where pedestrian scale persists throughout*

19 *Bos Park, Amsterdam. Integral spaces set in large wood*
20a, 20b *Restaurants set sensitively by Serpentine—an example of multi-use zoning (swimming, rowing, sailing)—but still car has not been tamed. (Hyde Park Restaurant Patrick Gwynne)*

18

echoed at Birmingham's Bull Ring. Today, us experience is now tending towards controlled environments with their own particular landscapes (see para 3).

Open spaces
Permanent
2.07 Stockholm and Amsterdam epitomise the best of recent decades in large urban open spaces with Stockholm's Norr Malarstrand **18** as an excellent example of a linear park, while Amsterdam's successful Bos Park **19** consists of integral spaces for rest and leisure set in a new wood. In this country there are no examples as yet of integral leisure areas.

2.08 As in New York's Central Park, London's Royal Parks are now slowly changing their faces for modern requirements. In London's Hyde Park, restaurants by the Serpentine **20**—excellent but for car parking arrangements —pop groups entertain in the cockpit and an art gallery opens. Unfortunately there is no cohesive landscape policy and poor St James's Park continues to be butchered.

2.09 *Linear parks* The potential of canals, rivers and old railway lines is only now slowly being realised as at Regent's Park Zoo **21** and at Farmers Bridge, Birmingham (page 126), and Stoke-on-Trent.
Large new spaces The Lee Valley progresses slowly while Liverpool's Everton Park and Newcastle's Town Moor press on at an even slower rate.

Temporary or 'fun' landscape
2.10 Landscapes for pleasure or exhibition have always been a feature from the Vauxhall and Cremorne gardens for the 19th century 'toffs' to today's Tivoli gardens (Copenhagen) for the *hoi polloi*. The first glimpses in this country

20a

of a new urban landscape was at the 1951 South Bank exhibition and its lighter-hearted twin at Battersea Park. Ephemeral and evanescent, both have been butchered by the GLC into pale shadows of themselves. Abroad, harder and tougher landscapes have been emerging through the excellent German International Garden Exhibitions (IGA) from Hamburg in 1963 through Stuttgart and Karlsruhe to Hamburg again in 1973, and at Zurich in 1959. Often the result of open competitions, they differ from British examples (Chelsea Flower show!) in that permanent urban parks were left for the cities to use. Note the varied and intelligent use of water, a German speciality in these examples from

20b

Stuttgart **22** and Karlsruhe **23**.
See also technical study 5 and information sheet 11 para 3.04
for Essen.

Incidental spaces
2.11 'Left-over' spaces are what make an urban landscape.
An intelligent appreciation of scale is all that is needed
especially in our latest problem of urban motorways where
success depends on pedestrian scales being designed independently of the motorway superstructures.

These impacts have been handled well in Germany and
Sweden **24** but hardly touched upon in this country.
Bristol's Cumberland Basin is weakly handled, research in
depth has been undertaken on Liverpool's motorways while
arguments rage over the afterthoughts to London's
Westway.

3 Future trends

Socio-economic influences
3.01 General trends are towards better and longer education,
higher living standards and shorter working weeks; to
greater leisure, mobility and adaptability. All these influence
the urban scene.

Mobility (both physical and social) and adaptability
3.02 *Flexibility* will cause the greatest problems in that
changing uses and disposable dry building forms will have
to be accommodated within slow-maturing wet and organic
landscapes. This could mean greater reliance on inorganic
or hard forms of enclosure and flooring with 'instant
planting' within urban complexes with major linear groupings of undisturbable plant material (large trees) in
between. It has even been suggested that forests should be
planted now in which new developments could be sited—in
the same way that early settlements were carved out of
virgin forest.

3.03 *Impatience* People are not so prepared to wait twenty
to twenty-five years for landscape to mature and will pay
more for 'instant work' in hard expensive materials. The
present so-called semi-mature tree industry could well
move upwards to providing those big trees that Baron

21
21 *A really urban/rural landscape of water/walkways/bridge,
with gravel and ground covers of neighbouring Regent's
Park Zoo*
22, 23 *Examples of permanent parks created as result of
biennial horticultural exhibition held in Germany in different
major cities: Stuttgart in 1961* **22**, *Karlsruhe in 1967* **23**

22   **23**

24 *Tullgarden, Sweden. Relaxation and calm, by and yet right away from elevated road systems*
25 *Is this the future pattern of leisure? Industry (left) cheek by jowl with children's play area and industrialised leisure pattern of future in caged golf driving ranges (right) (Tokyo)*
26 *Midland Arts Centre, Birmingham (Jackson & Edmonds). Integration of arts and sport. Full circle to Greek ideas of full integration of mind and body*

Haussman used in Paris in the eighteenth century. Meanwhile planting design will have to adapt to providing other shorter lived plants.

3.04 *Personalised transportation* Increasing numbers of cars, bubble cars, gyros, will lead to increasingly introverted layouts, with sterilisation of large areas for car parking.

Higher living standards
3.05 Rising labour costs should desirably lead to higher standards of design with robust finishes and low maintenance (that is, if current cost accounting methods can be changed). It could even mean that in high-density redevelopment, obliteration or relocation of existing organic landscape elements and their replacement by new materials could be more economic, although possibly undesirable on other grounds.

Leisure explosion
3.06 The horrifying pressures on spaces for leisure combined with increases in population densities are shown vividly in Tokyo where caged three-decker golf driving ranges are now the norm **25**, and every leisure activity is swamped by ant-like hordes. Multi-use of land is now considered essential using all available space on decks below ground and on roofs. There is also a much closer integration of buildings and outdoor spaces, and of functions, eg multi-use of water areas or school recreational facilities. These all lead to multi-purpose landscape plans.

3.07 Integrated leisure complexes include: Billingham forum (but with no integration of landscape—see AJ 22.11.67 and 27.8.69); Midland Arts Centre, Birmingham **26** which shows integration of indoor cultural activities with outdoor pursuits; Aviemore leisure centre used both in winter and summer; and Monaco development *below* beach level (see AJ 2.9.70).

Educational and social awareness
3.08 This awareness results in an increased social consciousness, an increasing desire to be involved in a healthy environment. Coupled with greater mobility (day trips to historic sites and so on) places like Longleat and Woburn could lead to a greater emphasis on history and continuity, and a more active involvement on the part of the visitors. Landscaping of conserved areas will grow and adaptation will continue of hitherto wastefully used external spaces for more intensive use.

Increasing public ownership
3.09 More public ownership of open spaces could lead to even more design for hard wear and defence against vandalism, as well as for increasingly low maintenance.

4 Technical advances

Mesoclimate and microclimate
4.01 Major advances can be expected in knowledge of this field as applied to urban design. Research is now beginning to be applied in depth at the BRS and university research units.

Wind
4.02 Wind is possibly the biggest factor on external comfort conditions in this country. Wind tunnel testing is being used increasingly to determine optimum shapes and sizes for buildings, especially for tall blocks, and for barriers. It is also being used in the design of open air leisure complexes.

Heating and cooling
4.03 Much has already been done in the US on heating of outdoor spaces: pedestrian ways, outdoor entertainment areas, shopping malls and so on. Apart from some pioneer installations for ramps and covered ways little work has been done in this country, probably because of higher power costs. Cooling techniques will be studied further for hot climate situations **28**.

Artificial light (*outdoors*)
4.04 The effect of artificial light on plants has been noted but no definitive data has yet been evolved; this is another field in which some advances can be expected.

Controlled environment
4.05 All this leads to the ultimate in climate control—the completely controlled environment as suggested by Buckminster Fuller for New York and practised on a smaller scale as in some shopping malls overseas and notably in the Ford Foundation building in Manhattan **27**.

Materials
4.06 There is likely to be far greater usage of pavings with possibly more research into wear and non-slip properties. Substitute materials for plants are also likely.
Inorganic materials are being increasingly used for playing surfaces while some cheaper German derivatives are being imported. Though expensive they may well become more economic with increasing requirements for multi-use of space, and manufacturing costs could drop with increased demands. Grass is an obvious candidate for substitution, taking into account its relatively poor wearing qualities and maintenance requirements in high density usage situations. Considerable advance in grass technology is now taking place and various other ground covers will offer increasing opportunities—especially as mass production techniques take over in nurseries.

4.07 Purpose-bred plants are being increasingly used in other countries for urban situations and further advances will be necessitated by the use of plants in controlled climate zones.

4.08 Containerisation of plants, combined with increasing use of anti-dessicants, are extending planting seasons dramatically. Further developments are inevitable as are the uses of inorganic materials such as glassfibre mulches. More drastically we can expect a greater increase in the science of hydroponics to cut out soil as a growing medium.

4.09 Most plant material industries (growth, supply, planting and design) in this country are still very much in the horse and buggy era and increasing rationalisation and industrialisation will have to accelerate to keep pace with the industrialisation of building processes. Battery production processes, of organic materials with mechanisation of growing and planting processes, are inevitable to meet the growing demands of society.

27 *Ford Foundation Building, NY (Roche, Dinkeloo & Associates; landscape: Dan Kiley). Completely controlled environment can bring its own problems of pest control. Difficult to determine optimum conditions for men and plant life*

28 *Architects' Consortium offices, Los Angeles (Architects: Smith & Williams; landscape architects: Eckbo, Dean & Williams). Expanded metal screening overhead and permeable screens around, provide pleasant comfort conditions for freestanding office units below*

27

28

6 *Monadnock building from Federal Centre, Chicago. Brick building radiates heat at night. Mies' glass façade, magnificent from within, is less effective climatically outside*
7 *St James's Park. People in the lunch hour enjoying narrow microclimate induced by grass cooling air in contrast with sun*
8 *Cross-section (north-south) through Trafalgar Square, London. High buildings on the south side of square would largely destroy usefulness of space*

3.27 In urban areas, the sun provides not only direct heat but radiation and heat storage. Earth-based materials are most effective radiators. South-west facing corners enclosed by masonry capture sunshine, store it and radiate it back into a sheltered space, the process continuing into the night **6**. Radiation from the ground is governed by the material of the surface. Grass is so delightful in summer because it creates a cool microclimate a few millimetres high in contrast to the megaclimate of hot sunshine **7**.

Noise
3.28 Vegetation is useful in combating noise and air pollution. On Earth as a whole, it prevents life from being rapidly extinguished in a world of carbon dioxide. In towns, foliage has little measurable oxygenating effect but one can detect the slight freshness of air over vegetation, always emphasised by a slightly lower temperature.

3.29 There are conflicting claims about tree and shrub barriers as effective deadeners of noise. Theoretically they can have little effect in diminishing volume, but they do make practical use of the space needed between noise source and hearer. The fact that the source is visually screened is said to lessen its offensiveness. However, there is evidence that grass and thick herbaceous ground cover attenuate sound intensity by sound absorption, whereas water and hard pavings do not, and may even increase the apparent loudness by reflection.

3.30 Background noise could perhaps be introduced to make traffic noise acceptable. Trees with fluttering leaves, such as poplars, produce several decibels in wind. Splashing water might be more effective. Trafalgar Square with its starlings and fountains is again an example **8**.

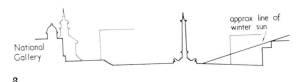

8

9a

9b

9 *Killesburg car park, Stuttgart.* **a** *General view and* **b** *detail. Note preference for shaded position and actual character of 'grass' ie mainly rank weeds. This type of treatment could not withstand heavy use every day but heavy use every weekend would not damage it*
10 *Hemel Water garden, Hemel Hempstead, cross section. Although there is only a narrow space between car park and shops each space has ample room for its function*
11 *Hemel Water garden. Screening of cars from pedestrians*

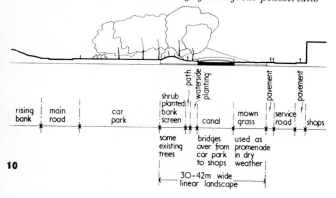

rising bank | main road | car park | shrub planted bank screen | path | waterside planting | canal | mown grass | service road | pavement | pavement | shops

some existing trees | bridges over from car park to shops | used as promenade in dry weather

30-42m wide linear landscape

10

Action, storage and movement

3.31 Comfortable conditions alone do not make outdoor spaces satisfactory: they must be *planned* to work well. Once they work they attract activities and access is required. But it is essential not to regard roads and paths as the dominant component of space between buildings. Spaces between buildings function very similarly to theatre foyers: they are for occupation and circulation. To design them as corridors is to kill them.

3.32 Buildings are very specific in their use and this tends to classify and sift users. Some are for exchanging goods, some for exchanging ideas and some for administering these exchanges. Others house people, buses, books and so on. People stream out from their entrances and intermingle in the space between buildings. Places for lingering and mixing are essential and the presence of cafés, leaves, birds, the scents of markets, all help to make them more inviting and work more efficiently.

3.33 Storage is as important as action. Sometimes storage points are interchanges between two scales of movement, eg car parks. Other types are for rubbish and waste or for storing 'urban freshness' in the form of plant and bird life. These uses are essential to the function of urban areas, even though they appear unused or 'ripe for development'.

3.34 Car parks are often, in essence, pieces of derelict land suitable for leaving temporarily unused objects. Urban freshness arises from land which is alive, but which is derelict from the point of view of urban use. There seems no reason why by storing cars in urban nature conservation areas, these two uses should not be combined **9**.

3.35 Effective urban spaces are very often small. Modern towns tend to have unusable space: too much to maintain and too much to use effectively; not truly space around buildings but rather 'space *around* space around buildings'. The cross section through Hemel Water gardens **10** shows the narrow distance between car park and shops. Yet each part is fully used and there is ample room for each function. Cars are screened behind an embankment completely

11

12a

12b

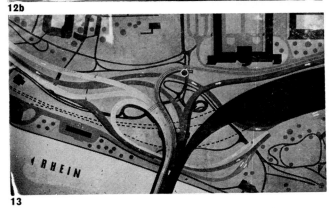

13

12 *Dusseldorf Autohochstrasse* **12a** *General view of structure*
12b *Flyover descends to ground level across right of picture,
with planting screen*
13 *Plan of Mannheim Bridgehead showing how footpaths are
a system forming part of overall layout plan. At no point is it
necessary for a pedestrian or cyclist to go up and then down
again. Curved ramps rise up to level of footpath over bridge*

covered with vegetation, creating a place with an air of
mystery **11**. Enough horizontal space is left for bank and
planting. A narrower space, ample for promenading, runs
along the waterside. It is long in one direction and there are
long views across the bank at chosen points.

3.36 When a road is considered as a route through a space
in use, there is more hope of a satisfactory design, for then
there must be a more controlled layout and not a jumble of
useless triangles scattered through the urban area. A road's
alignment is only one of several factors. Indeed its proportions can be modulated according to the requirements of
traffic density, parking, passing, turning and service to
buildings. The flyover in the centre of Dusseldorf **12** demon-
strates how every space is treated as valuable.

3.37 Pedestrian movement is just as important as vehicular
movement. Two attitudes tend to predominate in this
country. One completely ignores pedestrian needs until all
other routes have been laid out, then a tangled route is
threaded through (usually including several right angle
turns) with dark stinking flights of steps and unsavoury
underground passages and a plethora of railings. The second
attitude operates on spaces. These are criss-crossed by
desire lines, which eliminate the usefulness of the area.

3.38 Control of pedestrian movement needs as much care as
that of vehicles, but different criteria **13**. People are very
mobile, they can accelerate rapidly and turn suddenly, but
are prepared to take the most effortless route regardless of
safety—though willing to be diverted twice the distance for a
little stimulation.
Therefore movement of people is best achieved by sustaining
interest and suspense, and setting buildings at varied angles
and relationships to each other. Routes should pass around
the edge of activity areas and by disposing obstructions
and objects of interest, a longer route can be made to
appear the most natural. The faster people are moving, the
less space they need. A narrow alley is enough to guide a
crowd into a market place **14**. But leisurely movement needs
much more space—friends walk five abreast and mothers
let the children out of the pram to dawdle on both sides.

14 *Centre of Banbury showing wide space in park converging
to narrow alley which slips into market square. Larger
spaces have functions other than movement*
15 *Pedestrian underpass, Dusseldorf. Ramp is very gentle
and bridge is as wide as path. On one side ground hardly
rises after underpass*

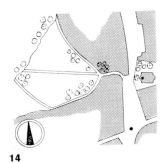

14

15

16

3.39 Pedestrian routes over or under roadways are a difficult problem. To prevent people braving traffic, easy flow of space to crossings is essential, with gentle ramps and wide underpasses to create confidence. The essence of pedestrian layouts is to understand that the mind has to be won over **15, 16, 17**.

Inadequacies of present technique
3.40 As urban space structure slackens (para 1.03) administrative problems arise, leading to slack design. Town mapping techniques are very crude and usually do not show changes of level or continuity of spaces which are small in relation to the total land area.

3.41 Plans showing different land uses with different colour or texture draw maximum attention to problems and interest at boundaries. For instance, at the junction of open land and woodland, the border strip is ecologically the richest. Yet the administrative machine which executes these plans gives least attention to such areas, usually ignoring them like the unused land between east and west Europe. Even at the smallest scale, units are studied in isolation rather than as part of their surroundings **18**. Building elevations do not show their neighbours and housing areas stop arbitrarily. Such techniques actually prevent coherent design of spaces around buildings. Perhaps inadequacies of existing practice are caused by doubt about the aims of organising urban space.

References
1 FAIRBROTHER, N. New lives, new landscapes, London, 1969, Architectural Press, £3.75 [O8]
2 Handbook of building environment Architects' Journal Information Library (AJ 2.10.68–13.8.69) see especially section 1 Climate and topography (AJ 2.10.68 and 9.10.68)
3 METEOROLOGICAL OFFICE MO 488 Climatological atlas of the British Isles, 1952, HMSO [(E7) sfB (1961): Aa9] o/p

17a

17b

16 *Pedestrian underpass, Stuttgart centre. Ramps here are steep and occur on both sides of road. To alleviate this, footpath grows wider as it falls and underpass is at the widest point*
17 *Footbridge over road, Schlossgarten, Stuttgart (city centre).* **17a** *Footbridge rises very slowly over road and branches. Space between rising of bridge and road is filled with vegetation shutting off roadway.* **17b** *Method of lighting handrail which avoids mass of lamp standards*
18 *Cumbernauld Seafar. Great skill has been shown in design of this area, but houses in distance are in another housing area. Retaining wall holds up a 'between area' which breaks continuous flow of pedestrian system. Steps lead up to roadway beyond which another sort of footpath starts in another position. Enclosure and shelter of each housing area is dissolved in space where two areas meet*

12

13

☐ Existing building

■ New building

▨ Landscape areas extended into adjoining existing areas

14

12 *Natural expression of individuality beyond the threshold of the dwelling effectively extends residents' zone of responsibilities*
13 *Modified boundaries of private and communal responsibilities as basis of rehabilitation project (Birmingham city architect's department)*
14 *New landscape shown taken out beyond boundaries of redevelopment area to promote rehabilitation and selective renewal*

and forcibly experienced on their edges—for these are the lines along which differences of use and ownership occur. Well cared for private land that is visible from the public realm is an asset, and vice versa, but this is not so where land in one or other of these realms is uncared for due to a failure in identifying ownership, of neglect in a discharge of responsibility for care, or a basic incompatibility of adjacent uses.
The junction of concurrent edges needs to be made into a positive asset, for this is precisely where deterioration most readily sets in.
The problem of the junction is indeed one common to building also; identifying and dealing with the edge condition seems similarly to be the crux of the problem of urban landscape—it certainly is central to that of housing. For this reason the physical form, function and identification of the edge conditions of spaces have been regarded as the best basis of the approach to the analysis of external spaces which is adopted in information sheet 25, page 155.

New forms of housing and layout
4.06 If the problems of financing management and maintenance can be overcome, new methods of communal layouts could be devised. Some of the many possibilities may follow naturally from current work, for example at Milton Keynes, where the ideas of freedom of choice and flexibility which underlie the philosophy of the new city should be able to lead to different forms of house ownership and of construction methods providing this future flexibility, perhaps in the form of do-it-yourself construction. The latter in particular would pose entirely new problems that might greatly benefit the landscape, especially in the immediate area of the dwellings.

4.07 Unless the landscape implications are fully understood and realistically tackled there is a risk of visual and physical disorder; at its worst, a junkyard of partially developed land and unfinished buildings. Lack of an appropriate system of land husbandry could result in large areas of uncared for space—neither specifically public nor private—used or misused by everybody and with no clearly defined responsibilities for ownership or upkeep.

Existing housing layouts and rehabilitation
4.08 Similar measures could be applied to vast areas of existing towns where ambiguous boundaries between private and public ownerships and responsibilities discourage a well cared for environment. Thousands of miles of Britain's streets are lined with dreary, unending rows of terraces or dotted with semi-detached houses, which are featureless, treeless and depressing. Transformation of these drab wastelands must start with administrative arrangements, ownership agreements, management costs and firmly defined responsibilities. A re-examination of these matters could well lead to adjustment of highway and path widths, stopping roads, and providing communal open spaces perhaps by absorbing front gardens. Residents' and other management groups could be established.

4.09 An AJ article on rehabilitation[3] stressed '. . . the need to balance internal and external amenities . . .' for there is '. . . little point in modernising a home if outside the front door there is only roaring traffic, a mile long walk to a bus stop and nowhere for the children to play. . . .'

4.10 Quite modest changes can have great value: selective demolition and clearance, adjusting garden sizes (both front and back) and moving boundaries to improve public open space provision. Even the reuse or sale of under-used backland for new infill housing can benefit the environ-ment if new development is skilfully done. Sale of council houses can be accompanied by obligations on new owners to carry out, or at least contribute to, environmental improvement.

4.11 At present, when dereliction, depression and form-lessness become intolerable, people either stop caring—leading to neglect, vandalism and delinquency—or, to quote Habraken, if they have retained the ability to care, they move on like nomads, instead of staying put and improving their habitat. It is like a game of musical chairs in which people must adapt to what is offered in order to meet their real social needs instead of themselves initiating change.

4.12 Continuity of existing communities in new housing is important, whether rehousing is partial or total. On the Winstanley Road, Battersea, site where a new housing estate was introduced, an unusually low cost for making good after vandalism to the landscape is credited largely to the considerable housing management skill by which people already living in the area were rehoused quickly with the minimum of disturbance. Residents sensed the social continuity and responded by feeling involved in the new estate. In this phased housing scheme, great care was taken to ensure that the landscape and buildings were finished at the same time so that residents lived in a com-pleted environment from the start. Integration of existing older dwellings with new development makes for physical and social continuity. It can also enable private initiatives—with or without financial assistance—to contribute to varied forms of ownership.

4.13 New development should allow changing the status of existing roads and rights of way to produce a new and better integrated system of movement—eg by culs-de-sac, nar-rowing roads and so on. Division of responsibility for cost and maintenance is too often permitted to become a stumbling block. New tree planting beyond development area limits could support new development and act as an arm of conservation **14, 15**.

4.14 An integrated arrangement of this sort will enable changes in house type and ownership to occur more readily: this could greatly increase flexibility of choice in response to change in family needs as well as a family's varying capacity to contribute financially at different stages of its life. Older buildings, often too large for small family occupa-tion, can be made to provide flexibility through internal rearrangement. This again illustrates the biological analogy of a multi-cellular organism's ability to increase its stability through change.

4.15 A multiple system of private and public initiatives and ownership could eliminate the conflict between the two and enable them to complement each other. For instance, in areas of privately owned dwellings public rights of way could be treated, maintained and financed as extensions of the communal spaces within adjacent housing. The housing landscape could thus interweave between the various privately and publicly owned components, with interlocking arrangements for responsibility and involvement **16**. This reasoning leads at least in the private sector to a flexible arrangement capable of adapting itself to a do-it-yourself, privately owned and initiated, layout whose spaces—

15

	Public open space		Vehicle space
	Private open space		Existing building
16	Group private space		New building

15 A missed opportunity to expand landscape routes outwards from new developments (in background—a situation frequently resulting in demolition of adjacent old housing instead of rehabilitation
16 Interpenetration of ownership: diagram of housing landscape interweaving across private and public areas

integrated with the communal landscape—would be of high quality, otherwise difficult to achieve.

Shared facilities
4.16 Integration needs to extend to facilities also. Large communal spaces may be less necessary in a housing layout immediately adjacent to open land, wood or public open space. Equally, facilities of adjacent users—especially schools—should be available to housing schemes. Hard play and kickabout spaces are often provided in housing layouts, when those of a nearby school site could so readily be used. Despite pleadings and official sanctions in DES and MHLG joint circulars, the ideas of multiple use of school and communal facilities has received very little attention and scarcely any action.

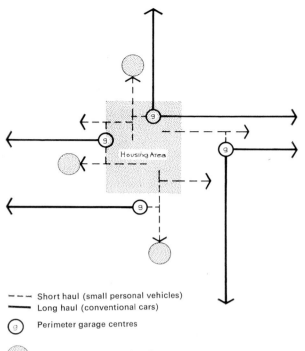

- - - Short haul (small personal vehicles)
——— Long haul (conventional cars)

ⓖ Perimeter garage centres

Local magnet (shool, shops)

17

18

17 *The vehicle for the job: possible new route system inside housing area, with conventional cars exchanged for small new means of personal transit for short journeys from perimeter garage centres*
18 *The therapeutic value of the relatively simple inexpensive elements of townscape—grass banks, trees, controlled space (Winstanley Road, Battersea: architect—George, Trew, Dunn; landscape architect—Michael Brown)*

4.17 It seems ludicrous to allow purely administrative difficulties or local government departmental rivalries to sabotage obviously sensible policies, which could form a very significant asset to housing estates and greatly influence their layout. Territorial rivalries between competing departments in local authorities frequently aggravate the situation. Difficulties of control, maintenance, and finance are not insoluble. One of the most compelling considerations is that the timings of different needs complement each

other so perfectly. In studies of universities, much has been made of the fact that sophisticated facilities remain idle for a very large proportion of the year when they could be giving a fruitful return on investment. Applying this rationale of cost effectiveness at the other end of the educational scale could indirectly increase resources needed for housing landscape.

4.18 The multiple-use principle should be applied to other things, such as parking and garage space. If this is provided on the edge of housing schemes it can frequently be available to people living, working or shopping in adjacent areas, offering a better return on initial investment.
Rationalisation of even one-third of the total parking provision could transform almost every housing scheme in the country. It would also give public transport a much needed fillip and help to eliminate extravagant use of land by cars **17**.
There are already new technical possibilities which more than compensate for the disadvantages of not having traditional motor vehicles on the doorstep of every dwelling. An intermediate technology is needed to solve problems of scale and compatibility of the types of vehicles suited to be close to the dwelling.

4.19 Another advantage of balanced as opposed to single-use development is the opportunity it gives for variations of character close to where people live. This can help to provide visual and social variation and interest for residents, as well as greater liveliness which has obvious social and economic benefits. Shops, libraries, primary schools, club rooms, pubs, open spaces and so on can enormously improve an otherwise unvarying townscape. The therapeutic value of relatively simple, inexpensive elements of townscape, **18** compared with the detrimental, costly, sterile ones that frequently displace or exclude them, make the benefits of a humanised, enriched urban landscape irrefutable.

5 Cost of housing landscape

5.01 An analysis of the cost effectiveness of what makes our towns good to live in will undoubtedly reveal how unstrategic use of resources has led to gross distortion in the direction of effort **19**.
Any significant existing assets—buildings or natural features—must be regarded as items whose removal may result in greater expense to make good their loss. Where buildings, individually, or in groups, can contribute to the new development after rehabilitation, they should be regarded as, if not irreplaceable, at least capable of giving some maturity which may well be totally missing from new projects, or can at best take several decades to develop. The retention of existing trees, hedges or water courses may be costly, but the expense of replacing them with new amenities may be much greater. New trees may need twenty or thirty years to acquire anything near the landscape value of large mature trees which have been removed.

5.02 A site's natural or man-made advantages and disadvantages affect its social and economic value. Unfavourable orientation, difficult topography or poor drainage all vitally affect housing layout **20**. Indeed some sites may well have such cost implications or constraints on their use as to rule them out for housing development. But if there is little choice, as sometimes happens, we must be sure that the total cost of meeting the difficulties justifies the choice that has to be made. It is not enough to expect that the ordering of land uses, assuming it to be on the right basis,

19

20

19 *Assets comparable with these Finnish trees and rocks seldom exist in this country, but conservation of existing natural features is especially vital and can offer economies in capital costs as well as contributing immeasurably to the sense of maturity and identity of new projects: Housing in Finland*
20 *Greek roofscape. Primitive buildings fitted into a hillside site unconsciously produce variation and interest in routes and spaces*

will automatically produce appropriate landscape. As Nan Fairbrother has pointedly observed in *New lives, new landscapes*[6] the relationship of planning and landscape is a bit like ordering a restaurant meal—the order is sent in but someone then has to do the cooking!

5.03 The best (or worst) example of cost effectiveness is the disproportionate management of resources, both of land and capital, given over to the motor car. In most housing layouts the proportion of land involved is seldom less than twelve to fourteen per cent and is frequently fifteen to twenty per cent of all site uses.
These percentages frequently equal or exceed the amount of hard pedestrian space. The cost of providing vehicle space is only exceptionally twenty per cent and more normally fifty per cent to seventy per cent of all externals costs—a staggering expenditure on large projects. Reconsidering disposition of resources would lead to much greater social and environmental benefit. The strikingly low allocation of funds to hard and soft landscape where motor vehicles' share of resources is high is clearly significant.

Housing investment
5.04 It is seldom realised how small is the total investment in the fabric of the building after land costs, rates, maintenance and loan costs have been taken into account. How much smaller it must therefore be for the visible externals where cost is seldom more than ten to twelve per cent or so of the total building costs.
Referring generally to the question of investment in housing and in particular to the views of the Parker Morris Committee, Lewis Womersley stated that our dilemma consists in '. . . deciding at what level to pitch housing standards when living standards generally have risen and are still rising substantially; and yet building costs are also rising fast and interest rates are about the highest of all time . . . it seemed that the way out of this dilemma . . . was being sought in the direction of producing dwellings of a quality that was quite inadequate . . . in comparison with our standard of life generally—our acquisition of (the) luxuries of mid-twentieth century life'. He doubted '. . . whether many architects and the public generally realise how limited the physical building cost is in relation to the gross cost paid for a dwelling on mortgage or loan repayments. . . .'
'. . . Regardless of the fact that government grants and tax relief considerably ease the financial burden of interest payments on the tenant or the owner the fact remains that the portion on which the architect is continually asked to make economies represents considerably less than one-fifth of the total cost of a dwelling.'
It is thus '. . . quite futile to talk about housing standards and costs in terms of architecture and building without relating them to the basic background of housing finance and to standards of living generally. . . .'
5.05 In 1963 Lewis Womersley reported the detail breakdown of the economic rent of a three-bedroom house, with 6 per cent interest rates and 60 year repayment period as follows:

Interest payments ..	53 per cent
Cost of building ..	17 per cent
Land	3 per cent
Rates	15 per cent
Maintenance	12 per cent

By 1969 the cost of building item had fallen to 11 per cent. Based on the later, ie 1969, figures if the external costs average say ten per cent of most total project costs—and these include underground services which are environmentally invisible—this would average only around £1·70 for every £100 spent on buildings. By 1980 what then will they be?

The truth is that seen in relation to the real costs of housing development the best possible landscape would cost only a quite trivial sum, say one-tenth of the eleven per cent referred to, yet it can and does make an overwhelming difference between a good place to live in and an environmental disaster.

These facts must surely put into perspective the idiotic and irresponsible policies which continue to deny adequate investment sums to making a decent environment.

5.06 Unfortunately, the depressant effect of the housing cost yardstick as currently operating has hit hardest at the less quantifiable aspects of housing and tragically the landscape has suffered most, and continues to do so. Although the Parker Morris report concerned itself principally with the arrangement of the dwelling itself, the importance of the setting was strongly implied.

Its main recommendations being already watered down, yardstick controls often make it increasingly difficult and sometimes impossible to achieve even these reduced standards in spaces outside dwellings.

Surely we cannot continue to spend countless millions every decade in building houses that are situated in environmental slums even at the time they are built? What then will they be like by the end of each of these decades?

The misuse of opportunity and the distortion of real values is nothing short of criminal.

Recent work by DOE's R & D section on residents' reactions shows that people do respond positively to well laid out housing estates where investment is adequate and management good. It may eventually be possible to prove as persuasive a case for the intangibles of landscape as for the more obvious demands of drains.

References

1 CHERMAYEFF AND ALEXANDER. Community and privacy
2 CHERMAYEFF AND TZOMIS. Shape of community
3 HABRAKEN, N. J. Supports: an alternative to mass housing. London, 1972, Architectural Press £1·50 [05]
4 GEDDES, P. Cities in evolution. London, 1968, Benn, £2·50 [052]
5 New homes for old. AJ 10.6.70 and 1.7.70 [81 (W6)]
6 FAIRBROTHER, N. New lives new landscapes. London, 1969, Architectural Press. £3·75 [08]
7 LEWIS WOMERSLEY. Productivity for what

Technical study
Landscape 5

Urban landscape review: Recreation

A more sensible sharing of sports and recreational facilities between educational establishments and town is urged by G. A. PERRIN *in this article. He also shows, by illustrating foreign examples, how we might revolutionise our parks and turn them into comprehensive recreation centres*

1 Introduction

1.01 Two previous AJ studies—*Designing for leisure* (in 1964[1]) and *Community recreation centres* (in 1967[2]) reviewed urban landscape with particular reference to sport and recreation. The latter described the important function of the Sports Council and regional sports councils, and the possible implications of their policies on facilities such as sports/recreation centres, and joint-use projects based upon school premises.

1.02 Between then and now there has been a seemingly unending economic squeeze, national expenditure has fallen to an extremely low level and construction costs have soared. Nevertheless general interest has quickened to an extent where it is estimated that there are now over 200 towns planning, or building, sports centres of one kind or another, plus an equal number of schools projects considering public use of their facilities outside school hours.

1.03 The underlying consideration at all levels is undoubtedly cost—value for money, analysis of costs in use, and general sensible husbandry. Co-ordination of effort is an important part of the day to day work of the regional sports councils. Minimising the fragmentation which still takes place among local government departments is another. The recent establishment of recreational offices, with recreation directors to guide their development, is a step towards a more effective and co-ordinated use of resources and effort.

1.04 Reports such as *Planning for leisure*[3] and the Sports Council's *Planning for sport*[4] have provided useful guide lines for those embarking on major recreational provision for the first time. But we are still unquestionably far behind our nearest neighbours in Europe (West Germany for example) who are currently spending up to ten times as much on comprehensive recreational programmes. In this country, the Maud Report indicates that recreational uses (under the block grant system) will have to fight for a share of whatever money is available and take their chance with all other urban users. Successive governments show little concern for increasing the present rate of progress.

2 Standards

2.01 Where and how can resources be used to their maximum potential? To take one example: grass pitches, on which this country has always depended so heavily, are badly in need of appraisal and re-evaluation. They offer limited use in poor weather, and cannot be used after dark without floodlighting. Hence the development of weekend sports fixtures with the pavilion used at most twice a week.

1 *Part of Bracknell Sports Centre, Berks. Changing rooms on right serve outdoor pitches and running track*

2.02 Floodlighting is expensive and can be associated with more than one playing area only with considerable trouble. If this area is laid using a hard porous surface, however, the use factor rises sixfold. Pavilions which previously needed to accommodate, say, ten teams on a Saturday afternoon, can be built smaller as games can be spread throughout the week—leaving players free for weekends with the family. On a town scale the saving in land allocation and capital cost would be appreciable, especially if it is accepted that one floodlit hard porous soccer pitch is the equivalent of up to six grass pitches.

2.03 This would have a considerable effect on the forty-five year-old 6 acre (2·4 hectare) standard for play space suggested by the National Playing Fields Association, which has so strongly influenced the planning of our immediate post-war new towns. *Planning for sport*[4] suggests that an area of 2·4 acres per 1000 people (approximately 1 hectare) might be more appropriate, but sensibly adds that no standard is capable of universal application. Obviously this latter figure would be more applicable to a central London borough than to a new town, but even the six acre standard could be pared to 4·5 acres (1·8 hectares) without detriment, providing a balance is established between indoor and outdoor facilities, grass and non-grass surfaces, and floodlit areas.

2.04 Pressure on urban space has led to the increasing provision of shared facilities, the best example being the sports centre. Thought of as a 'stadium' in the late fifties, ideas have progressed to the present arrangement of one large indoor nucleus surrounded by a number of outdoor playing facilities—on the lines of Bracknell **1**. Even these have altered in the space of the last three years to indoor-only provision of the kind now in use at Poole, Dorset (the Arndale Centre), and Basingstoke where facilities are part of the central area shopping precinct.

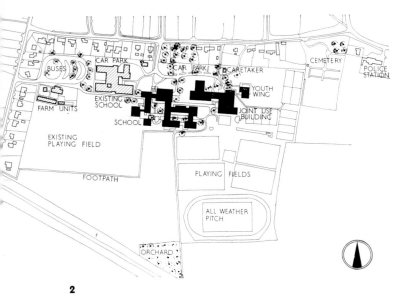

2

3 Future provision

3.01 Should Basingstoke set the pattern for future major indoor recreational provision, what is likely to be the future pattern of outdoor provision?

Better use of school facilities is one major area for reappraisal in this respect. The Sports Council has for many years been trying to persuade education and local authorities to combine their resources to make more effective use of land and capital. Bingham joint use school in Nottinghamshire **2** is one of the first examples where the public may use the school's excellent facilities after school hours **3**. This should not be considered an alternative in every case (especially in larger towns) to the 'town' sports centre which can be used in off-peak hours by schools. Many countries are now considering joint use of community schools, with extra facilities attached at an additional cost of between £50 000 and £60 000, and open to outside public use after school hours. Totnes Grammar School **4** is a typical example; others are coming into use in Hampshire and Essex.

3.02 Thus we are beginning to see the realisation of the three-tier planning forecast in community sports halls, published by the NPFA in 1965. Edinburgh is a good example of this on a city scale[6], with primary schools, secondary schools and town facilities in that order, providing overall sports coverage **5**. With the growth in popularity of some games—golf, water sports such as sailing and fishing, and climbing—the need has also arisen for practice and performance facilities—the former available in the home town, the latter probably some distance away. Consequently regional patterns are becoming established with the emergence of 'importing' and 'exporting' authorities: some with outdoor facilities enabling people to sail, climb, pony-trek, or play golf; others with good indoor provision for training purposes.

3.03 This arrangement could be a means of revitalising many seaside towns and holiday areas affected in recent years by society's increasing mobility, especially to other countries. The places around Lake Leman (Geneva), the Dolder open-air sports park in Zurich **6**, **7**, the Gruga Park in Essen **8**, **9**, **10**, **11**, the parks and water sports areas around Amsterdam, or even the ubiquitous Tivoli Gardens in Copenhagen, must inevitably influence the UK if this movement continues.

3

4a

4b

2 *Site plan of Bingham comprehensive school joint use buildings* (1:7500)
3 *The gymnasium forming part of a £200 000 + sports*

complex at Bingham, available to the public after school hours
4a 4b *Another smaller scale example of joint use school facilities, the sports hall at Totnes Grammar School.*

5

3.04 What many of these examples illustrate is the present obsolescence of most urban parks in this country, with their Victorian origins still firmly dictating present day use. Their only purpose has been to provide a green 'lung' in built-up areas which have failed to attract people sufficiently, The Gruga Park on the other hand, with many other Bundesgarten examples in West Germany provides a very wide range of facilities: heated outdoor 'Olympic' swimming and diving pools (including a surfing pool), tennis, miniature golf, boating pools, pony rides, an aviary, small zoo, tropical house, ice-rink, sports hall, exhibition hall, concert stand, museum, library, lakes, azalea gardens, Japanese gardens, and back-ground planting generally of the highest order **11**. Although a charge of four shillings is made for admission it is not inconceivable that there would be many in this country willing to pay for the same range of facilities.

5 *Meadowbank Sports Centre, Edinburgh, scene of the 1970 Commonwealth Games. The sports centre will eventually form the top rung of a hierarchy of provision starting at junior school level*
6 *Part of the Dolder open air sports park in Zurich*
7 *The 'surfing' pool in the Dolder Sports Park, Zurich. Artificially-made waves formed every thirty minutes during the summer are a big attraction for bathers*
8 *Children's free play area, Gruga Park, Essen*
9 *Gondola pool, Gruga Park, Essen*
10 *Concert stand, Gruga Park, Essen*

6

7

8

10

11

11 *Restaurant forming part of a water sports centre in Zurich. Note the quality of the landscape treatment at the water's edge*
12 *One of several pools forming part of the Gruga Park, Essen, and constructed in the last six years*

12

3.05 The Canon Hill Park project in Birmingham (otherwise known as the Midlands Art Centre, see technical study LANDSCAPE 2 fig 26) probably comes closest to being the first UK example of this trend towards fully-fledged 'recreational' parks. Whatever inter-departmental barriers in local government need to be broken down to achieve similar examples, the success of Canon Hill is beyond doubt.

4 Summary

4.01 Pressure on urban space, the high capital cost of providing major recreational facilities, and the expectation of future demands, have all contributed towards a general reappraisal of resources at local and regional level.

4.02 A measure of co-ordination is being achieved by regional sports councils through whom all projects requiring central government funds must pass. Their role may be uncertain if the Maud Report is put into effect. Similarly the role of such bodies as the Technical Unit for Sport just starting its work, may be equally unclear.

4.03 The better use of school facilities on the lines of Bingham, or the Cambridgeshire Village Colleges, appears to be inevitable, although meeting with the expected resistance from many headmasters. In this respect university sports centres should not be exempt, although at present—with the notable exception of Lancaster—most operate policies of exclusive use on the lines of their American counterparts. At least a dozen are as good as any in Europe.

4.04 Park design is another area for reappraisal within the same context. As an alternative to peripheral urban provision there seems no better solution in the foreseeable future. As planned at Essen or Canon Hill parks may well be a suitable answer to the need for new 'sports' centres, and as they already exist land purchase costs are avoided.

4.05 New techniques (floodlighting), new surfaces (hard porous materials) now much used in the western and wettest side of the country, new management techniques (eg the MSC course in Recreation Management at the North-West Polytechnic), and a new look at space standards (*play space* not to be confused with *open space*), are all contributing to make the next ten years the most interesting in recent times. It must be hoped that this message is gradually percolating through to government circles, and that they accept the quality of leisure time as investment justifying.

References

1 AJ Information Library: Designing for leisure: the future of sports facilities AJ 14.10.64 p891-896 [(95) CI/SfB]
2 AJ Information Library: Community recreation: the need for a wider view AJ 5.4.67 p853-857 [(95) CI/SfB 5]
3 DEPARTMENT OF EDUCATION AND SCIENCE, Planning for Leisure. 1969, HMSO £1·75 [5]
4 SPORTS COUNCIL Planning for sport—a report. London 1968, The Council [5]
5 NATIONAL PLAYING FIELDS ASSOCIATION Community Sports Halls, London 1965. The Association, £1.5 [562]
6 AJ Information Library Building studies: Royal Commonwealth Pool, Edinburgh AJ 16.9.70 p645-662 [541] Sports Centre, Meadowbank, Edinburgh AJ 23.9.70 p705-718 [661]
7 TOWN PLANNING INSTITUTE Open space in new towns—an appraisal by F. T. Burnett. TPI *Journal*, 1969, June [083]
8 REGIONAL SPORTS COUNCIL Appraisals of demand [5]
9 TOWN PLANNING INSTITUTE Working for recreation by D. D. Molyneau. TPI *Journal*, 1968, April [5]

Section 2 **Design procedure**

Design guide
Urban landscape

Scope

As explained in the introduction to this handbook, landscape work can be divided into separate types of landscape spaces in much the same way as building types. While several landscape types will be covered in the handbook, there is only one design guide, which attempts to provide a check list for the design of any landscape work which is a component of the urban scene. Although much 'urban' landscape will be executed as a subcontract to a building or civil engineering contract, this design guide follows the pattern of a main contract.

Form

The main stages of this guide are based upon the RIBA Plan of work, amended for landscape contracts and subcontracts, and shown in information sheet LANDSCAPE 2. The left-hand column is intended as a checklist; advice, information and cross references are given on the right.

References

References in the body of the guide are given a shortened title only. Full details are given in appendix C. References in SMALL CAPITALS are to AJ design guides, technical studies and information sheets. References of a more general nature and books for further reading are included in appendix C.

Brief and feasibility study

1 Inception and primary brief

The object of this stage (which corresponds with stage A of the RIBA Plan of work) is to establish sufficient information about client's overall requirements to allow feasibility of project to be assessed (see stage 2) and to set the broad framework within which architect and consultants are to work

Although the landscape designer should be appointed in time to contribute to the earliest thinking on the project, a feasibility study for a building or civil engineering project may have already been carried out, in which case such a study would form a large part of the primary brief

1.01 Scope of project

Physical scope

At this stage some assessment of size and character of project is needed, even though no brief has been given. Area of site plus client's financial commitment will probably be adequate. A preliminary visit, or even study of maps and air photographs, will be adequate to assess physical character

Functional scope:

If project is for use of land for a clearly defined purpose (eg sports centre, town park, and so on) preliminary studies can be based on similar projects executed recently, and on published critiques of such projects which analyse areas, accommodation, cost and so on

Is project
    improvement of existing
      land only?
    extension of existing land use?
    new use for the land?

Aesthetic considerations:

Is project
   wholly compatible with
     surrounding landscape?
   reasonably compatible, so
     that new landscape work can
     be easily married in?
   incompatible?   If project is incompatible, client must be warned that site is unsuitable; or that scheme may be rejected on planning grounds; or that extensive and expensive treatment involving land beyond limits of actual site may be necessary

1.02 Client

Type of client: There are four general types of client, as shown in left-hand column below:

   private   Usually for gardens and small work, but including private groups such as sports clubs

   developer   Usually intends to develop land for such uses as speculative housing, office buildings, industry or recreation

   'corporate body'   An impersonal committee or board of an organisation which finds itself with a 'land' problem incidental to a property project

   public   Acting at every level through central and local bodies, requiring the landscape treatment of schools, hospitals, public buildings, new towns, and so on

Relationship with client   Relationship may be direct, but is frequently through another professional adviser, staff member (eg estates officer, surveyor, engineer) or committee chairman. In dealing with a large organisation it is helpful to have a 'liaison officer' formally made responsible for external works

Client's brief   One is fortunate if the briefing comes through another professional, as some definite guidance may then be expected. If not, then brief might be negligible. Apart from specific uses (eg sports pitches, car parks) clients are notoriously vague about their need for, and use of, external space. In the majority of jobs the architect may have to write his own brief

Client's interest in site: Once type of client has been established, client's interest in site may be determined:

   absentee landlord   Investment interest only

   owner occupier   Direct user and financial interest

   tenant   Temporary user interest owner

Client's financial capacity   Determine at early stage whether client has financial capacity and intention to adequately finance project. If not, inform client that:
project is likely to be more expensive than he anticipated;
or whole of project cannot be done for anticipated expenditure;
or desired standard cannot be achieved

Client's management capacity   Client should be made aware that landscape work (even more than building work) needs competent maintenance for scheme to reach expected standard. Determine whether he has (or is prepared to recruit and pay for) suitable staff both to supervise and carry out maintenance work after completion of contract

1.03 User requirements

                        Determine uses to which external space is to be put

Physical   Determine physical restraints on such open space uses eg length and width (sports pitches); area (car parking); number of participants (swimming pool)

Aesthetic   Determine client's desires and taste (colours, plantings)

Other determinants   Eg client's interests (gardening, swimming); client's needs (privacy, social life); orientation, security, paid admission etc

Maintenance limit	Following on from client's management capacity above, determine precise design limitations imposed by capacity of client's resources to maintain project after completion

2 Feasibility

2.01 Appointment of consultants

Obtain client's agreement to the appointment of specialists, eg landscape architect (unless already running the project), civil engineer, quantity surveyor, hydrologist, ecologist, forester, horticulturalist, economist, traffic engineer, sociologist, soil scientist

Fees and services

Agree extent of services to be provided, and application of ILA, RIBA, or other scale of charges

Directory

Make directory list of: client's officers and staff concerned with project; all professional staff engaged; planning departments, service companies, control boards, legal agencies, and personal contacts, together with addresses, telephone numbers

2.02 Site investigation
Preliminary data

Obtain plans, maps, published data, and extract data from reference libraries, ministries and other organisations. See information sheet LANDSCAPE 1

Investigations made on site

Collect data from site by observations, photographs, measurements and testing procedure by own staff or specialists. See information sheet LANDSCAPE 1

Record data

By plotting or updating maps, plans etc, and by written reports and record data collected on site

2.03 Legal requirements

Ascertain constraints imposed on site (or on project) by legal requirements. See information sheet LANDSCAPE 2

2.04 Available areas

Study space standards laid down by statutory and/or advisory bodies, and exact space sizes required for various uses (see 1.03 above) and compare with availability of space on site. Decide on viability of brief

2.05 Preliminary planning decisions

Discuss with consultants, and with officers of local planning authority, likelihood of project meeting local planning regulations; note constraints to be taken into account in order to meet planning requirements. See information sheet LANDSCAPE 2

2.06 Early cost studies

Make approximate estimates (in consultation with qs, if appointed) on available project data, and collected cost analysis data, to initiate cost studies. See information sheet LANDSCAPE 3

2.07 Programming

Commence programming of project ('office' stages in detail and 'contract' stages in outline) by means of bar or network charts, critical path analysis or other management technique taking into account: availability of site; client's occupation date commitment; work load; staff capacity; phasing of project; re-locating areas within site to make other areas available for reconstruction; relations with other professions and specialists; labour supply; supply of materials; weather and planting season

2.08 Appraisal report

See information sheet LANDSCAPE 1

Evaluation

From preliminary data and site investigations (see record data above) evaluate site in relation to the project

Assets and liabilities

Establish which site elements are assets, to be kept, and which are liabilities, to be dealt with

Design potential

Evaluate design potential (genius loci) of the site and its application to the particular project

Report to client

Write report to client: appraising the site; appraising the problem; giving conclusions on relationship of site to problem; stating intended methods of proceeding with project; and appraising financial and management situations; expectation of planning approval; and probable programme. State, finally, summary opinion on feasibility of project

2.09 Metrication

Consider desirability of carrying out whole project in metric units. The official programme for the change to metric suggests that there should be very few new projects designed and documented in imperial terms after 1971. Type and suitability of project, availability of metric-sized products and components, and financial effect on client are factors which will influence decision

3 Secondary brief

At this stage brief is updated by client's reaction to feasibility report 2.08, and by receipt of more precise information on user requirements, by consultants' demands and by results of research into particular problems revealed by feasibility study

3.01 Detail user requirements
3.02 Further site investigation data
3.03 Programme demands from other specialists
3.04 Other constraints brought to light

Because these stages refer to specific sites, and specific project-types, it is not possible to detail them in this general design guide. Much of the thinking will, however, be found in the information sheets covering various landscape spaces later in this handbook

Design stage

4 Outline proposals

At this stage a definite scheme begins to take form, even though in broad pattern only. It is important not to go on to stage 5 *Scheme design* until agreement has been reached with client, and all consultants, on the suitability of these outline proposals

4.01 Zoning

The site appraisal 2.08 will have revealed certain areas of the site which are suitable, because of levels, climate, location etc, for certain purposes. By relating these to the user requirements 1.03, outline zoning plan can be produced for site

4.02 Site planning
Communications

Apply user requirement data 1.03 to site appraisal conclusions to produce communication pattern linking the areas on the zoning plan

Access

Ensure that layout meets access requirements for deliveries, furniture removal, ambulances, refuse collection and fire fighting services

Checks

Use association chart, string diagram or linear programming to check and confirm the relationship of zones to each other, and validity of flow pattern

Buildings (where landscape layout is associated with a building project)

Agree with architect on relationship of site zoning and circulation diagrams to outline building proposals to ensure unity of internal and external flow patterns

Services

Agree with civil and mechanical engineers on relationship of zoning and circulation diagrams to outline proposals for services, drainage, roadworks, river works, bridges etc

Other activities

Ensure adequate allocation of space for clothes drying, children's play areas, telephone kiosks, and similar ancillary items

Other factors

Study likely effects of noise, overlooking etc and adjust proposals to mitigate their effects

4.03 Revisions

As a result of 'give and take' process with other professionals and specialists, amend outline proposals to co-ordinate spaces, routes, levels, drainage, services

4.04 Statutory approvals

Submit for outline planning approval at this stage, unless already obtained

5 Scheme design

5.01 Creation of spaces

Masses and voids

If project incorporates buildings or civil engineering structures, consider:
1 siting of individual buildings or structures, in relation to existing topography; contours; existing trees and other vegetation; drainage pattern; enclosure, shelter and screening

2 siting of groups of buildings or structures in relation to each other to define external spaces; to create vistas and close views; to avoid wind tunnels, frost pockets etc

5.02 Circulation

Examine site

Movement of vehicles, pedestrians and objects between zones, between individual building units, and between building units and site entrance. Consider volume of flow, intensity and periodicity

Select form of horizontal traffic channels

Eg roads on, above or below ground level; paths on, above, or below ground level; paved areas (adjacent to or separate from vehicle routes); conveyor systems

Select form of vertical traffic channels

Eg slopes, ramps, parking elevators for vehicles; ramps, steps, staircases, elevators, escalators for pedestrians

Consider junctions and interchanges

Eg crossings, branches, gyratory intersections, overpasses and underpasses

Consider static areas

Eg parking spaces, paved areas, loading bays

Determine sizes of traffic channels

Consider: flow; direction; junction capacity; emergency use; peak loading; control points
Determine: minimum widths; radii; gradients; levels; height clearances

Plan control elements

Eg surface controls, fences, screens, rails, gates, doors, lifting barriers, cattle grids, hazards; signals and notices

5.03 Visual linking

Some spaces to be visually linked

Consider vistas, views

Some spaces to be visually separated

Consider privacy, concealment and surprise

5.04 Ground modelling

Consider features needing attention to ground shaping

Eg pools and reservoirs, tanks, spectator banking, flyovers, underpasses

Consider existing topography

Consider using: rising ground for views; hollows for privacy, concealment, water; slopes for seating, changes of level
Consider existing site water levels

Determine new ground modelling

For circulation gradients; essential changes of level; meeting building levels; controlling surface water run-off; offering or restricting views; creating interest on flat sites

5.05 Surface treatments

Decisions to be taken 'in principle' only at this stage

To encourage movement

Hard, near-level surfaces to vehicular standards
Hard surfaces to pedestrian standards
Semi-hard surfaces for casual walking (including grass)
Concealed hard surfaces, eg fire paths

To discourage movement

Hard, rough surfaces: ridged, stepped, cobbled
Semi-soft surfaces: ballast fill, thick gravel, sand
Soft surfaces: rough grass and planting

5.06 Enclosure

Decisions to be taken 'in principle' only at this stage

Consider need for enclosure

Eg physical boundary; legal boundary; privacy, security, control; demarcation only; wind shelter

Consider degree of enclosure	Eg complete, partial or slight enclosure; physical but not visual enclosure; visual but not physical enclosure; filtering; aural
Consider permanency of enclosure	Eg permanent, temporary, ephemeral
Consider character of enclosure	Eg insuperable, domestic, psychological only

5.07 Shelter

Some forms of 'shelter' are large enough to be considered as separate building types, in which case reference should be made to the appropriate AJ design guides

Consider need for shelter	Staff shelter (eg ticket office, booth) Players' shelter (eg changing rooms, clubhouse) Spectators' shelter (eg grandstand, covered seating) Animal shelter (eg aviary, kennels) Public shelter (eg bus shelter, park shelter) Vehicle shelter (eg garage) Materials, equipment store Pedestrian shelter (eg pergola, covered way) Casual shelter (eg awning, blind etc)
Consider degree of shelter	Eg against wind, rain, sun, view; overhead only or total
Consider degree of permanency	Eg permanent, temporary, ephemeral
Consider character	Eg fully private, domestic, open for view, public, functional, ornamental
Select location	According to need, purpose, pedestrian access, vehicle access, levels; avoid 'undesirable' locations in public areas

5.08 Planting (structural)*

Planting design is an art which does not lend itself easily to classified procedure; the following is intended only as a general checklist

Consider purpose of planting	Eg space enclosure; space division; boundary enclosure; linking buildings; punctuation; focal point; shade; shelter; screening; windbreak; acoustic filter; filter to dust
Decide form and density of structural planting	Eg woodland; shelter belts; screens; avenues; hedges; copses; clumps; groups; single trees; covert

5.09 Statutory approval
Building regulations	Submit for approval to appropriate bodies If applicable
Planning approval	Always needed unless gardens and site improvements only, with no structure above 2ft (610 mm) high, and no change of use
Other authorities	As relevant to particular project type, eg county fire service, river board; alkali inspector

6 Detail design

This stage deals with the preparation of working drawings for detail design and construction. Where they are specific to a particular landscape type, they will be dealt with in later information sheets. The design guide is only a brief check list of items common to all landscape work

6.01 Surfaces
Hard surfaces	Select materials and construction for surfaces to drive on; to walk on; or to discourage walking. Select combinations of different materials for large and small scale surface patterns
Soft surfaces	Consider materials and construction for soft surfaces
Junctions	Consider junction of each surface material with each adjoining surface Consider insertion of objects and materials into various surfaces
Trim	Consider which surface materials need edge trim; which materials need edge protection
Margins	Consider which surfaces need margins and mowing margins

*Non-structural planting is dealt with in para 6.08, which also gives more detailed guidance on plant selection than para 5.08

6.02 Changes of level
Construction	Consider method of changing level (eg ramps, steps)
Drainage	Consider levels with relation to surface water drainage
Slope surfaces	Consider face-surface of level-change (eg ramps, revetments, rock walls)

6.03 Enclosure
Construction	Consider form which enclosure will take (eg walls, fences)
Levels	Consider enclosure in relation to ground slopes
Openings	Consider openings in enclosure and means of closing them
Juxtaposition	Consider detail construction in changing from one form of construction to another
Space-division	Consider form of enclosure construction to act as space division
Planting-enclosure	For planting as a form of enclosure see information sheet LANDSCAPE 36

6.04 Shelter
Siting	Consider exact siting of sheltering elements; consider also in relation to levels
Materials	Consider materials in relation to function, durability, colour and so on
Construction	Select method of construction Consider possibility of ready-made, or prefabricated construction

6.05 Artefacts and site furniture
Focal points	Consider location, form and construction or purchase of fountains, sculpture, plant containers, masts, flag poles
Site furniture	Consider location, form and construction or purchase of seats, tables, litter baskets, signs

6.06 Water and rock work
Location	Consider location in relation to levels, function, access, water supply, drainage, overhanging trees
Shape	Decide shape in relation to available space, function, appearance
Construction	Select method of excavation and soil disposal; method of construction Consider method of marrying edge to levels, and detail of edge treatment
Water supply	Consider inlet, outlet, water supply, circulation, aeration, natural balance, maintenance
Rockwork	Study suitability of site for natural rockwork or constructed rockwork Consider type of rock, location, form, method of construction, levels, marrying in to surroundings, vehicle and crane access

6.07 Services*
	The following is a check list of main points to discuss with the appropriate specialists
Drainage	Modify surface levels to fall to collection points Consider effect of gulleys, manholes and so on upon surface pattern Consider effect of any other drainage elements upon surface pattern Investigate needs for subsoil drainage. Design subsoil drainage system
Water supply	Investigate possible sources of supply Consider needs for wells, pumping, tank storage Determine head, pressure, consumption, maximum demand storage capacity needed Prepare circuit layout

*Further information and guidance on the planning of these services may be found in the various sections of the AJ Handbook of building services and circulation (collectively classified under CI/SfB (5–)), published in the AJ between 1.10.69 and 7.10.70

Electricity supply	Consider electricity requirements for lighting, floodlighting, power take-off, pumps, fountains, and so on Determine voltage and phase supply needed Consider intake cable route, substation position Consider internal circuit layout; overhead and underground
Gas supply	Consider any requirements for gas supply Consider intake point and meter housing Consider internal pipe layout and outlet positions
Telephones	Consider telephone requirements Consider intake point and private branch exchange (if needed) Consider extent to which overhead wires are acceptable Consider underground duct circuit Consider effects of junction chambers on paving layout
Other services	Consider the effect of other services either to the site or crossing the site, upon the landscape layout
Maintenance areas	Decide size of maintenance area(s) needed Select location with reference to aspect, access, concealment Plan working yard, buildings, frames, lights, staff quarters, storage bunkers, glasshouses Include for all supply services and drainage, heating and ventilation

6.08 Planting (non-structural)*

Consider purpose of planting above eye-level	Eg area demarcation; space division; small scale screening, shelter, windbreak
Consider purpose of planting below eye-level	Eg underplanting; low covert; ground cover; pattern, colour, seasonal interest
Decide location of non-structural planting	
Decide form and density	Eg main shrub planting; shrub groups; shrub beds; specimens; borders (shrub, heather, herbaceous perennials, biennials, annuals); climbing, trailing, and wall plants; alpine and rock planting; water and waterside planting; bulbs; indoor planting
Prepare planting plan	Select plants according to factors given in information sheets LANDSCAPE 5 to 10. It is essential to check plants chosen for availability and cost against nurserymens' catalogues. The Institute of Landscape Architects publishes a list of recommended plants for landscape work
Grassing	Allocate grass areas Adjust width and levels to suit mowing Decide whether to seed or turf

*For structural planting see 5.08

Documentation and subsequent stages

7 Documentation

7.01 Working drawings

7.02 Specifications

See information sheet LANDSCAPE 3. Plants are usually included in specifications in the form of schedules stating number, genera, species and variety; height; and particular habit desired, with priced rate per 1000, per 100, per dozen or each

7.03 Bills of quantities

Required for landscape contracts of value of £4000 and over, and would be useful for contracts of £2000 upwards. Should follow elemental classification order described for specifications (information sheet LANDSCAPE 3)

8 Tender and contract stage

8.01 Tender procedure

See checklist in information sheet LANDSCAPE 4

8.02 Contract procedure

See checklist in information sheet LANDSCAPE 4

8.03 Subcontract procedure

Checklist on contract procedure describes situation in which the landscape work itself is the subject of a main contract. In many instances, however, the landscape work is a subcontract to a building or civil engineering main contract. When this is so, adopt following procedure:
1 Compile list of suitable firms, including client's and main contractor's nominations; check financial status and references, and visit nursery
2 Send out letters of invitation and receive acceptances
3 Send out tender documents, including drawings, specification, bq, form of tender, return envelope and covering letter
4 Receive back tenders, reject late submissions and those which fail to meet tender requirements
5 Pass to qs for cost check; notify unsuccessful tenderers
6 If value of tenders modifies total value of contract, inform client; if necessary negotiate revised figures with lowest tenderer
7 If desirable, place advance order with successful subcontractor to enable plants to be reserved, but warn that he must be willing to enter into a subcontract with main contractor, in the same terms as the main contract (enclose copy of relevant clauses)
8 Instruct main contractor to enter into contract with subcontractor
9 Agree dates for commencement and completion of work, and length of defects liability period

8.04 Plant supply

It is sometimes felt desirable to have a separate nominated supplier for plants, or a separate subcontract for 'supply and plant' as a way of ensuring that plants will be available in the right numbers and quality, and obtained from a reputable grower. It is desirable to visit the nursery and select personally the larger specimens—particularly of on-grown trees in large sizes

Appendixes

A Definitions

While the work of the BSI subcommittee on landscape work and definitions is not complete, there are about 650 terms defined in BS 3975 Parts 4 and 5 which are relevant to this design guide.

A few technical terms which are essential to the understanding of this guide are:

Genus (pl genera)
A group of closely related species possessing certain morphological characters in common, by which they are classified and distinguished from all others.

Species
A subdivision of a genus consisting of plants which have the same constant and distinctive characters, and which have the capacity to interbreed.

Variety
A subdivision of a species, consisting of plants which differ in some heritable characters such as form, colour or season, from what is regarded as typical of the species. It is also applied to a member of a hybrid group.

Cultivar
An internationally agreed term for a cultivated variety.

Perennial
Any plant which lives for more than two years (including trees and shrubs).

Herbaceous perennial
A plant with herbaceous stems and foliage and perennial roots.

Half-hardy annual
An annual, or a plant commonly treated as an annual, which cannot be grown in the open before the warm season of the year; usually of plants raised from seed under glass for summer display in the open.

Hardy
Able to thrive in a given climate all the year round without special protection.

True to type
Having all the characteristics typical of the original plant.

True to name
Consistent with the name under which it is described.

Hydroponics
The method of growing plants without soil in water to which the necessary nutrients are supplied (loosely applied to all forms of soilless cultivation).

Containerised
Of plants, having been transferred at some stage of development into containers for purposes of sale, transport or decorative effect.

Tilth
The state of the upper layers of the soil, in respect of size of aggregations, resulting from cultivation and/or weathering.

Firming
Any method of lightly consolidating the surface of the soil.

Lifting
The loosening and raising of the root ball of a tree or plant by the action of frost (FROST HEAVE), or wind (WIND ROCK).

Habit
The natural mode of growth and the general appearance of a plant.

Spread
The diameter of the head of a tree or shrub.

Feathered
1 Having lateral growths on the main stem. Used of a young tree with a single main stem.
2 Having lateral growth on the main stem, some or all of which have been shortened back to stimulate growth.

Standard
A plant with an upright clean stem supporting a head. Plants in standard form are described, in descending order according to height of the clear stem, as TALL STANDARD, STANDARD, ¾ STANDARD, and ½ STANDARD (INTERMEDIATE STANDARD and SHORT STANDARD are deprecated).

Large standard
A standard tree which has been grown several years beyond the size normal for nursery sale.

Topping
Of grass, lightly mowing. The first cut on newly sown or newly turfed grass areas.

Gapping up
Filling gaps in planted areas by replacing plants that have failed to thrive.

Beating up
Replacement of failures in a newly planted tree crop, normally done at yearly intervals after planting.

Tree work
The care and repair of trees.

Guying
The securing of a tree in an upright position by means of ropes or wires fastened to supports driven into, or buried below, the ground. Usually of newly transplanted trees.

Root bracing
The securing of a tree in an upright position by means of wire ropes and boards, or scaffold poles, tensioned across the root-ball below ground level, and fastened to supports buried in the ground. Usually of newly transplanted trees which cannot be secured by normal guying methods.

Modified forestry planting
The planting of larger-than-normal size transplants by forestry methods for the rapid establishment of woodland and belts.

B Organisations

Institute of Landscape Architects, 12 Carlton House Terrace, London SW1

Town Planning Institute, 26 Portland Place, London W1

Royal Institute of British Architects, 66 Portland Place, London, W1N 4AD

Royal Institute of Chartered Surveyors, 12 Great George Street, London SW1

Institution of Civil Engineers, Great George Street, London SW1

Institute of Park and Recreation Administration, The Grotto, Lower Basildon, nr Reading, Berks

Forestry Commission, 25 Savile Row, London W1

Nature Conservancy, 19 Belgrave Square, London SW1

Countryside Commission, 1 Cambridge Gate, London NW1

Building Research Station, Garston, Watford, WD2 7JR

Arboricultural Association, The Secretary, 36 Blythwood Gardens, Stansted, Essex

British Waterways Board, Melbury House, Melbury Terrace, London NW1

Civic Trust, 18 Carlton House Terrace, London SW1

National Playing Fields Association, 57b Catherine Place, London SW1

Association of British Tree Surgeons and Arborists, 11 Wings Road, Upper Hale, Farnham, Surrey

Association of Swimming Pool Contractors, 75 Marylebone High Street, London W1

Association of Tree Transplanters, Secretary, 100 Colney Hatch, London N10

British Association of Sportsground and Landscape Contractors Ltd, 76 Marylebone High Street, London W1

Horticultural Trades Association, Roman Wall House, 1 Crutched Friars, London EC3

National Association of Agricultural Contractors, Garden Section, 140 Bensham Lane, Thornton Heath, Surrey

National Association of Groundsmen, 108 Chessington Road, Ewell, Surrey

C Selective bibliography

Essential references

WEDDLE, A. E. Techniques of landscape architecture. London, 1967, Heinemann, £4·50 [08]

BEAZLEY, E. Design and detail of the space between buildings. London, 1960, Architectural Press, £2·10 [08·90]

NATIONAL PLAYING FIELDS ASSOCIATION Selection and layout of land for playing fields and play-grounds. London. Out of print [085]

MINISTRY OF EDUCATION Building bulletin 28: playing fields and hard surface areas. HMSO, 1966, 2nd edition [560]

MINISTRY OF HOUSING AND LOCAL GOVERNMENT Design bulletins 10 and 12: Cars in housing 1 and 2. 1966/67, HMSO [810]

Design bulletin 5: landscaping for flats. 1963, HMSO [08·816]

Trees in town and city. 1958, HMSO, £1·00 [Yx1]

Background reading

COLVIN, B. Land and landscape. London, 1970, Murray, 2nd edition [08]

FAIRBROTHER, N. New lives, new landscapes. London, 1970, Architectural Press, £3·75 [08].

HURTWOOD, LADY ALLEN OF Planning for play, London, 1968, Thames & Hudson [083]

BROOKES, J. Room outside. London, 1969, Thames and Hudson [084]

CROWE, S. Garden design. London, 1968, *Country Life*, £2·63 [084]

HURTWOOD, LADY ALLEN OF, and S. JELLICOE The new small garden. London, 1956, Architectural Press [084]

GIBBERD, F. Town design, 5th edition, London, 1970, Architectural Press, £4·20 [05 (G)]

INSTITUTE OF LANDSCAPE ARCHITECTS The urban scene; symposium report 1960
Organisation of space in housing

neighbourhoods; symposium report 1961 [06: 8]
Private enterprise housing and landscape design; symposium report 1962 [08: 8]
Landscape maintenance; symposium report 1963 [08 (W1)]

MONO CONCRETE LTD Paved areas (current edition) [08]

CEMENT AND CONCRETE ASSOCIATION Paving patterns. London, 1959, *Concrete Quarterly*, vol 43, 1959, Cement and Concrete Association [90]

DAWSON, R. B. Lawns. London, 1960, Penguin/Royal Horticultural Society [(90·42)]

MANLEY, G. Climate and the British Scene. London, 1962, Fontana [(E7)]

RUSSEL, E. The world of the soil. London, 1961, Fontana [00 (E4)]

Specialist references

CABORN, J. M. Shelterbelts and windbreaks. London, 1965, Faber & Faber [083]

AIR MINISTRY Climatological Atlas of the British Isles. London, 1952, HMSO O/p [(E7) (Abr)]

E & OE Planning. London, 1959, Illiffe, 8th edition [(E1)]

MORLING, R. J. Trees in towns. London, 1954, *Estates Gazette* [Yx1]

CONOVER, H. S. Grounds maintenance handbook. New York, 1958, Dodge Corporation, 2nd edition, £4·18 [087 (W1)]

MINISTRY OF AGRICULTURE, FISHERIES AND FOOD Leaflet 44: Mole drainage for heavy land. HMSO, 1960 [(11)]

MINISTRY OF AGRICULTURE AND FISHERIES FOR SCOTLAND Administrative leaflet 5: Shelterwoods or belts. HMSO, 1959 [083]

CENTRAL ELECTRICITY GENERATING BOARD Design memorandum on the use of fences. London, 1966, The Board [(90·21) (A3)]

INSTITUTE OF LANDSCAPE ARCHITECTS Plant. London, 1967, *ILA Journal* [Yx]

SUDELL, R. and WATERS Sports buildings and playing fields. London, 1957, Batsford [56]

Action	Subsidiary action
Agree measurement, re-measurement and daywork procedures	
Continue day-to-day supervision by c of w and regular (fourteen days or less) visits by professional-in-charge	Examples of items to be noted in supervision: Clean stacking of top soil and other materials; storage of materials liable to deterioration.
Inspect and approve samples*	
Inspect and approve samples* in-situ (eg plants, turf, examples of workmanship)	
Study of c of w reports	Take progress photographs
Make reports of own visits	
On receipt of valuations by qs, issue interim certificates	Copies of interim certificates to: client, contractor, qs, file
Keep client informed on progress	

Check list 5: completion procedure

Action	Subsidiary action
Prepare maintenance drawing and notes to accompany drawings	
Submit to grounds maintenance officer	
In advance of completion date, instruct contractor to be ready for inspection	
Inform client of date for handover meeting	Insurance by client from handover date
Arrange pre-handover inspection	Contractor's agent, foreman, c of w to attend Inspect; list defects and outstanding work
Instruct contractor to rectify defects and deficiencies and complete outstanding work by date of handover	
Hold handover meeting	Client, contractor, grounds maintenance officer attend Inspect site; client takes keys. Agree on maintenance by contractor or by client or his grounds maintenance officer, or by maintenance firm appointed by client

Action	Subsidiary action
Issue maintenance drawing and notes to grounds maintenance officer	
Agree date of expiry of defects liability period	Agree dates for takeover of maintenance functions
Instruct contractor to remedy any defects noted at handover meeting	
Issue certificate of practical completion	Copies to client, contractor, qs, file
Agree with client, then contractor, on payment of bonus, or claim for liquidated damages	
Receive confirmation from qs that all outstanding accounts have been paid to sub-contractors, suppliers, etc	
Issue interim certificate for the release of part of retention fund	
If maintenance work is by the contractor, supervise this work at regular intervals (probably monthly)	(Eg watering, weeding, firming in, grass cutting, pruning, hedge cutting)
Before end of defects liability period make a preliminary inspection	Client and c of w to attend Make a list of defects
Inform contractor of date of final inspection and send list of outstanding work and list of defects held to be his responsibility	Plants which have *died* should be listed for replacement. If plants are *missing*, establish whether or not contractor is responsible
Carry out final inspection to ensure that all outstanding work is complete and all defects made good	
Qs to prepare final account	
On confirmation by qs that no bills are outstanding, issue certificate releasing rest of retention fund	
Instruct contractor again (if necessary) to make good	
Receive final account and final valuation from qs	
Issue final certificates	Copies to client, contractor, qs and file

* Plants should be supplied *certified* as true to name and quality as this can **only** be checked when they begin to grow.

Section 4 **Basic plant data**

Information sheet
Landscape 5

Physical conditions affecting plant selection

In this sheet ALLAN HART *notes climatic conditions and site characteristics which limit selection of trees, shrubs and plants. Suitable types are listed in Information sheets* LANDSCAPE 6 *to* 9

1 Climatic conditions

Wind
1.01 Prevailing winds stunt growth on windward side of plants by reducing or killing new leaves and shoots. A sacrifice line of planting should be used to protect tender species. Sycamore, ash, and austrian pine are wind-hardy.

Frost
1.02 Many attractive shrubs and exotic tree species are more subject to frost attack when planted in areas other than south and west England*. Ground hollows and pockets of land between buildings trap frost; this inhibits less hardy species, but they can be grown if sheltered by walls or south-facing buildings.

Shade
1.03 Very heavy shade—either from buildings or dense foliaged trees—inhibits many plants, particularly discouraging flowering. Periwinkle and ivy provide ground cover and evergreen colour in shade. Box, holly and elder will form a shrub layer. Partial or dappled shade is beneficial for species such as rhododendrons, azaleas. Small or fine leaved trees (birch, rowan, false acacia) are ideal for providing light and shade, and cool, airy conditions for underplanting. Branch and leaf arrangement of certain trees allows sunlight through, eg indian bean, which has large leaves, but open angular branching.

Atmospheric pollution
1.04 Smoke, fumes and town grime restrict plant growth. Sycamore, ash, plane and poplar tolerate some pollution*. Conifers and evergreens are not recommended.

2 Soil type and natural drainage

General guide
2.01 Types of trees growing locally are usually a wise guide as certain trees have affinity with certain soils. This applies less to cultivated shrubs, but the soil's composition and chemical reaction are important*.
Where soil conditions are extreme (very dry, waterlogged, acid or shallow) seek expert advice before final selection. (See Information sheet LANDSCAPE 10.)

3 Water requirements and root systems

Water requirements
3.01 Poplar, ash, elm and willow are 'greedy-rooted', probably consuming at least 50 000 litres of water a year.

On shrinkable clays in south and east England, these trees may endanger buildings by depleting ground water. Other trees (willow and alder) have been adapted to growing near or in water. Small-leaved trees generally require much less water.

Root systems
3.02 Each tree species has a distinctive root system, usually of 1 m maximum depth. Poplars on clay may send out roots 90 m to tap water during drought. Upward branching (fastigiate) varieties of oak, beech, false acacia can be planted nearer to buildings than common varieties, but some fastigiate trees are unsuitable (lombardy poplar with greedy roots, cypress with dark, dense foliage).

4 Proximity of buildings, roads and services

Damage
4.01 Trees and shrubs have a continuing growth change, above and below ground. Damage to buildings, roads and drains may be caused by roots of certain species.

Shrinkable clay
4.02 On shrinkable clay, faster growing species (poplar, elm, ash) should not be planted within 60 m, and all other trees within 9 m of buildings and roads. On heavy soils in south and east England avoid poplar, ash, elm within 15 m of buildings and roads. After removing trees from clay, ground may absorb water slowly and swell for many years. At least one whole winter should elapse before building begins, to avoid uplift and distortion. There may also be subsidence through decay of old roots.

Damage to drains
4.03 Allow for maximum future root spread when planting trees and shrubs near drains. Otherwise, encase the length of drain in concrete at least 75 mm thick.

Nuisance
4.04 Nuisance from trees close to buildings and roads through shading and leaf fall is often exaggerated. Trees form wind breaks and filter dust and noise, which compensates for any nuisance. Common and red-twigged lime trees should be avoided adjacent to paving and roads as they become heavily infested with aphids which excrete 'honey dew' onto the ground beneath.

Sight lines
4.05 Only low growing shrubs and slender clear stemmed trees should be planted within road sight lines.

*Refers to tables in Information sheet Landscape 6 to 8 for details on tender planting, suitability in conditions of atmospheric pollution and planting soil type requirements.

Common name	Botanical name	Spread m	Soil type	Notes	Foliage
Conical (Broadly fastigiate)					
elm	*Ulmus viminalis*	9	1	T	DG
holly	*Ilex aquifolium*	6	1 2 3	(E)	DG
poplar	*Populus alba richardii*	9	1		PG
whitebeam	*Sorbus aria*	12	1 2		grey-green
mountain ash	*Sorbus discolor*	9	1 2 3		DG (berries in autumn)
Columnar					
(Narrowly Fastigiate)					
blue lawsons cypress	*Chamaecyparis lawsoniana alumii*	6	1 2 3	(E)	blue green
golden lawsons cypress	*Chamaecyparis lawsoniana lutea*	6	1 2 3	(E)	golden
crab	*Malus trilobata*	6	1 2 3		MG (white and pink flowers—fruit in autumn)
Tracery					
gold bark ash	*Fraxinus excelsior aurea*	15	1 2 3	f T	MG
swedish birch	*Betula pendula dalecarlica*	9	1 2 3		MG
rowan (mountain ash)	*Sorbus aucuparia*	45			DG (berries in autumn)
willow	*Salix vitellina britzensis*	12	1	f	PG (red bark)
swedish whitebeam	*Sorbus aria intermedia*	12	1 2 3	T	grey-green
honey locust	*Gleditschia triacanthos*	7·5	1 3	t T	PG (spring—yellow in autumn)
japanese pagoda tree	*Sophora japonica*	24	1 3	t T	DG (yellow in autumn)
laburnum	*Laburnum vossii*	6	1 3		MG (poisonous seeds—yellow flowers in spring
Picturesque					
Weeping					
weeping elm (grafted)	*Ulmus glabra pendula*	6	1 2		DG
weeping ash	*Fraxinus excelsior pendula*	7·5	1 2		MG
Spreading					
strawberry tree	*Arbutus unedo*	15	1 2 3	(E) t S	DG (white flowers)
indian bean tree	*Catalpa bignonioides*	18	1 2 3	t T	PG
golden indian bean tree	*Catalpa bignonioides aurea*	18	1 2 3	t T	golden leaves
mulberry	*Morus nigra*	18	1		DG
yew	*Taxus baccata*	18	1 2 3	(E)	DG

Table III. Small trees: Height 4.5m plus

Round					
almond	*Prunus amydalus*	7·5	1 2	T	DG (pink flowers in spring)
siberian crab	*Malus baccata*	9	1 2 3		MG (pink and white flowers in spring)
winter cherry	*Prunus subhirtella autumnalis*	6	1 2 3		MG (white flowers in autumn)
snowy mespilus	*Amelanchier laevis*	6	1 2 3		MG (white flowers in spring—AC)
hawthorn	*Crataegus oxyacantha plena*	7·5	1 2 3		DG (red flowers in spring—AC)
Columnar					
(Narrowly Fastigiate)					
yew (irish)	*Taxus baccata fastigiata*	3	1 2 3	(E)	DG
golden irish yew	*Taxus baccata fastigiata aurea*	3	1 2 3		yellow
juniper	*Juniperus communis hibernica*	3	1 2 3	(E)	blue-green
cherry	*Prunus Ama-no-gawa*	3	1 2 3		MG
Tracery					
willow leaved pear	*Pyrus salicifolia*	7·5	1 2		silver-grey
japanese maple	*Acer japonicum*	7·5	1 2 3		MG (AC)
willow	*Salix daphnoides*	6	1 2 3		blue-grey
golden box elder	*Acer negundo auratum*	9	1 2 3		
silver box elder	*Acer negundo variegatum*	9	1 2 3		white-green
mountain ash	*Sorbus vilmorinii*	7·5	1 2		DG (berries in autumn)
Picturesque					
Weeping					
willow leaved pear	*Pyrus salicifolia pendula*	6	1 2		silver-grey
birch	*Betula pendula youngii*	4·5	1 2 3		MG
willow	*Salix purpurae pendula*	6	1 2 3		blue-grey
Angular					
corkscrew hazel	*Corylus avellana contorta*	6	1 2 3		DG
judas tree	*Cercis siliquastrum*	9	1 2 3		MG (purple flowers in spring)
Spreading					
sumach	*Rhus typhine (female)*	7·5	1 2 3	f g T	(AC)
fig	*Ficus carica*	6	1 2 3	t	MG (yellow in autumn)
cockspur thorn	*Crataegus crus-galli*	6	1 2		DG (AC)
strawberry tree	*Arbutus unedo rubra*	6	1 2 3	(E)	DG
mop-head	*Robinia pseudoacacia inermis*	4·5	1 2 3		MG (yellow in autumn)
Open and arching					
cherry	*Prunus subhirtella pendula*	4·5	1 2 3		MG (pink flowers in autumn)
scotch laburnum	*Laburnum alpinum*	4·5	1 2 3		MG (yellow flowers in spring)
ash	*Fraxinus mariesti*	6	1 2		MG
flowering dogwood	*Cornus florida rubra*	4·5	1 2 3	t	MG (flowers in summer)
cotoneaster	*Cotoneaster frigida*	6	1 2 3	(E)	DG (berries in autumn)
	Cotoneaster cornubia	6	1 2 3		DG (semi-evergreen)

Information sheet Landscape 7

Section 4 : **Basic plant data**

Shrubs, ground cover and grass

In this sheet ALLAN HART *discusses the functions and uses of shrubs, ground cover and grass; describes their maintenance; and lists readily available species and varieties*

1 Introduction

Functions of shrubs, ground cover and grass
1.01 Shrubs, ground cover and grass should always be used in accordance with a predetermined plan.

Uses
1.02 Shrubs, ground cover and grass have many uses:
1 To cover ground not covered by hard materials
2 To relate buildings to the site and to each other, and to link external spaces
3 To demarcate boundaries and areas **1**
4 To accommodate changes in level and ground modelling
5 To give privacy, screening and visual barrier
6 To shelter from wind, dust, strong sunshine and to some extent—from noise
7 Structurally to create external spaces by enclosing or breaking up areas
8 To direct pedestrian circulation
9 To channel views to or away from buildings or objects **1**
10 To provide contrast in form, texture or colour, with buildings, paving or water
11 To contrast with or complement sculpture **2**

2 Shrubs generally

Planting
2.01 Shrubs are best planted in groups or massed together either informally laid out, in or adjoining grass, or formally, against walls, in raised boxes or in paving patterns.
Few shrubs have sufficient character to be used as single specimens. For maximum effect and to avoid duality or row effects, groups should consist of odd numbers and of only one species or variety, with single plants included only for special emphasis or contrast.
Width of shrub beds is important when viewed from above. The 'gardenesque' planting detail of smallest plants in front, rising in height to the rear should be avoided in larger scale planting; bold massing is needed to contrast with open areas or buildings. Changes in height are more effective when infrequent and between large groups of similar height plants.

Planting distances
Shrubs should grow to cover all bare soil. To achieve this quickly, spacings of 1 per sq m should be aimed at for most species, and even closer spacings for less vigorous lower growing types. It is possible that stronger growing shrubs could be thinned and transplanted to other sites as they develop. For ease of maintenance, shrub beds should not exceed 6 m across and rarely less than 2·5 m.

Height
2.02 The critical height is related to eye level. Plants which reach above eye level form a visual barrier enclosing space; planting below eye level is seen as either additional surface pattern or as a directional hazard if dense and prickly.
Shrubs vary in height from prostrate to 4·5 m to 5 m and may include those smaller trees which are many stemmed from the base (japanese maples, willows, mespius).

1 Shrubs, ground cover and grass in formal layout demarcating boundaries between areas and channelling view
2 Grass and background shrubs complement sculpture

Character

2.03 Because of the wide range of character, factors such as habit, flowering effects, breadth (in proportion to height) and whether foliage is evergreen or deciduous, help to distinguish different species and varieties of species. There are ten basic characteristics of shrubs and some species combine several characteristics **5**:
1 Bare stems **a**—all foliage and flowers are carried at the top of the plant in the light. These can appear gawky but stems can be hidden by
2 Facers **b**—shrubs with a complete cover of foliage from base to top (barberry, ceanothus, cotoneasters).
3 Stems with character **c** are very useful for vertical effect, bamboo, jew's mallow, flowering nutmeg, all with vertical green stems, and dogwoods with green, yellow and red stems.
4 Bushy spreading shrubs **d** which form a complete dome of foliage are useful. Planted singly or in small groups in confined areas (rock rose, broom, plumbago, daphne).
5 Shrubs with a distinctive arching habit **e** (tamarisk, *Rosa rubrifolia*) are best planted singly or in groups with under-planting of low growing species.
6 Columnar **f** shaped shrubs are best treated as scaled down columnar trees and used with discretion; similarly
7 Picturesque **g** shrubs (corkscrew hazel—with contorted branches, *Hydrangea villosa* with spreading lush foliage, the weeping *Buddleia alternifolia* and angular chinese juniper are best used as a single specimen, at a focal point of interest.
8 Large leaf shrubs **h** can be used for exotic effect, make an excellent foil against plain surfaces (fig, fatsia, aralia). Certain tree species if stooled at ground level will produce very large leaves eg false acacia, pawlonia, indian bean tree.
9 Prostrate **j** and creeping shrubs are useful for covering ground as they spread round stems etc (periwinkle, rose of sharon). Some prostrate growing shrubs (creeping junipers, fish-bone cotoneaster) are good as individual specimens.
10 Shrubs grown specially for large flowers **k** (hydrangeas, hybrid rhododendrons, azaleas) are best kept for massing with similar species and preferably 'contained' by walls or hedges.

Colour

2.04 In naturally occurring species and many cultivated plants, colours blend, but hybrid varieties often have harsh unsubtle primary colours. Stronger colours may be used successfully by grouping similar varieties and planting grey and white foliaged plants between giving a background for the bright colours. Very strong colours should not be allowed to interrupt vistas and should be used only sparingly in carefully chosen situations **3**. Flower colour is subject to seasonal change, weather and sunlight—conditions of infinite variety.
Carefully chosen shrubs can provide colour in various forms throughout the year. These range from different shades of evergreens, which may be variegated with silver or gold edging, gold, white spots or blotches (holly, aucuba), to deciduous species (deutzia, veronica, kerria), which can also be variegated, but these should be used with restraint and for effect. In addition to all shades of green, leaf colour includes red, purple, copper, brown, grey, and blue (glaucous).
Stems can also be coloured and can be effective in winter (dogwoods, brambles, birch, willow have stems of red, yellow, white and orange). Berries (firthorn, cotoneaster, viburnums) add winter colour with flowers (wychhazel, wintersweet, jasmine) supplementing green and gold evergreens.

Texture

2.05 At close quarters different textures of shrub can be used to complement and contrast with different species, hard paving and walling **4**. Texture can apply to stems and branches as well as leaves.

Ground cover planting

2.06 Ground cover plants can be used under taller shrubs or as low growing carpet. Essentially they are ground hugging species whose growth helps to suppress weeds. However, it is essential that before any planting begins, the soil is free of weeds, particularly perennial, strongly rooted types (thistle, couch grass). There should be a thorough maintenance of bare ground between individual plants, until a complete cover is formed. These types of

3 *Strongly coloured shrubs used in grass area for visual effect*

4 *Different textures of shrub*

a **Bare stems**

f **Columnar**

g **Picturesque**

b **Facers**

c **Stems with character**

h **Large-leaved-shrubs**

d **Bushy spreading shrubs**

j **Prostrate**

e **Arching habit**

k **Large flowers**

5 *Basic characteristics of shrubs*

6 *Ground cover suppress weeds, while costing less to maintain than grass*

plants (rose of sharon, cotoneaster, periwinkle, ivy, pachysandra) have to be planted closely together—as many as nine per square metre and therefore the initial cost is high, but once established should cost little to maintain **6**.

Plants for specific purposes

2.07 Shrubs are commercially obtainable for:
hot and dry sites (lavender, rosemary, heathers)
chalky soil (quince, daphne, barberry)
sunless positions (ivy, holly, jasmine, dogwoods)
moist ground (bamboos, willows, golden elder)
scent (lilac, lavender, mock orange, honeysuckle)

Planting for temporary effect

2.08 To produce a mature effect quickly, it may be necessary to introduce temporary measures:
1 Planting at greater densities for thinning out later. The success of this method depends on ensuring that subsequent thinning is carried out. It is expensive unless thinnings can be used elsewhere.
2 Positioning cheaper plants between the permanent planting, to be cleared at a later stage. Cheap plants are usually vigorous though coarse and difficult to remove.
3 Quick growing plants can be used as a background for permanent planting which will eventually obscure them. This method can be very effective, but care must be taken to ensure that the slower growing plants do not suffer through competition for light and nutrition.
4 Quick growing climbers will scramble over metal and timber fences giving vertical emphasis and screening.
5 Some quick growing tree species (leyland's cypress, lombardy poplar, willows) can be planted in large tubs to give temporary height. It is vital that they should receive ample water, preferably by some form of irrigation.

Planting on a temporary site

2.09 When a site is available for a limited time and will be put to some other use in the future.
Most of this type of planting should be recoverable for further use. To facilitate subsequent shifting it should be grown in large boxes or wire cages preferably sunk below ground to conserve moisture. Smaller growing ornamental trees can also be used in this way, care being taken to turn them round every year to prevent roots forming outside the container. Herbaceous plants can be planted directly into the soil as they are normally lifted, divided, and replanted every three or four years like turf. Topsoil can be lifted and relaid for further use if additional fertilisers are added.
Good seasonal colour can be gained with annuals and half-hardy bedding plants, which can be grown in tubs or other containers, particularly where little topsoil is available. This type of planting is relatively expensive owing to the

plants short life. Success depends on the displays being changed as soon as the flowering period is finished.

3 Maintenance of shrubs

3.01 During the first years of establishment, it will be necessary to keep planting weeded and watered during periods of drought. Soil around plants should be firmed after periods of high winds or frosts, and given an annual feeding with a general fertiliser at the rate of 120 g/m².

Pruning

3.02 The select list of shrubs has been chosen to exclude those which need skilled, detailed pruning—any pruning needed should be for the following reasons only:
1 Removal of dead, diseased, damaged branches
2 Removal of shoots alien to the character of the plant
3 Removal of old or weak growth
4 Removal of dead or damaged shoots
Immediately after planting, it is good practice to reduce shoots by one half to help to compensate for loss of roots during lifting and transplanting.
Where old shrubs have outgrown their area, branches should be systematically removed, perhaps by a third annually.
Suckers should be removed from the base of roots or they will grow again.

Maintenance programme

3.03 Future maintenance programmes should encourage shrubs and ground cover planting to spread as quickly as possible to reduce competition from weed growth.
Ground-cover planting should be weeded and watered. Most planting requires mulching with weed-free compost and ericaceous plants (genus of plants including heather) require mulching with peat. Plants such as ivy and periwinkle should have their new growths pegged to the soil with galvanised wire pins to encourage them to cover bare ground. Dead flowers should be removed annually.

4 Select list

Notes to tables I, II and III

4.01 It is important that these lists are not regarded as a substitute for professional knowledge of plants and plant groupings. They should be used only for preliminary selection. Plants listed have been chosen for tolerance, hardiness, good growth without much pruning, and to be commercially available at reasonable cost.

Key to abbreviations
Soil types
1 Medium loam (neutral)
2 Light alkaline
3 Light sand (acid)

Notes
T suitable for town smoke or industrial fumes
S suitable for coastal conditions and salt spray
N suitable for waterside planting (ie needs moist soil)
E Evergreen
t Tender (to be grown south of a line from Aberystwyth to Thames Estuary only, unless specifically sheltered)
f fast growing
Foliage:
PG pale green
MG mid green
DG dark green
AC bright autumn colouring

Common name	Botanical name	Soil type	Notes	Foliage

Table I Tall to medium shrubs: Height 2.5m to 4.5m

Arching

Common name	Botanical name	Soil type	Notes	Foliage
barberry	Berberis stenophylla	1 2 3	semi-E	
buddleia	Buddleia alternifolia	1 2	t	grey-green (mauve rosy-flowers)
cotoneaster	Cotoneaster salicifolia floccosa	1 2 3		MG (berries in autumn)
	C. dielsianus	1 2 3		
	C. simonsi	1 2 3		MG (berries in autumn)
escallonia	Escallonia pink pearl	1 2 3	E	MG (berries in autumn)
forsythia	Forsythia suspensa	1 3	f	MG (yellow flowers in spring)
weeping pear	Pyrus salicifolia pendula	1 2		
sorbaria	Sorbaria aitchisonii	1 2	f	grey-green (white summer flowers)
stephanandra	Stephanandra incisa	1 3		MG
rose	Rosa rubifolia	1 2 3		blue-green (pink flowers in summer)
tamarisk	Tamarix pentandra	1 3		PG (pink flowers in summer)

Stems

Common name	Botanical name	Soil type	Notes	Foliage
buckeye	Aesculus parviflora	1 2 3		MG (white flowers in summer)
dogwood	Cornus alba	1 2 3		MG (red stem)
	C.a. gouchaultii	1 2 3		MG (yellow stems)
	C.a. sibirica Westonbirt variety	1 2 3	t	MG (red stems)
	C.a. spaethii	1 2 3		MG (gold variation in leaves)
	C.a. variegata	1 2 3		MG (white variation in leaves)
	C.a. stolonifera flaviramea	1 2 3		MG (yellow stems)
hazel	Corylus maxima atropurpurea	1 2 3		purple (white flowers in spring)
chokeberry	Aronia arbutifolia	1 2 3		DG (red stems)
nutmeg plant	Leycesteria formosa	1 2 3	f	MG (sea-green stems)
jew's mallow	Kerria japonica	1 2 3	f	DG (yellow-green stems)

Picturesque

Common name	Botanical name	Soil type	Notes	Foliage
corkscrew hazel	Corylus avellana contorta	1 2		PG
corkscrew willow	Salix matsudana tortuosa	1 2 3	W	PG
sumach	Rhus typhina	1 2 3	f	DG
japanese maples	Acer japonicum	1 3		MG
judas tree	Cercis siliquastrum	1 3		PG
fig	Ficus carica	1 2 3		MG
mahonia	Mahonia japonica	1 3	E	MG (yellow flowers in spring)

Bushy

Common name	Botanical name	Soil type	Notes	Foliage
barberry	Berberis darwinii	1 2 3	Ef	DG
	B. Barbarossa	1 2 3		MG
	B. thunbergii	1 2 3		MG
	B. t. atropurpurea	1 2 3		red
deutzia	Eleagnus discolor major	1 2 3		variegated
eleagnus	Eleagnus commutata	1 2 3		silver
	E. pungens		E	
spindle	Euonymus europaeus	1 2		
veronica	Hebe. Midsummer Beauty	1 2	E	MG (blue flowers in summer)
daisy bush	Olearia haastii	1 2 3	E T	grey-green
firethorns	Pyracantha angustifolia	1 2 3	E T	(orange berries)
	P. atalantoides	1 2 3	E T	(crimson berries)
	P. coccinea lalandii	1 2 3	E T	(orange-red berries)
buckthorn	Rhammus alaternus	1 2 3	E T	MG
	R. cathartica	1 2 3		DG
viburnum	Viburnum carlcephalum	1 2 3		DG (fragrant)
	V. henryi		E	DG
guelder rose	V. opulus	1 2 3		GM (red berries)
	V. rhytidophyllum	1 2 3	E	DG
laurustinus	V. tinus	1 2 3	E	DG
snowy mespilus	Amelanchier canadensis	1 2 3		MG

Table II Low shrubs: Height 1.5m

Bushy

Common name	Botanical name	Soil type	Notes	Foliage
barberry	Berberis candidula	1 2 3	E	PG
	B. x. erwinii	1 2 3	E	P to MG
	B. thunbergii atropurpurea nana	1 2 3		red
caryopteris	Caryopteris clandonensis	1 2 3		grey
rock roses	Cistus silver pink	1 2 3		grey-green
herringbone	Cotoneaster horizontalis	1 2 3		MG (berries in autumn)
cotoneaster	C. rotundifolia	1 2 3		MG (berries in autumn)
spanish gorse	Genista hispanica	1 3	E	grey-green
dyer's greenwood	G. tinctoria	1 3	E	DG
veronica	Hebe pageana	1 2 3	E	
	H. Marjorie	1 2 3		MG
st john's wort	Hypericum patulum henryi	1 2 3	E	PG
lavender	Lavandula spica and varieties	1 2		blue-grey
shrubby potentilla	Potentilla arbuscula	1 2 3		PG
	P. fruticosa beesii	1 2 3		silver
	P. f. farreri	1 2 3		PG
bramble	Rubus cockburnianus	1 2 3		grey-green (white stems)
	R. thibetanus	1 2 3		grey-green (blue-white stems)
rue	Ruta graveolens	1 2 3		glaucous blue
david's viburnum	Viburnum davidii	1 2 3	E	DG

Picturesque

Common name	Botanical name	Soil type	Notes	Foliage
juniper	Juniperus sabina pfitzeraina	1 2 3	E	PG (branches at 45° angles)
chinese juniper	Juniperus chinensis	1 2 3	E	DG
european scrub pine	Pinus mugo pumila	1 2 3	E	DG

Common name	Botanical name	Soil type	Notes	Foliage

Table III Ground cover plants

The term ground cover planting used here refers to plants which naturally creep over ground and cover all bare soil to exclude future weed growth. Plants chosen are the 'easiest' of this group of plants which contains many hundreds of species, both shrubby and herbaceous

Common name	Botanical name	Soil type	Notes	Foliage
himalayan cotoneaster	Cotoneaster congesta	1 2 3	E	PG (berries in autumn)
bearberry C.	C. dammeri	1 2 3	E	DG (berries in autumn)
small leaved C.	C. microphylla	1 2 3	E	DG (berries in autumn)
willow leaved C.	C. salicifolia	1 2 3	semi-E	DG
	Herbstfeur	1 3	prostrate form f	
wintergreen	Gaultheria procumbens	1 3	E	DG
ivy	Hedera helix and varieties	1 2 3	E	DG
st john's wort	Hypericum calycinum	1 2 3	semi-E	MG
creeping juniper	Juniperus horizontalis and varieties	1 2 3	E	DG
tamarix juniper	J. sabina tamariscifolia	1 2 3	E	
oregon grape	Mahonia aquifolium	1 2 3	E	DG
pachysandra	Pachysandra terminalis	1 3	E	PG
dwarf periwinkle	Vinca minor	1 2 3	E	PG
creeping spindle	Euonymus fortunei	1 2 3	E	
	E. radicans		E	variegated
arrow broom	Genista saggitalis	1 3	E	DG
heathers	Erica in variety	1 3	E	certain species can be grown in alkaline soils; shades of grey, yellow and red

7

7 *Grass areas, with varying degrees of maintenance to demarcate path*
8 *Clear stemmed tree trunks allow easy access for mowing*

8

9

10

11

9 *Formal cutting regime to grass on hill—rough maintenance by pond*
10 *Grass 'naturalised' with daffodils*
11 *Power driven gang mower*

8 Grass
General
8.01 Grass as a surfacing material should be fully exploited, and not regarded merely as a convenient finish for space left unplanned. Because British climatic conditions are very favourable for the growth of grass, and because it is comparatively cheap as a surface material and for maintenance, it has developed as a major element in landscape design.

Use
8.02 Grass can be used either naturally in large areas with varying degrees of maintenance **7**, or as an uninterrupted spread of close-mown turf with neat edges clearly defining the area in relation to other surfaces. Its smooth texture emphasises land form and contouring, though care must be taken not to destroy the flowing character of the land form and the eye should be allowed to pass freely over the surface without interference from obstructions such as signs, structures, isolated beds of shrubs or plants cut into the grass. Clear stemmed tree trunks allow grass spaces to flow around them **8**.

Colour and texture
8.03 Grass colour and texture can give a restful effect, picking up all the nuances of light and shade, shine of raindrops, effect of breezes blowing over it. Colour and texture are dependent, as are the species of grass, on soil type and cutting regime **9** eg the pale blue green of fescue on well drained chalk soils, with harebell, orchid species, sheep's bit scabious, forming a well knit short turf, compared with the leafy appearance of meadow grasses on heavy damp soils.

Mowing and obstructions
8.04 Generally grass appears very smooth when closely mown and this can be effectively contrasted with less frequently mown grass, especially when wild flowers and bulbs are naturalised **10**.
For efficient mowing, multi-gang machines are used **11**. They are about 2·66 m wide, and need a turning circle of 10 m. Grass areas should therefore be not less than 3 m wide and there should be 3 m between obstructions. Where spaces are necessarily confined, a 750 mm motor mower

8 Grass

Seeding of grass areas
8.01 General procedure for seeding grass areas:

Lightly and uniformly firm the surface by foot or roller
Rake or chain harrow to provide a fine tilth
Remove all large stones greater than 50 mm
One to two weeks before seeding, apply pre-germination fertiliser at 90 g/m² lightly raked in. This enables rapid establishment of grass seedlings
Sow grass seed at rate of 20 g to 30 g/m² for fine sward
Sow grass seed at rate of 15 g/m² in general areas
Sow equal quantities of seed from two directions
Rake or chain harrow. Roll and cross roll with lightweight roller on light sandy or chalk soils.

Seeding seasons
8.02 Seeding season is best in late summer when soil is warm, air temperature is high and there is plenty of moisture available. This enables grass to become established before winter. Grass is an evergreen and will continue to grow slowly during mild spells in winter. Observe the following seasons for best results: North England and Scotland: mid August. South and West of Britain and coastal districts: end of August to early September. Spring sowings—generally April to May—often suffer from drought or drying winds which reduce resistance to pests and diseases.

Turfing
8.03 Turfing is more expensive than seeding but provides a quicker effect. Turf is sometimes used, in single rows, to provide an edge to perimeters of seeded areas. The level of the seed bed should be married into that at the turf edging. The component grasses of the turf should approximate those of the seed mixture eg fine or coarse.
All turf should be to BS 3936. Areas for turfing should be well firmed and have 75 g/m² of fertiliser containing bonemeal, sulphate of potash and superphosphate raked in.

Laying turves
8.04 Turves should be laid with broken joints in stretcher bond **17** with finely sifted topsoil well brushed into joints. Unevenness caused by local formation levels and differences in thickness of adjacent turves is best adjusted by raking or packing with fine soil. Do not roll humps and hollows. Standard size of turves: 300 mm × 900 mm (S. England), 300 mm sq (N. England and Scotland).

Turfing season
8.05 Turfing is best carried out in autumn to early winter, if it is to become established. Do not lay turf during frosty weather, drought etc.

Turfing to banks
8.06 Turves should be 60 mm thick if possible and laid horizontally or diagonally in stretcher bond etc as described, and secured with wooden pegs 200 mm long or with galvanised bent wire pins 200 mm long. On very steep slopes, wire or hessian netting can be laid over the turf and pegged down.

9 Waterlilies and aquatics

Planting waterlilies and aquatics
9.01 These are grown in soil which must be contained in order to:
1 Make planting easier
2 Enable plant groupings to be easily rearranged
3 Control growth
4 Reduce amount of soil needed
5 Prevent fish from stirring up mud on bottom of pool
Containers must be porous to allow soil to remain moist.

Preparing container or plant bed
9.02 Plant bed or container should be lined with turf, grass side outward, coarse hessian or plastic netting. This is then filled with good garden soil, fibrous loam chopped turf, clay and heavy soil **18**. Do not add any fertilisers, peat, leaf mould etc which are likely to cause discoloration of the water, also avoid acid sandy soils and chalk soils. Leave 25 mm to 50 mm between top of soil and top of container. Plant firmly and cover with 25 mm to 50 mm of gravel to prevent soil washing away.

Water level
9.03 If the pool is empty, gradually raise water level as the leaves of waterlilies etc develop. If full, lower container gradually so that the leaves are never completely submerged. This can take up to a couple of months **19**.

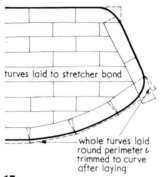

turves laid to stretcher bond

whole turves laid round perimeter & trimmed to curve after laying

17

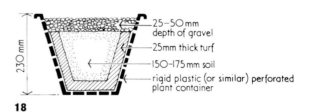

230 mm

25–50 mm depth of gravel
25mm thick turf
150–175 mm soil
rigid plastic (or similar) perforated plant container

18

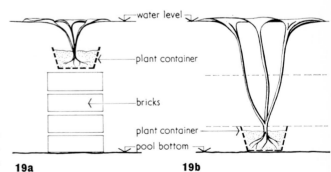

water level

plant container

bricks

plant container

pool bottom

19a   **19b**

17 *Turves laid to stretcher bond are not likely to be disturbed and, on steep banks, they can be further secured with metal or wooden pegs*
18 *Method for preparing planting containers to be submerged*
19 *Foliage of most aquatic planting cannot be submerged:*
a *If the pool is full, the container, on bricks, should be lowered gradually as the leaves develop*
b *If the pool is empty, the water level should be gradually raised as the leaves develop*

10 Compost for plant containers

10.01 Planting in containers, window boxes, planting beds in courtyards etc usually suffer from lack of water during dry spells, unless arrangements are made for irrigation to be carried out. A prepared compost which will hold moisture and still drain freely should be used. Depth of compost should be a minimum of 400 mm and as deep as 800 mm for trees. The following specification meets the requirements for water retention and is also solid enough to stabilise plant roots.
A lightly consolidated bed of compost consisting of:
Seven parts by bulk of good fibrous loam top spit soil
Three parts by bulk of coarse peat
Two parts by bulk coarse sand or grit.

All materials should be free of weeds and other extraneous matter. The topsoil should be within the pH range for the plants to be grown. After planting 120 g hoof and horn and 120 g bone meal should be added to the surface and lightly forked in.

11 Hydra seeding

11.01 A technique used to establish grass or other vegetation on steep banks, poor soils or inaccessible areas. It is also used to control erosion.
Seed and fertilisers are mixed with water and sprayed on to the soil by high-pressure hoses **20**, the surface is then sprayed with either wood pulp or chopped straw, mixed with bitumen, to form a thin mulch on the surface. Alternatively the area can be sprayed with latex, emulsion or glass fibre, all of which bind soil particles, fertiliser and seed together. Moisture is absorbed, but transpiration is reduced by the protective layer.
It is preferable to carry out normal cultivations before the mixture is sprayed on. If possible this enables plant roots to develop into the ground material more easily.

12 References

The following are recommended as further reading for Urban Landscape Section A, Basic plant data:

BEAN, W. J. Trees and shrubs; hardy in the British Isles. London. John Murray. 8th edition in 4 volumes. £8·00 each
THOMAS, G. S. Plants for ground cover. London. 1970 Dent (J. M.) & Sons Ltd. 1st edition. May. £3·00
GREENFIELD, I. Turf culture. London. 1962, Leonard Hill Books. 1st edition. £4·10
PERRY, F. Water gardening. London. *Country Life*. Out of print.
LE SEUR, A. D. C. Hedges, shelterbelts and screens. London. *Country Life*. Out of print.

20 *Hydra seeding bank too steep for conventional seeding techniques. In this illustration, seeded surface is being sprayed with a mulch of chopped straw*

Section 5 **Parks and open spaces**

Parks and open spaces: General

Many existing parks and sports centres are under-used at present, and represent poor value for money on highly priced urban land. In this sheet GERRY PERRIN *and* TIMOTHY COCHRANE *briefly sketch the historical background to Britain's urban parks and then go on to examine new planning trends and new methods of increasing the attraction of parks and open spaces. They analyse three examples of urban open spaces to illustrate the principles involved, and conclude with a list of key points for future design*

1 Historical background

1.01 Except in new towns, Britain's parks and open spaces are largely the legacy of urban evolution in the late nineteenth and early twentieth centuries. Central area parks in particular owe much to Victorian and Edwardian leisure patterns, tending to be places for Sunday afternoon perambulation, picnics, and boating, where people could observe nature (often their only chance to do so) and other people.

1.02 Between the two world wars suburban growth mushroomed, leaving pre-1914 parks to ossify, and creating a need for subsidiary parks, amenity spaces and—for the first time—organised play space.

1.03 Play space areas have for almost 40 years been based on an empirical standard of 2·43 hectares of play space per 1000 population, including 0·20 hectares for children's playgrounds. Such standards have been partly responsible for the loose-knit structure of the first eight new towns built around London after the second world war.

1.04 Recently, however, the increasing use of hard surfaces and floodlighting for outdoor sports areas and the increasing use of indoor recreation facilities, all of which tend to lead to more intensive use of space, have caused the appropriateness of these figures to be questioned. Some authorities have even advocated the abandonment of such standards altogether, believing that provision should be related to individual circumstances instead. Studies[3] indicating (*a*) frequency and patterns of use in urban parks, (*b*) time and money spent, and (*c*) catchment areas, are likely to become increasingly important as a basis for future provision, in place of the old empirical standards.

Future trends
1.05 With the value of land at a premium, attention needs now to be directed towards improved usage of open space; increasingly parks, play spaces, amenity space, and school grounds will be regarded as part of an integrated pattern of provision.

1.06 Co-ordination of management bodies and rationalisation of land use will be essential to avoid wasteful duplication of facilities. Where existing open spaces in central areas permit, leisure parks will be combined with intensive recreation areas (indoor and outdoor) providing maximum choice of activity—recreational, cultural, entertainment, social.

Such facilities will require spaces suitable for a large number of activities and, even more important, spaces within which new activities and impromptu happenings can be generated when the demand arises. In town centres, land values may often preclude large areas of open space, and indoor leisure centres in the town centre could be complemented by outdoor facilities in outer areas.

1.07 Industrial concerns are also beginning to combine with local authorities to provide facilities for the whole community whereas before they provided, on their own, facilities for their own employees. Surveys show that people apparently prefer to spend their leisure time at places which are open to all.

Similarly, universities are beginning to encourage sports associations to make use of their sports centres. Community schools are under-used assets with great scope for accommodating a wide range of leisure pursuits, but their management and organisation are not geared to developing their full potential as evening and weekend leisure centres.

However, there are some examples of this idea working, especially in Scotland; in such cases the schoolchildren have access to better standards of provision than they could normally expect.

2 Leisure in towns

2.01 The main types of open space in and around towns are the following*:

2.02 *Linear recreation spaces* Parks must be accessible from and linked to the rest of the urban area. The old concept of parks with finite boundaries is being replaced by that of a series of linear parks, for both active and passive recreation, linking all outdoor and indoor recreation facilities together like beads on a chain—shops, social facilities, recreation centres, and peripheral open spaces. Old railway lines, rivers, streams and canals offer natural routes for linear ways. Water has strong visual attraction, and can be used for boating and fishing, while disused railway lines can be used for footpaths, cycle tracks and bridleways.

* See also fig 1, information sheet LANDSCAPE 1

1

2.03 *Central open spaces* Shopping malls, squares and so on. These should be capable of accommodating multi-usage **1**—eg symphony concerts held in Mondawmin shopping centre, near Baltimore, Maryland; and demonstrations in Trafalgar Square. Covered shopping areas facilitate such use of space, while multi-level centres for intensive use of space in centres are coming in (eg Cumbernauld, and The Cannery, San Francisco).

2.04 *Recreation orientated housing developments* Housing grouped around recreation facilities such as a lake or golf course is a growing trend for first as well as second homes—eg Reston, us. Each group of houses has a distinguishing feature giving it its own separate identity. On a smaller scale, too, the sharing of communal recreational facilities by near neighbours gives a more positive unit than merely sharing a patch of open space.

2.05 *Sports centres* contain a number of indoor and outdoor games facilities grouped together. Usually include a sports hall with hard-porous floodlit games and training area. The following are the main types:
1 Commercially sponsored leisure centres—high entrance charges (eg Aviemore and Isle of Man).
2 University sports centres (eg Exeter).
3 School sports facilities.
4 Community sports centres (eg Harlow **5**).
5 National recreation centres (eg Crystal Palace **2**, **3**, and others specialising in particular sports).

Water sports centres are a special category and must be as versatile as possible to cater for both active and passive recreation. Such centres could either combine their natural competitive function with that of a holiday centre (eg Cotswold water park) or have a local and regional catchment (eg Holme Pierrepont—see information sheet LANDSCAPE 20, AJ 13.1.71). Notice that at both of these places activities are diversified and not confined to water sports.

2.06 *Rest and leisure parks* Combined sports, arts and social centres originated in West Germany (eg Gruga Park in Essen—see para 3.04). The idea is to give people the widest possible choice of things to do, **7** to **11**. If there is something to attract everyone the park will be more intensively used. The main requirements are:
Informal open spaces with children's play areas.
Indoor and outdoor sports, cultural and social facilities.
Spectator/audience viewing facilities with refreshment facilities and ancillary accommodation.
(See 4.03-4.06 for details)

1 *Multi-usage is becoming increasingly important in urban open spaces, where land value is at a premium. For example shopping street used for fair (Harrow)*
2, 3 *Parks are no longer restricted to catering for activities such as perambulation and picnicking. Cities also need recreation centres such as Crystal Palace, which can accommodate for example, dry skiing and motor racing*

2

3

Section 6 **Recreation: sport**

Information sheet
Landscape 12

Sports centres:
Priorities and planning
strategies

In this information sheet GERRY PERRIN *briefly notes the problems inherent in providing adequate sports facilities. He describes various types of sports centre, with particular reference to the advantages of large central sports centres and proposes a series of long-term, staged planning strategies for different sizes of population*

1 Present situation

1.01 Shortage of funds is seen to be responsible for the low priority with which the government rates sport and recreation. Our current annual expenditure of £5m on capital works for indoor sports centres—compared with that of West Germany (£48m), France (£35m) and Sweden (£21m) is in need of revision.

Regional sports councils and the DES technical unit for sport
1.02 Until 1 April 1971* all projects requiring loan sanction or grant aid will be 'priority-graded' according to need by the appropriate regional sports council[1]. Plans are then assessed in detail by the Technical Unit for Sport, a department within the DES, before going to the Department of the Environment for capital assistance.

2 Dispersal or centralised centres?

Dispersal system
2.01 *Planning for sport*[2] is a document closely followed by regional sports councils when assessing projects, and in it a case is argued for small facilities—a 25 m indoor swimming pool and a one-court sports hall **1**—which is interpreted as a pattern of dispersion on the assumption that many small centres thinly distributed over the country are more effective than a few larger centres. The report also strongly supports the provision of 'dual/joint use' projects, based on school complexes, shared by the public after school hours[3].

Implementation of dispersal system
2.02 This policy has been implemented in a number of counties, with sports centres costing about £250 000 serving basic needs of a catchment area of about 25 000 population. These normally contain a 25 m indoor swimming pool, a one-court sports hall for badminton, tennis, netball and basketball, refreshment/social accommodation, and often provide some indoor and outdoor 'specialist' features such as squash courts, an athletic track, diving facilities, or additional outdoor tennis courts, with grass pitches a low priority.
For a population approaching 100 000 at least two such units would be required, and they would be supported by about six small units (see para 3)—ie with a one-court sports hall and a training pool—costing under £50 000 each **3**. Before the second large unit could be implemented, there would be an interim period of limited facilities, possibly for 10 years.

* The Department of the Environment Circular *2/70* (HMSO 2s 6d) states that as from 1 April 1971 all projects (apart from the very large) will receive consideration for loan sanction at county council, not ministry, level.

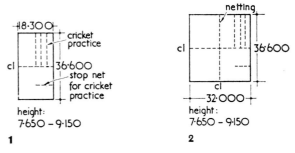

1 *One-court sports hall.*
Called a one-court hall because it can accommodate to tournament standard either one tennis court, one basketball court, one netball and one volleyball court, or four to five badminton courts. (Netting positions normally seen in practice are shown dotted.) It is worth noting that the French equivalent is 44 m × 24 m × 9 m, and the German 42 m × 26 m × 7 m
2 *Two-court sports hall.*
Doubles the number of courts listed for the one-court sports hall. Top class competition is normally staged in centre of hall with seating (usually of the bleacher variety) arranged around as required

Disadvantage of dispersal system
2.03 Studies of costs in use indicate several weaknesses in this policy. Most units report severe overcrowding within a year of opening, with no hope of expansion for up to ten years. Capital costs are two-thirds of those for facilities twice the size, yet the smaller centres require the same

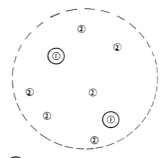

① dispersal' sports centre

② pavilion units

3 *Decentralised system of sports facilities for a population between 50 000 and 100 000 in a town catchment area of about 10 km diam. System would have two sports centres, each with a 25 m indoor swimming pool, a one-court sports hall and a limited range of outdoor facilities; and up to six pavilion units, each of which possibly serving a dual use function with local schools, and contain a training pool, a one-court sports hall and grass pitches*

amount of support area (car parks, circulation space and services), and as many staff, as the larger units. Pre-contract work (mainly committee procedure in negotiations between regional sports councils, ministries, client committees, and other authorities) is repeated for each project (see para 2.07).

Many small units operate at a considerable loss, whereas a number of larger units make a profit. Also, the favourable impact of large units on the public should be considered in conjunction with the general reluctance, where alternative facilities are available, for people 'to go back to school to play'.

Centralised system

2.04 An alternative approach already in practice[4] has been to build one large unit (a 25 m or 33⅓ m indoor swimming pool, a two-court sports hall **2** and a range of outdoor facilities that would include up to six grass pitches) to act as a 'generator' servicing a catchment area in excess of 50 000. As overcrowding occurs, or if the catchment area approaches 100 000, the 'generator' facilities would be relieved by about six small units (with a one-court sports hall and a small indoor training pool—see para 3) costing under £500 000 each, scattered within a 5 km radius of the 'generator' **4**. Such an example is Harlow with a population of 90 000[4]; a similar approach on a city scale is now being implemented by Edinburgh[5]. However, comparison should be made with West Germany where, for example, Bochum with a population of 370 000 has one international size sports centre, four district sports centres (each containing a 25 m indoor swimming pool and a '1½ court' sports hall) 28 local sports centres, and 56 very small, school-based facilities.

Running costs

2.05 The difference between the two strategies described in para 2.01 to para 2.04 is the annual running cost. This is over ten years (by which time new projects may be at the point of construction), the 'dispersal' method could cost up £250 000 more than the centralised 'generator' type of approach.

Other factors which should be considered at the pre-planning stage are as follows.

Land purchase
2.06 Land purchase for a double unit dispersal system is considerably more expensive than the purchase for one large unit.

Committee procedure
2.07 Each centre can occupy many months of pre-contract negotiations with regional sports councils, county councils, local council and related subcommittees (recreation, parks, education, baths and so on), the ministry, and other bodies such as sports organisations, neighbouring authorities and so on. The average time between inception of primary brief and completion of contract is up to five years.

User participation
2.08 Sociological research indicates that large centres generate a more intense atmosphere than smaller units. This seems to be partly responsible for the greater degree of participation that occurs in larger centres.

Planning for individual circumstances
2.09 The centre should suit individual requirements of the catchment area it is to serve. Difficulties occur when planning norms or ministry strategies dictate a particular approach whatever the catchment area, growth rate or socio-economic situation. Therefore each factor must be

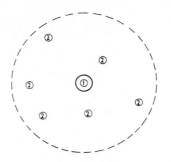

① 'generator' centralised sports centre

② pavilion units

4 Central or 'generator' system of sports facilities is for a population between 50 000 and 100 000 in a town catchment area of about 10 km diam. System would have a 'generator' or central sports centre with a 52 m or 33⅓ m indoor swimming pool, a two-court sports hall, outdoor training facilities, grass pitches and some specialised facilities; and up to six pavilion units, each of which possibly serving a dual use function with local schools, and contain a training pool, a one-court sports hall and grass pitches

weighed against the other (in the form of a feasibility study if possible) before a formal presentation is made to the client committee.

3 Sports pavilions

Function

3.01 Sports pavilions are intended as support units for the major sports centres of a central or dispersal sports facilities system. These units could be coupled with local schools and provide a dual use function until the schools or the recreation authority receive more money.

Description

3.02 (*a*) A typical sports pavilion described in table II item 1 would contain a two-badminton-courts-sized multi-purpose sports hall (18 m × 12 m approx), two squash courts, a cricket practice gallery, refreshment/social accommodation, floodlit hard porous training area, up to four grass pitches and optional tennis courts.

(*b*) A typical sports pavilion described in table II item 2 would contain a one-court multi-purpose sports hall, two squash courts, a cricket practice gallery, refreshment/social accommodation, an optional training pool, floodlit hard porous training area, up to six grass pitches and optional tennis courts and bowls greens.

4 Indoor only sports centres

4.01 Some recent sports centres have sacrificed outdoor facilities in preference for a location in the heart of the town centre[6].

Advantages

4.02 The advantages of indoor only centres are accessibility from most parts of the town by car and public transport; late closing hours (23.00—24.00) can generate activity in a part of the town which very often 'dies' after 17.30; and services (heating, drainage and public utilities) can be shared with other town centre buildings.

Disadvantages

4.03 Central areas are the most expensive to develop; if it is difficult for sports centres built there to expand to meet future demands; and there is the problem of car parking at weekends when town centres are at their busiest.

5 Recreation parks

5.01 The trend for urban recreation space to become more difficult to acquire in the centre of towns, favours the concept of indoor-only facilities, or those combining indoor provision with existing open space on the lines of the Gruga Park example referred to in Information Sheet LANDSCAPE 11 para 2.06. This new form of 'recreation park' could well supersede the more 'traditional' concept of dispersal or centralised sports centres, especially in urban areas where the only available space is in large existing parks, which are usually close to town centres. There is also a case for providing commercial facilities such as dancing, eating, drinking and gambling to offset 'loss leaders', publicly financed, recreation facilities provided as a non-profit making service.

References

1 CENTRAL OFFICE OF INFORMATION The sports council—a report. 1966, HMSO [E2p]
2 CENTRAL COUNCIL OF PHYSICAL EDUCATION Planning for sport—a report. 1968, CCPR bookshop [E2p] *Price 25p*
3 Comprehensive school at Bingham. Building study, AJ, 1969, June 18, p1645-1662 [sfB (87): CI/sfB 713]
4 Sports hall at Harlow. Building study, AJ, 1964, September 30, p769-780 [sfB (95): CI/sfB 562]. Building revisited, AJ, 1967, April 24 [sfB (95): CI/sfB 562]
5 Sports centre at Edinburgh. Building study, AJ, 1970, September 23 [561]
6 Billingham forum. Building revisited, AJ, 1969, August 27 [561]

Table I Cost comparison between dispersal and centralised systems

Dispersal system	Costs (£)	Centralised system	Costs (£)
For catchment area of 100 000, capital cost for two large sports centres (equivalent to one generator or centralised unit) costing about £250 000 each	500 000	For catchment area of 100 000, capital cost for one centralised 'generator' sports centre (varies between £350 000 and £580 000)	500 000
Increase in building costs over, say, five years before second centre is implemented at 10 per cent pa	125 000		
Capital cost for six small sports centres at £50 000 each	300 000	Capital cost for six small sports centres at £50 000 each	300 000
Total capital costs	**925 000**	**Total capital costs**	**800 000**
Annual running costs for two large centres at £30 000 + per unit		Annual running costs for generator unit (varies between £30 000 and £35 000)	
Annual running cost for six small centres at £1000 per unit		Annual running costs for six small centres at £1000 per unit	
Total annual running costs	**65 000**	**Total annual running costs**	**40 000**

Table II Planning strategies

Type of community	Population	Capital cost of facilities proposed (£)	Facilities and comment
1 Local community centre or village sport centre	1000—5000	30 000—50 000	Pavilion unit (see para 3.02)
2 Large village or growing suburb	5000—15 000	75 000—100 000	Pavilion unit (see para 3.02(*b*)) or two pavilion units as described in item 1
3 Small town, neighbourhood or large suburb	15 000—25 000	250 000	Pavilion unit (see para 3.02(*b*)) and a 25 m indoor swimming pool
4 Average town or small new town	25 000—50 000	350 000	One pavilion unit and indoor pool as described in item 3 and up to four pavilion units as described in item 1
5 New town or expanding town	54 000—65 000	350 000—500 000	Two-court sports hall, indoor pool and up to six grass pitches as described in para 2.04
6 Large town or town with expanding suburban catchment area	65 000—100 000	45 000—600 000	As for facilities described in item 5, (or double the facilities described in item 3) and up to four pavilion units described in item 1
7 Large town or new city	100 000—250 000		Up to four times the facilities described in item 3 (or double the facilities described in item 5) and up to eight pavilion units as described in item 1

Information sheet Landscape 13

Section 6: **Recreation: sport**

Sports centres: Planning and costs

In information sheet LANDSCAPE 12, GERRY PERRIN *dealt with long-term programming and types of facilities. In this information sheet he describes those facilities in greater detail, paying particular attention to costs*

1 Planning

Demand for indoor facilities

1.01 After the 'stadia period' following the 1948 Olympics, the need for running tracks and grand stands has decreased. Demand for further similar centres has been small, and present needs are mainly for more training facilities, particularly those associated with field events and sprinting. The demand for indoor facilities, however, has increased considerably. As provision for floodlit hard porous training areas has greatly extended the use of outdoor facilities, and the development of minimal maintenance surfacing materials allows their economical inclusion with proposals for indoor sports centres (indoor swimming pools and sports halls), such centres invariably receive a high priority grading when being considered by regional sports councils.

Function of indoor sports centre

1.02 The indoor sports centre provides the nucleus for management of all subsequent facilities and around it other playing units will grow. It should eventually become the focus for all major sports fixtures in the town and be required to liaise with other sports organisations such as schools, private clubs, the services etc.

1.03 Indoor facilities usually consist of a 25 m swimming pool, a training pool, a two-court sports hall, squash courts, secondary activity spaces, and refreshment/social accommodation.

Planning sports centres

High-intensity use facilities with floodlighting
1.04 Hard porous training areas (tennis, basketball, netball courts) should be closely related to the indoor centre **1**.

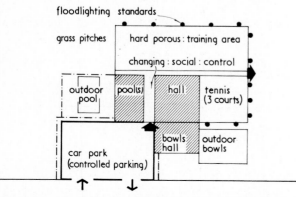

1 *Hard porous training areas should be closely related to the indoor centre for control and changing. Floodlighting is essential for optimum use*

Ancillary facilities
1.05 These usually consist of:
1 Groundstaff quarters, equipment and plant storage, and repair depot.
2 Secondary pavilion(s) for additional changing and showering provision.
3 Amenity areas—grass banks, surrounds, general planting and landscaping, children's play area, car parking and water facilities.

Grass pitches
1.06 Provision is usually made for grass pitches in 'traditional' sports centres, though indoor-only centres and indoor centres with only limited outdoor facilities as noted in para 1.04 have proved, after cost in use analysis, to be economically viable as well as desirable— see information sheet LANDSCAPE 12 para 3.
1 Two soccer pitches—one for training and minor league fixtures (in addition to the hard porous training area referred to in para 1.04).
2 Two hockey pitches—in many cases these are positioned on either side of a cricket table.
3 One cricket table—this should be large enough for one game a day to be played throughout the season.
4 Space for lacrosse, croquet, pitch-and-putt.
5 Two bowling greens.

Athletic training facilities
1.07 These facilities are often associated with a floodlit, hard porous training area (see para 1.04).
1 Two high jump areas and pits.
2 Two long jump areas and pits.
3 One triple jump area and pit.
4 One sprint straight.
5 Hammer, discus and shot-put circles, nets, cages. See information sheets LANDSCAPE 14 and 15 for details of sizes, construction and layout.

Facilities based upon local demand
1.08 These are often arbitrary, but frequently include the following:
1 Artificial ski slope(s).
2 Outdoor climbing facilities.
3 Water-based activities.
4 Outdoor pool(s).
5 Riding—including stabling and an indoor riding school.
6 Outdoor roller and ice skating (usually on the Continent).

Space requirements
1.09 Table I gives approximate land areas required for types of sports centres listed.

Section 7 **Recreation: general**

Information sheet
Landscape 18

General leisure facilities

After a brief survey of trends in leisure today, TIMOTHY
COCHRANE *describes the various types of facilities required to
satisfy these needs. Relevant legislation is listed in an
appendix*

1 Trends in leisure

1.01 Leisure (christened the 'Fourth wave' by Michael
Dower in his article in AJ 20.1.65) is one of the greatest
growth industries of modern civilisation. The following
definition has been proposed by the International Study
Group on Leisure and Sciences:
'Leisure consists of a number of occupations in which the
individual may indulge of his own freewill—either to rest,
to amuse himself and improve his skills disinterestedly or
to increase his voluntary participation in the life of the
community after discharging his professional, family and
social duties.'

1.02 More spare time and more money generate more leisure;
and the scope of leisure activities is constantly being
increased by the growth of mobility and education.

1 *Types of recreational supply needed to serve urban region.
Intensively used local facilities within city (eg linear
recreation spaces), and sub-regional facilities in and around
city (eg sports centres; rest and leisure parks), absorb*

1.03 Increasing mobility also means that accessibility is
now becoming time-based rather than distance-based;
many of the activities noted in para 3 are well within reach
of weekend, day, or even evening trippers, even though
being some distance away from population centres.

1.04 There is a great unfulfilled need for recreational spaces
accessible from urban areas, for both passive and active
recreation, not only to satisfy user demand, but also to ease
the pressure on vulnerable rural areas **1**.

1.05 An indication of the kinds of recreation demanded by
people may be gained from the ORRRC report[1] published in
the US, which noted that driving for pleasure topped the
preference chart, followed closely by picnicking, climbing,
riding and birdwatching, camping and caravanning, and the
more expensive winter sports. The popularity of traditional

*largest number of people. Regional country parks, picnic
sites and so on absorb most of remaining demand; national
parks, conservation areas and wilderness areas are therefore
relieved of excessive pressure. See also table I*

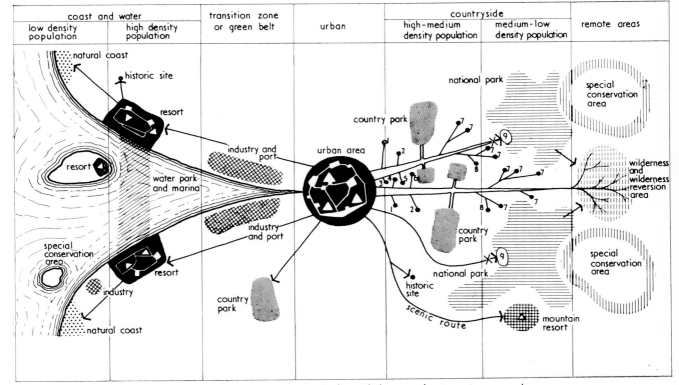

1. playing fields 2. golf 3. race course 4. water sports 5. show ground 6. athletics 7. picnic spot 8. beauty spot 9. car park

△ indoor recreation centre   X access control point

2 *Crystal Palace sports centre, example of subregional centre which attracts large numbers of users because it offers varied facilities and activities*

team recreations (eg football, cycling and cricket) is fairly static. The BTA in their predictions for the future that golf and sailing have the greatest unsatisfied demand, while swimming, riding and fishing also have great growth potential[2], [3].

1.06 The increasing popularity of active forms of recreation, requiring a lot of room, is exerting great pressure on regional and rural recreation spaces. This pressure can to some extent be lessened by the use of artificial recreation aids such as climbing walls, golf driving ranges and practice machines, rowing and canoe tanks, artificial ski slopes and so on, which enable recreational activities not previously associated with the urban scene to become part of it (see para 4).

1.07 Many of those preferring more passive kinds of recreation, such as driving out into the country, would also be happy to keep near the town if there were attractive places to go to. These need not necessarily be spectacular—as demonstrated by the depressingly ordinary places where the motorised hordes choose to picnic.

2 Financing and organisation of leisure

Commercial leisure facilities
2.01 These have to include revenue-earning activities such as gambling, eating, drinking and dancing, to balance losses made by other facilities such as swimming pools, which help to attract people to the centre as a whole but lose money ('loss leaders'). Private developers may be eligible for grants from the Exchequer, under the Countryside Act, for the development of country parks or picnic sites.

Publicly financed leisure facilities
2.02 These could learn valuable lessons from commercially financed facilities on how to pay their way, or at any rate defray costs. Savings can result if sports and cultural facilities can be combined, and joint planning by local and education authorities can help maximise the use of facilities*. Also several local authorities may join together to finance a project for the use of their communities, particularly where a development in a rural area is intended primarily for use of the adjoining urban area. Local authorities in rural areas are comparatively poor and can hardly be expected to pay for the recreation of their urban neighbours.

* See MHLG circulars 31/66 and 42/55.

3 Supply of leisure facilities

3.01 Leisure facilities can be grouped broadly into a hierarchy of four categories, as shown in table I. These categories overlap, and clear definitions or classifications are not possible except theoretically. This does not matter as long as a hierarchy of recreation areas of varying intensities of use is established.

Local spaces
3.02 The main types of local open spaces for leisure and recreation are the following. They are described in more detail in information sheet LANDSCAPE 11.

1 *Linear recreation networks:* parks, recreation centres, social centres, peripheral open spaces and so on linked together in a continuous, easily accessible chain of varied facilities **3, 4, 9**.

2 *Central open spaces:* parks, shopping malls, squares etc.

3 *Recreation-orientated housing developments:* a rapidly growing trend.

4 *Playgrounds and playing fields:* See information sheets LANDSCAPE 12 to 17.

Subregional spaces
3.03 Subregional open spaces include the following types:

5 *Sports centres:* Complexes containing several indoor and outdoor games facilities grouped together **2**. See information sheets 11 to 17.

6 *Rest and leisure parks:* Combined sports, arts and social centres catering for interests of wide variety of users. Gruga park in Essen is a good example; the idea has not yet been fully put into practice in this country. See information sheet LANDSCAPE 11.

Regional spaces
3.04 Regional leisure facilities include open spaces such as country parks and picnic sites, regional parks, and weekend and annual holiday areas, situated on or near the urban periphery. For example:

7 *Country parks and picnic sites*
Detailed criteria are outlined in the Countryside Commission's booklet[14] setting out policy on park and picnic sites. Country parks are loosely defined as sites over 10 hectares; picnic sites are under 10 hectares. The purpose of *country parks* is to draw off recreation seekers who might otherwise

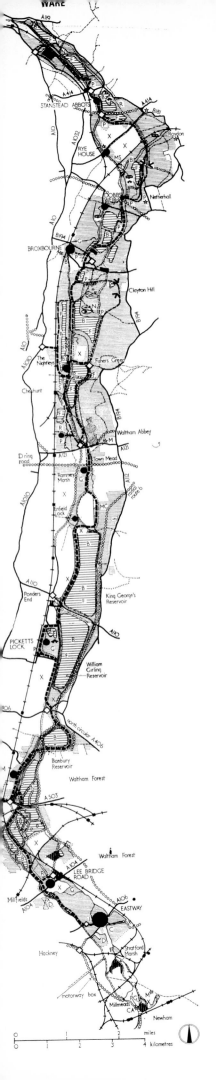

KEY
park road and intersections
car parking
viewpoints
existing roads
major road proposals
and intersections
footpaths
bridleways
nature trails
railways and stations : BR
: LTB
water
extension to flood relief channel
major recreational facilities
playing fields, open space, woodland
industrial areas
other built-up areas
golf course   G
pitch and putt course   PC

athletics   A
motor sports   MS
motorcycling   MC
cycling centre   C
dog racing   D
chalets caravans
camping
riding   R
nature reserve   N
swimming   S
fishing   F
boating   B
playground   PG
cultural activities   CA
museum   M
historic building   ☆
information centre   I
public utilities   X

3 *Proposals for Lee Valley regional park, an attempt to provide wide spectrum of outdoor recreational facilities within easy reach of city dwellers*

4 *Lee Valley already provides Londoners with some opportunity to enjoy riverside relaxation; such facilities will be made available to many more as development proceeds*

5 *Intensive and quiet uses at Elvaston Castle Country Park are buffered by dense existing woodland*

Table 1 Hierarchy of spaces for recreation

Category	Types of space	Examples
Local (urban)	Linear recreation networks Central open spaces Recreation orientated housing developments	Craigavon Dronton Agora Reston, Va. USA
Sub-regional (urban and semi-rural)	Sports centres Rest and leisure parks	Harlow Gruga park, Essen; Bos park, Amsterdam
Regional (urban-rural)	Country parks and picnic sites Regional parks	Elvaston country park Lee valley
National (urban-rural)	Weekend and annual holiday areas	Aviemore
National (rural)	National parks Forest parks Nature conservation areas	Not covered by Handbook of Urban landscape

drive out into the countryside, adding to rural congestion, and focus them into areas designed to absorb them. This eases the pressure on more remote recreation facilities as well as on agricultural or other rural interests.

Associated with the 'growth sports' (see para 1.05) and therefore often with water areas, country parks can provide for intensive outdoor recreation and education in the use of the countryside. Exchequer grants of up to 75 per cent of approved expenditure can be obtained.

An example is Elvaston Castle Country Park, **5**, which opened in March 1970, attracting 4500 visitors in the first four days. Close to Derby (with $\frac{1}{2}$ million people in a 16 kilometre-radius catchment area) this country park comprises 77 hectares of park and woodland with 81 hectares of agricultural land. A riding school, field studies centre and countryside museum are proposed for the future. Established landscaping allows a large influx of people without generating feelings of overcrowding.

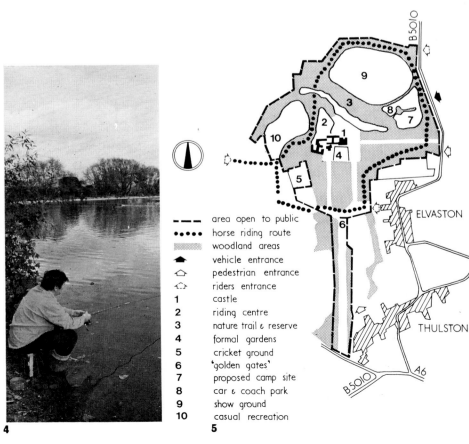

```
----  area open to public
••••  horse riding route
      woodland areas
▲     vehicle entrance
⬠     pedestrian entrance
⬡     riders entrance
1     castle
2     riding centre
3     nature trail & reserve
4     formal gardens
5     cricket ground
6     'golden gates'
7     proposed camp site
8     car & coach park
9     show ground
10    casual recreation
```

4

5

Another example is Emberton Park, Olney, Bucks. The original derelict wet gravel pits were converted into a recreational area in 1965-69 at a cost of £100 000. It was designed on a rather *ad hoc* basis, and on a shoe string, but its new status as a country park will probably attract grants for a proper realisation of its undoubted potential. The policy is to encourage those who want to picnic and wander freely, while also making provision for boats in the large lake.

London has many such areas—Hampstead Heath, Epping Forest, Wimbledon Common, Putney Heath and Richmond Park, for example, though none of these has as yet been much developed to provide for more intensive recreation and therefore to absorb more people.

Picnic sites can be classed in two groups. Transit sites provide for short breaks (half an hour or so) near the roadside; recreational sites provide a destination for day-trippers, often forming part of a larger recreational complex. Car parking should allow for picnicking away from, as well as close to the cars.

8 Regional parks
The Lee Valley Regional Park is the first and classic example of this category **3, 4**. Covering an area of 4000 hectares and 37 kilometres in length, it will provide for a broad spectrum of activities linked by the river Lee and a proposed new link road. It is more fully described in AJ 23.4.69.

9 Weekend and annual holiday areas
These are, in general, not urban areas, and therefore fall outside the scope of this handbook. See, however, information sheets LANDSCAPE 19 and 20.

4 Specialised recreation facilities

4.01 It has already been stated in para 1.05 that active forms of recreation are increasing in popularity. Data on the design of sports facilities is given in information sheets LANDSCAPE 14 to 17. The following paragraphs give planning data on a few other facilities which could form part of the urban landscape.

A comprehensive list of recreation facilities forms appendix c to this information sheet, this lists the facilities required for each recreation type, and gives the name of the relevant National Association to be consulted for further information.

Riding centres
4.02 Basic criteria for a covered riding school are outlined in *Basic requirements for a riding centre* (published by the British Horse Society) from which the following data has been abstracted:

1 Access should be available to countryside and bridlepaths; and buildings should include stables and associated facilities, offices, lavatories, car park and accommodation for night guard.

2 Minimum size of track is 30 × 15 m; 60 × 25 m for dressage and show jumping.

3 Outdoor menages should have an all-weather surface (sand and wood shavings) and be fenced all round; minimum size 40 × 20 m.

4 Grass paddocks should be ½ hectare minimum.

Artificial ski slopes
4.03 Slopes may be formed by artificial ramps (eg Thornaby Sports Centre), mounding or natural gradients, or a combination of all three. Mean incline about 1:3 (1:2 maximum

6 *Orienteering: a fast-growing sport which taxes both mind and body and ideally requires undulating wooded country*

to 1:5 minimum). Minimum useful length 15 metres; minimum width 8 metres plus 0·3 m for every metre of length over 15 m.

The slope should not achieve length at the expense of width. Ideally, it should be wider at the bottom than the top. If it is very long a number of starting points should be arranged. A startpoint (consisting of an adequate area of level ground, or platform) must be provided at the top, with easy access for people carrying skis. Main ski-ing area gradient should be about 1:3, with steeper gradients at the upper end and with the lower end levelling off to the horizontal finish area. Changes of gradient should not be too severe. Slope margins, particularly in the centre and lower sections, should allow for a smooth turf pull-out area free from solid obstructions. On the upper section where speeds are low a barrier, not less than 1 metre high, can be used.

A resilient surface such as turf is necessary as a foundation. Rock, sand, cinder, gravel or fresh soil are not suitable. Excessive growth can be inhibited by laying the matting on pvc sheet or hessian.

Severe irregularities in the natural profile should be graded out, filled or artificially bridged.

Finally, the slope should be protected from pedestrians, children and livestock and sited away from deciduous trees; and features such as floodlighting, partial weather protection, changing accommodation, equipment store and mechanical hoist will be required.

Artificial climbing walls
4.04 These can be outdoor (preferably) or indoor. Outdoor climbing walls need some sort of security to prevent access by unauthorised persons. They can be portable or form part of a structural wall. Proprietary climbing towers are available for use on outside walls.

Appendix A: legislation

Civic Amenities Act 1967
Strengthens previous legislation dealing with preservation of areas and buildings of architectural or historic interest. It also makes it obligatory for developers to preserve and protect trees, and gives compulsory powers to clear rubbish (such as old cars) away.

Countryside Act 1968 (Scottish version of Act passed 1967)
Sets up Countryside Commission to replace the National Parks Commission. Extends rather than supersedes previous legislation. Makes it possible for local authorities to

set up 'country parks' (over 10 hectares), to provide picnic sites (under 10 hectares) and camping sites, and generally to provide for better enjoyment of the countryside.

Town and Country Planning Acts—relevant legislation:
1962 Act   Major Act governing planning today.
1963 & 1969 Acts   Planning control etc.
1968 Act   Covers acquisition of land—also covers conversion of 'highways' to footpaths or bridleways for amenity purposes.

Appendix B: Organizations
Bodies concerned with recreation and tourism
Countryside Commission 1 Cambridge Gate, Regents Park, London, NW1
Countryside Commission for Scotland Battleby, Redgarton, Perth
They were formed from the old National Parks Commission and are the central source of reference and advice for local authorities setting up Country Parks, picnic sites and camping sites. They select and designate National Parks and areas of outstanding national beauty, and draw up proposals for long distance footpaths and bridleways. They also publish Research Registers which list all research with countryside and leisure problems.

The English Tourist Board 26 Chapter Street, sw1
The Scottish Tourist Board 2 Rutland Place, Edinburgh
The Welsh Tourist Board High Street, Llandaff, Cardiff
The boards encourage people within their respective countries to spend their holidays there. They are not concerned with promotion overseas, but they are concerned to establish a framework within which the tourist industry can function and develop, including provision and improvement of appropriate tourist amenities and facilities and to ensure that future demand and supply in the tourist industry are kept in balance.

The British Tourist Authority Queen's House, 64 St James's Street, sw1
Works closely with the Tourist Boards. It handles all promotion overseas (i.e. the Beefeater image!) and advises the government on all matters to do with the UK as a whole. It also conducts research and development projects (ie Pilot National Recreation Surveys—see bibliogr.).

Bodies concerned with sports
The international working group for the construction of sports facilities (Internationaler Arbeitskreis Sportstattenbau e. V. s. Koln-Mungersdorf, Carl-Diem-Weg, Federal Republic of West Germany)
Research into sports facilities, exchange of results and information at international level. Publishes bi-monthly magazine on recently completed sports/recreation facilities in Europe and America.

The Sports Council 26 Park Crescent, w1N 4AJ
Has been given powers under a Royal Charter to take over from government depts the job of developing sport in Britain, by improving facilities and thereby increasing participation.
It is no longer an advisory but an executive body, and will be joined by the Technical Unit for Sport of the DES.

Regional sports councils
Their function is consultation and priority-grading of facilities requiring loan sanction or grant aid. They en-

7 *A climbing wall: an urban facility for weekday practice for activities which take place in open country at weekends*

8 *Archery is typical of target sports requiring specialised ranges*

courage local authorities to provide better facilities for sports and recreation.

Central Council for Physical Recreation 26 Park Crescent, w1N 4AJ
Negotiations are in progress for a proposed merger of the CCPR with the Sports Council.

9 *A water and pedestrian network penetrating to the heart of a city from the country outside. James Brindley Walk, by the canal at Farmer's Bridge, Birmingham.*

Sports Council for Scotland, Edinburgh
Sports Council for Wales, Cardiff
Have similar powers in their respective territories.

School sports associations
Specialist schools sports associations are run by school teachers. The Associations aim to develop a basic interest in sport and to lay the foundations of skill in participation. National councils co-ordinate sports at school level, organise competitions and make representation on problems of school sport.

Local sports advisory councils
The councils help to co-ordinate voluntary sport and local authorities. They encourage local authorities to provide better sports facilities at town level.

Local authorities
Provide sport and recreational facilities in their areas, sometimes with other authorities and other bodies.

Local education authorities
Provide school and youth facilities.
'Dual use' provision by LEAs and LAs is becoming more common and is being actively encouraged by the Sports Council.

The National Playing Fields Association 57 Catherine Place, sw1
A voluntary organisation registered as a charity. It aims to encourage the provision of recreational facilities for all age groups, particularly with reference to village communities. To provide technical advice, information and research on planning design and construction of indoor and outdoor facilities and sporting activities. To specialise in recreation for children and young people. To raise funds and make grants and loans in furtherance of these objects. To co-

operate in saving threatened recreational facilities.

Insitute of Parks and Recreation Administration
The Grotto, Lower Basildon, Berks.
Concerned with management and design of parks. Runs courses for their exams.

Bodies whose primary interest is elsewhere, but who provide for recreation

The Nature Conservancy 19-20 Belgrave Square, sw1
A grant aided body, established in 1949, it is now part of the Natural Environment Research Council. Its primary function is to advise on conservation, while it surveys sites of special scientific interest and is concerned with the protection of natural environments. It provides research and study facilities, and carries out its own research. It manages the National Nature Reserves and helps to set up local and forest nature reserves, wildfowl refuges, and non-statutory reserves to which the public have varying degrees of access.

The National Trust 42 Queen Anne's Gate, sw1
A voluntary body registered as a charity concerned with the preservation and conservation of places of historic interest and natural beauty. It owns holiday cottages and promotes cultural events at its properties.

The National Trust for Scotland
The Trust has the same functions, in Scotland, as the National Trust above. In addition it runs interpretive courses, information centres and camp sites.

The Civic Trust 18 Carlton House Terrace, SW1
Concerned with high quality of townscape and to protect countryside. Advises on trees.

Forestry Commission 25 Savile Row, w1
The Commission's primary aim is the production of timber. They have set up forest parks on their land for public recreation. These may contain information centres and museums, hides and towers, camping sites, barbecue sites, picnic sites, nature trails. The Commission also manage the New Forest—not a forest park—also arboreta.

British Waterways Board* Melbury House, Melbury Terrace, nw1
Management of Waterways (canals). Under the Transport Act 1968 the bwb have a duty to maintain some 1780 km of cruising waterways in a state suitable for cruising, fishing and other recreational purposes.

The Association of River Authorities* 15 Great College St., sw1
This body represents the 29 river authorities of England and Wales formed in 1963, who are concerned with the management and maintenance of rivers, the conservation of water, the maintenance of water levels and the control of pollution. Most authorities provide facilities for fishing, boating and sailing, although quantity and quality varies with the authority concerned.

Water Resources Board exercises planning and advisory powers over the River Authorities.

The Arts Council of Great Britain Hayward Gallery, Belvedere Road, sw1, and 105 Piccadilly, w1.

* Negotiations are in progress for the separation of these two bodies into nine Regional Water Authorities: there is, however, strenuous opposition to the dismantling of the British Waterways Board.

10 *Pony trekking is typical of sports which need specially surfaced tracks if in or near urban areas and are intensively used*

Appendix C: Outdoor sports and recreations

This has been prepared by Timothy Cochrane with the aid of Fiona Wilton's thesis for Edinburgh University on recreation.

Selection of activities for the chart:

aims to be fairly comprehensive without getting too esoteric. It is based on the CCPR's list with additions to cover all activities which could be expected to take place outdoors in or near urban areas.

In this last context it is important to note that many country-based activities rely increasingly on urban-based training facilities i.e. climbing walls for mountaineering, many indoors, but which can be located outdoors in the urban landscape.

References are made mainly to other sources in this book; additionally three other major sources of reference are made to particular issues of the Architects' Journal. Photocopies of these should be easily obtainable from good libraries.

National Associations. For the sake of simplicity only British and English associations are shown. Many have equivalent Scottish and Welsh associations which have not been listed. Addresses—unless otherwise noted are in London.

OUTDOOR SPORTS AND RECREATIONS   *Including recreational activities which can be both outdoor and indoor*

Key: ■ indoor facilities   ◘ indoor/outdoor facilities   ○ outdoor facilities

Recreation type	Facilities			National Associations	Notes and Cross-references Bold nos. refer to information sheets in this book Nos. preceded by IS refer to pages of Indoor sports spaces (AJ 30.9.64) Nos. preceded by SH refer to pages of Sports halls (AJ 5.4.67)
	Local	Regional and subregional	National		
A Casual Recreation					Need for scenic routes and honeypots, 15-35 km average pleasure drive, wooded sites absorb most cars and people **18**
Informal games	○				
Motoring	○	○	○	Automobile Association / Royal Automobile Club / see section G for racing	
Picnicking	○	○	○		
Sitting and sunbathing	○				
B Environmental study					
Sightseeing	◘	◘	◘	British Tourist Authority	
Photographing and painting	◘	◘	◘		
Natural history, zoos history, archaeology	◘	◘	◘	Council for Nature	
C Entertainments					
Fairs, shows, displays	◘	◘	◘		Flattish, well drained, with vehicular access
Festivals, concerts, plays, exhibitions	◘	◘	◘		215 × 130 m flat grass with banking round
Meetings and happenings	◘	◘	◘	Various clubs and societies	
Chess, draughts etc.	◘			British Chess Fed. St Leonard's, Sx	
D Social activities					
Dancing and folk dancing	◘	◘	◘	Royal Academy of Dancing English Folk Dance and Song Society Royal Scottish Country Dance Society Welsh Folk Dance Society	
Folk singing	◘	◘	◘	English Folk Dance and Song Society	Enclosed 0·40 ha with banking
Parties	◘				

OUTDOOR SPORTS AND RECREATIONS (*continued*)

Key: ■ indoor facilities □ indoor/outdoor facilities ○ outdoor facilities

E Children's play

	indoor	indoor/outdoor	outdoor		
Playgrounds, adventure playgrounds		□	□	Various : see information sheets	**21, 27**
Model engineering		□	□ ○		

F Activities requiring access to the open countryside

	indoor	indoor/outdoor	outdoor		
Walking and hostelling			○ ○	Ramblers' Association	Needs green networks (old rail lines, canals, etc.)
				Youth Hostels Association	
Camping			○ ○	Youth Camping Association of GB and Ireland Cheshunt, Herts	**19** Big requirement for urban sites
				Camping Club of GB and Ireland	
Caravanning			○ ○	Caravan Club	
				National Caravan Council Ltd	**19** Big requirement for urban sites
				Motor Caravanners' Club Ltd	
Cycle touring			○ ○	Cyclists' Touring Club Godalming, Surrey	Additional networks needed away from main roads
Orienteering			○ ○	English Orienteering Association	2·4-16 km course length. Wooded and well configured area needed
				British Orienteering Federation, Edinburgh	
Cross-country running			○ ○		
Riding including pony trekking			○ ○	British Horse Society, Stoneleigh, Wwks	**18** Riding centres in urban areas with access to open country
				Pony clubs	
Motor rallies			○ ○	Royal Automobile Club	Normal roads : public and private
Autocross			○ ○	Royal Automobile Club	2 ha sufficient. Unmetalled surfaces : fields, etc
Driving tests		○		Royal Automobile Club	Any surface. 182 m max straight
Motorcycle scrambling			○ ○	Autocycle Union	Rough open country, heaps, pits
Cyclocross			○ ○	British Cyclo-cross Association, Solihull, Wwks	Rough tracks 16-24 km length 1·6-3·2 km circuit ideal
Hunting, shooting, stalking, beagling			○ ○	British Field Sports Society	Open country and woods
Birdwatching			○ ○	Royal Society for the Protection of Birds	**20** Private or controlled areas needed
Wildfowling			○ ○	Wildfowlers' Association of GB and Ireland, Sandy, Beds	

G Activities requiring specially constructed facilities

	indoor	indoor/outdoor	outdoor		
Athletics				British Amateur Athletic Board	**13-16,** IS 1286
				Amateur Athletic Association	
				Women's Amateur Athletic Association	
				Modern Pentathlon Association of GB	
Archery		□	□	Grand National Archery Society, Chelmsford, Essex	**16,** IS 1285
Shooting : small-bore rifles and pistols		□	□	British Field Sports Society	**IS** 1285
				National Rifle Association, Bisley, Surrey	100 m long
				National Small-bore Rifle Association	Pits and quarries ideal sites
clay pigeon			○ ○	Clay Pigeon Shooting Association	
Skittles	■			Amateur Skittle Association	
Tenpin bowling	■		■	British Tenpin Bowling Association	
Golf and putting			○ ○	Golf Development Council, Wimbledon, Surrey	**16-17**
				Royal and Ancient Golf Club of St Andrews, Fife	18 holes : 40-60 ha : 6000 m course length
				Ladies' Golf Union, Sandwich, Kent	18 hole pitch and putt : 3 ha sufficient. Driving range : 200-250 m × 100-200 m wide
Dry skiing and tobogganning		□	□		15, 15, 18, IS 1285 ; see also skiing, section L
Motor racing			○ ○	Royal Automobile Club	No minima required : existing circuits :
					Formula 1 : 4-4·8 km
					Club : 1·6-4·4 km
Artificial hill climb				Royal Automobile Club	Mean of existing facilities is : 400 m-2 km × 60-300 m height
Karting			○ ○	Royal Automobile Club	
Autocycle racing			○	Autocycle Association	
				Autocycle Union	
Motorcycle speedway			○	Amateur Motor Cycle Association	
Cycle racing			○	Cycling Council of GB Godalming, Surrey	
				British Cycling Federation	
Horse racing : flat			○	Jockey Club Newmarket, Suffolk	IS 1286
steeplechase			○	Jockey Club	
showjumping			○	British Show Jumping Association	
Greyhound racing			○	Greyhound Racing Association Ltd	

H Individual sports

	indoor	indoor/outdoor	outdoor		
Badminton	□	■	■	Badminton Association of England	
Batinton	■				**IS** 1275 (revised 26.4.67)
Bowls		○	○	English Bowling Association Bournemouth, Hants	IS 1276
				Crown Green Bowling Association Huddersfield, Yorks	**14, 16,** IS 1283
Boxing	■	□	□	Amateur Boxing Association	IS 1282
Croquet		○	○	The Croquet Association	32 × 26 m
Fencing	■	■	■	Amateur Fencing Association	IS 1277
Gymnastics	■	■	■	British Amateur Gymnastic Association Slough, Bucks	IS 1287
Judo	■	■	■	British Judo Association	IS 1282
Karate	■	■	■	British Karate Control Commission	
Keep-fit	□	□		Keep-fit Association of England and Wales	
				Women's League of Health and Beauty Thames Ditton, Surrey	IS 1286
				Medau Society of GB and NI	
Padder tennis	■			Slazenger Ltd for details of rules	IS 1279
Roller skating				National Skating Assn. of GB	**17**
Squash	■	■	■	Squash Rackets Association	IS 1284, SH 1492
				Women's Squash Rackets Association	
Table tennis	□	■	■	English Table Tennis Association	IS 1280 (revised 26.4.67)
Tennis	○	□	□	Lawn Tennis Association	**14, 16,** IS 1280 (revised 26.4.67)
Trampolining	□	■	■	British Trampoline Federation Northolt Middx.	IS 1286
Weightlifting	■	■	■	British Amateur Weightlifting Association Oxford	IS 1282
Wrestling	■	■	■	British Amateur Wrestling Association	IS 1282

comfort standards than camping. Until the regulations change mobile homes will have to fill the need (a pair of wheels, however small, gives exemption from regulations.)

Type of leisure homes
5.03 *Chalets, cabins, summerhouses* Basically one room, or one room with sleeping alcove accommodation. These could be treated in much the same way as static caravan sites for 'mobile homes'.

Individual houses, cottages, bungalows Buying up existing property often excludes local inhabitants from the property market. 'Individual' houses tend to develop into a sprawling mass of holiday homes.

Holiday house developments In the past, these have been badly sited, badly planned and sprawling. New developments must be sited with care, compact and integrated into the landscape.

Flats There are many examples in high-amenity urban areas on the French coast **8**.

Open space requirements for holiday homes
5.04 *Urban holiday and recreation area* Flats, holiday houses, chalets, caravan and camping. Requirements are minimal, owing to the many alternative outdoor and indoor recreation facilities available.

Rural holiday and recreation areas. As above; there should be open space all round the development, but the development itself should be kept compact to avoid sprawl and to minimise distance from house to facilities and open space.

Remote individual holiday cottages. Much enjoyment comes merely from living in rural surroundings, providing pleasant enclosures and opportunities for activities completely different from urban life. Unfortunately as more people become aware of this, the remote soon becomes unremote and subtopia sets in.

Low-density living has many advantages; how can it be reconciled with the need to conserve open spaces?

6 Legislation

Control
6.01 Caravan sites are controlled under the Caravan Sites and Control of Development Act 1960, which covers licensing and control of sites. Its successor, the Caravan Sites Act 1968, extends its scope and deals mainly with protection of dwellers and provision of facilities for gypsies.

6.02 Caravan operators must obtain planning permission, and a site licence from the local planning authority must be prominently displayed on the site. These are not required if caravans are used in conjunction with dwelling houses, are on the site for less than 28 days in a year and are under the auspices of an approved recreational organisation, or are used in connection with building or agricultural operations or travelling showmen. Local authorities themselves can provide caravan sites.

6.03 Camping sites for tents are controlled under the Public Health Act 1936 and the Town and Country Planning Acts.

Standards for caravan sites
6.04 *Permanent residential caravan sites* Requirements are as follows. Caravans should be at least 6 m apart and not less than 3 m from a carriageway.

Density should not exceed 50 caravans per hectare (considered by many to be much too low).

Roads should be at least 4 m wide (2·7 m for one-way traffic). Footpaths should be at least 0·7 m wide.

No caravan or toilet block should be over 45 m from a road.

Each caravan should have a hard-standing and refuse bin. Provision for fire-fighting equipment, water supply, drainage, sanitation and washing facilities are specified.

Lockable covered storage space, at least 2·8 m² per caravan, to be provided not less than 4·5 m from any other caravan, but separate from the caravan served.

Properly surfaced parking space for a minimum of one car for three caravan standings is specified. Other spaces, not necessarily surfaced, should bring the provision up to one parking space per caravan.

An area equivalent to one-tenth of the site area to be devoted to recreational purpose.

6.05 *Holiday caravan sites* (sites in regular summer use). Density should not exceed 62 caravans per hectare. Where densities are 30 to the hectare or less, no standing should be more than 5·4 m from a water stand pipe.

Standards of water supply, drainage, washing facilities, paving, footpaths, storage facilities and hardstandings are less stringent than those for residential sites.

References

1 BEAZLEY, E. Designed for recreation. London, 1969. Faber & Faber [083] *Price* £5·00

2 HOOKWAY, R. J. S. Leisure. London, 1970, Countryside Commission. [083(E2p)] *Free*

3 LYNCH, K. Site planning. Cambridge, Massachusetts, 1962, MIT Press [0] *Price* £3·75

4 WILSON, R. Mobility. *Architectural Design*, 1967, May, p217–223 [87]

5 KASPAR, K. Holiday houses. London, 1967, Thames & Hudson. [845] *Price* £5·25

6 CLOUT, H. D. Second homes in France. *Journal of the Town Planning Institute*, 1969, December, p440–443 [845]

7 Second home communities. *Architectural Record*, 1965, November p143–158 [845]

9 MINISTRY OF HOUSING AND LOCAL GOVERNMENT. Caravan parks—location, layout, landscape. 1962, HMSO. [87]

10 NATIONAL CARAVAN COUNCIL. A manual of caravan park development and operation. London, 1970, The council [87] *Price* £2·00

11 CARAVAN CLUB OF GREAT BRITAIN AND IRELAND. Caravans and the English landscape. London, 1957, The club [87]

12 BRITISH TRAVEL ASSOCIATION. Caravan and camping sites 1970. London, 1970, The association [87]

13 Caravan sites and control of development act, 1960, and model standards. HMSO [87(Ajk)]

14 Caravan sites and control of development act, 1960: Twin unit caravans Circ. 17/65. 1965, HMSO

15 Caravan sites and control of development act, 1960: Circ. 49/68, 1968, HMSO

16 NATIONAL CARAVAN COUNCIL/BTA. Report on short-stay conference. London, 1969, The council. £0·25

17 BRITISH STANDARDS INSTITUTION. BS CP 310, 1952, HMSO

Organisations

Camping Club of Great Britain and Ireland, 11 Lower Grosvenor Place, London SW1 (01-828 9235)

Caravan Club, 65 South Molton Street, London W1 (01-629 6441)

The Motor Caravanners' Club Ltd, 22 Chiswick High Road, London W4 (01-994 3158)

The National Caravan Council Ltd, Sackville House, 40 Piccadilly, London W1 (01-734 3681)

The Forestry Commission, 25 Sackville Road, London W1 (01-734 0221)

Information sheet Landscape 20

Section 7: **Recreation: general**

Water recreation

In this information sheet TIMOTHY COCHRANE *describes the principal sports and pastimes in, on and around water, lists their requirements and illustrates three examples of water sports centres*

1 Introduction

Water in the urban landscape scene
1.01 Though perhaps the greatest magnet in the urban scene and certainly the focal point of much recreation, water is only now beginning to be exploited properly. Use of rivers and canals as bases for linear park systems is growing, while water-based leisure complexes are being formed in the Lee and Colne valleys near London and by the Trent near Nottingham.

Multi-use
1.02 Inland water areas are subject to conflicting demands. On one hand is the day tripper's desire for at least a view of the water, if not for complete access for the increasingly popular participation in water sports. At the same time there is urgent need for more drinking water supplies, and increasing interest in wild life conservation. Multi-use is therefore inevitable and though some incompatibilities arise, they can be lessened by space zoning and time tabling (see tables I and II).

2 Water resources

Tables I and II show suitability and incompatibility of locations for water sport, and **1** shows types of inland water available.

Natural lakes
2.01 England's relatively few lakes have attracted visitors for many years, and areas such as the Lake District are now seriously overcrowded during the holiday season, whereas Scotland and Wales have many remote lakes far from population centres.

Artificial lakes
2.02 Though it is unusual for large lakes to be created for purely recreational use, existing water areas—mostly lagoons in old gravel or clay pits—are enlarged and reshaped as at the National Water Sports centre at Holme Pierrepont, Nottingham **2**.

Enlarged gravel pits
2.03 Appearing rapidly along river valleys, these have great potential, especially in helping to form large new parks such as the Cotswold water park and the Lee Valley and Colne Valley regional parks.

Canal feeder reservoirs
2.04 These reservoirs, which maintain the water level in canals, are usually owned by British Waterways Board, who may not, however, have riparian rights.

Compensation reservoirs
2.05 Most recreational uses are easily accommodated if the water is not to be drunk, eg on Snowdonia's Tryweryn compensation reservoir, which regulates the natural flow of the river.

Supply reservoirs
2.06 There is great variation in the policy of different water boards on permitting the use of reservoirs for recreation. Boards in Gloucestershire, Somerset and Derbyshire have been the most progressive. Usage depends on the water's natural purity and the consequent amount of purification required. Recreational use can obviously be allowed if the water has to be purified, but in highland areas such as

Table I *Compatibility of watersports*

	Fishing	Swimming	Subaqua	Wildfowl	Canoeing	Rowing	Sailing	Waterski-ing	Hydroplaning	Powerboats	Cruising
Fishing		X	X		PZ	PZ	PZ	X	X	X	PZ
Swimming	X			Z		Z	Z	Z	Z		Z
Subaqua	X					PZ	PZ	PZ	PZ	PZ	Z
Wildfowl		Z						X	X	X	
Canoeing	PZ					PZ	PZ	PZ	PZ	PZ	
Rowing	PZ	Z	PZ		PZ		PZ	P	P	P	PZ
Sailing	PZ	Z	PZ		PZ	PZ		PZ	PZ	PZ	Z
Waterski-ing	X	Z	PZ	X	PZ	P	PZ		PZ	PZ	N/A
Hydroplaning	X	Z	PZ	X	PZ	P	PZ	PZ			N/A
Powerboats	X		PZ	X	PZ	P	PZ	PZ	PZ		N/A
Cruising	PZ	Z	Z			PZ	Z	N/A	N/A	N/A	

Key X incompatible; P programming; Z zoning; N/A not applicable

Table II *Areas suitable for watersports*

	Lakes	Canal feeders and compensation reservoirs	Water supply reservoirs	Rivers	Canals	Sea
Fishing	X	X	X	X	X	X
Swimming	X			X		X
Surfing	X					X
Subaqua	X			X		X
Diving	X	X	X	X	X	
Wildfowl	X	X	X	X		X
Canoeing	X	X	X	X	X	X
Sailing	X	X	X	X		X
Waterskiing	X	X				X
Hydroplaning	X	X				
Powerboats	X	X				X
Cruising	X	X		X	X	X

Dartmoor, where water can be taken almost straight for drinking, purification entails considerable extra cost. In any case, additional roads and car parks, buildings, slipways etc are necessary. Water level may fluctuate.

Club membership is usually required for ease of control over fishing, sailing and canoeing. Water ski-ing, bathing and sub-aqua are rarely allowed.

Rivers

2.07 Freshwater rivers are controlled by the appropriate river authorities. Tidal rivers are often controlled by port authorities.

Uses: sailing, canoeing, rowing, cruising **6**. (Though water ski-ing does take place on rivers, it is discouraged as it causes bank erosion.)

Canals

2.08 Canals offer great potential for relieving overcrowding in popular waterways such as the Thames and Norfolk Broads. They could be made to pay by encouraging commercial as well as recreational traffic, and their use as water supply for irrigation and industry and as a permanent water 'grid'.

3 Recreations and their requirements

Sailing

Launching and mooring facilities

3.01 Dinghies need a hard beach or, preferably a slipway down which cars may reverse, allowing boats to be floated off trailers. Width must be enough to take car and trailer safely and allow room for persons helping launching. Slipways should extend to low water mark and are best set back into the bank to avoid obstructing navigation. Dinghies do not require moorings: for temporary tying up during sailing hours a slipway is adequate.

Keel boats need moorings or—particularly to facilitate winter storage and maintenance—some form of lifting device. Mooring must be to a jetty, or if there is considerable change in water level, a floating pontoon which will not foul the boat.

Building, car parks and storage

3.02 Lavatories and simple changing and washroom accommodation are essential. Sewage disposal near reservoirs must be into a public sewer or by means of a chemical process.

Parking space is needed for sailors' cars and trailers and for visitors' cars.

Boat storage sheds are advantageous but not essential. A shed and/or trestles is useful for storing spares. A covered store for other small equipment can be incorporated with other buildings.

Water requirements

3.03 *Area:* less than 4 hectares are used for competitive and recreational dinghy sailing, but the Royal Yachting Association recommends a minimum of 6 hectares. Boat density on inland waters may be in the order of one boat to 0·80 hectares, up to one boat to 0·20 hectares.

3.04 *Shape* is not very critical but the minimum area must not include small bays. A bank consisting of long smooth curves or straights is desirable. Islands are acceptable if they are at least 46 m from the bank.

3.05 *Depth* of water should be at least 1·50 m: 1·80 m is preferable. Shallows must conform to the same conditions as islands.

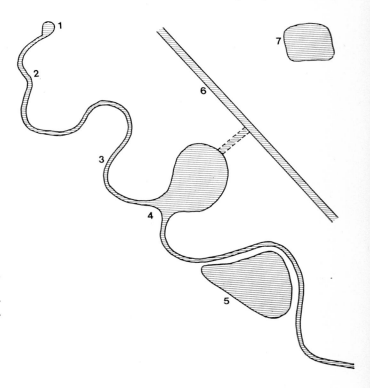

1 *Inland water recreation: potential sites*

Key:
1 Source of river: beauty spot, pool
2 Young river: brooks, rapids and waterfalls; footpaths, ponytrails, picnicking; basis for small country parks
3 River's middle reaches, meandering, wide, slow-flowing river; fishing and sailing; footpaths, pony trails
4 Lakes: all aspects of water sport; country parks
5 Former mineral workings, eg gravel pits: can be flooded and set aside for water recreation
6 Canals: linkage to river valley complex allows long distance tours, fishing, canoeing etc
7 Small lakes and pits: fishing, bird watching etc

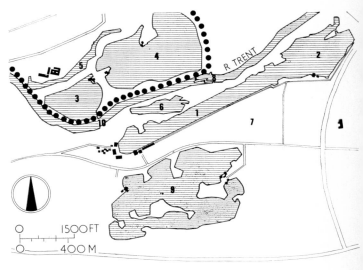

2 *National water sports centre, Holme Pierrepont, Nottingham*
Colwick Marina is within Nottingham city (boundary shown by large dots)

Key:
1 Rowing course
2 Water ski area
3 Colwick marina
4 Sailing lagoon
5 Pleasure boating
6 Nature reserve
7 Open space
8 Canoe slalom at Holme Locke
9 Public sailing and boating
10 Waterbus terminal

Rowing

Launching and mooring

3.06 Launching is by ramp or steps. Landing stage: 18 m long for sideways launching of 'eights'; if necessary, with ramp and pulleys for hauling up narrow frontage.

Buildings, car parks and storage

3.07 Clubhouse should be preferably in bay or sheltered inlet away from traffic.

Training

3.08 Training can take place in a rowing tank (12·6 m × 7·6 m for one 'eight'). As shells are easily damaged by obstructions and swamping by other craft, water must be sheltered. If also used by power boats, water areas must be zoned or subject to time tables.

Water requirements

3.09 Amateur Racing Association club competition standards require a stretch of water 1500 m long, not less than 1·83 m deep and 50 m wide (four lanes).
National and regional competitions (FISA* Standard c course) require 2000 m length, at least 50 m wide (four lanes) and 1·83 m deep.
Olympic or FISA men's championship course: 2000 m long, plus 100 m beyond the finish, 75 m wide (six lanes) plus 5 m between outside lanes and bank; not less than 3 m deep.

Canoeing (general)

Launching, mooring and buildings

3.10 Canoes can be launched almost anywhere, but a landing stage is useful. In addition, canoeists need a boat store and clubhouse.

Canoe touring

3.11 Water 0·23 m deep and 0·60 m to 0·90 m wide provides a possible route. Camping sites with portage facilities will be needed along waterways.

'White water' canoeing

3.12 The correct conditions and unrestricted passage are required.

Canoe racing

3.13 The international distances for competition sprint canoeing are 500 m, 1000 m and 10 000 m. A 1000 m straight course minimum depth 2 m and 45 m wide (six abreast) is required.

Canoe slalom

3.14 This takes place on fast flowing, turbulent water, There are penalties for any divergencies from the straight course.
The course should be not more than 800 m long measured through the gates. It may extend several hundred metres down a river, or take a more serpentine route in the restricted turbulent water below a weir. In the case of a hill river course it is a great advantage, even a necessity, if the river flow can be controlled by manipulating sluices at a reservoir higher up the valley.

Sea canoeing

3.15 *Surf canoeing* takes place in surfing areas. Beaches may have to be zoned for safety reasons.
Canoe touring usually takes place in sheltered coastal areas. Ease of transport allows club hqs to be sited some distance

*Federation internationale des sociétés d'aviron

away from water, but accommodation for changing clothes nearby is an obvious advantage.

Water ski-ing

Launching, mooring and buildings

3.16 Moorings and storage space for boats; clubhouse, ramp or hard beach, with jetties for dry starts.

Water requirements

3.17 As calm water is required, no designated area should be close to vertical or concrete banks which tend to build up a rebound wash. For this reason the sea does not provide the conditions necessary for competitions. Jumps and a permanent slalom course may need to be maintained. Zoning of water is important. Minimum dimensions of water for establishing a slalom course are 640 m × 182 m but 823 m × 1097 m to give greater clearance for turning and accurate speed approaches. A jump and figures course can be incorporated within a slalom course.

Powerboating and hydroplaning

3.18 Launching and mooring requirements on inland waters are as for sailing dinghies.
Larger power boats need the same facilities as keel boats. Boats can be stored outside under their own covers but engines need a lockable storage room. Fuel storage space is required. Lavatories, changing and first aid facilities are necessary and a clubhouse is desirable.
Car parking should include provision for spectators.

Water requirements

3.19 Minimum area of inland water required is 6 hectares. A large bay in a lake is desirable for 'pits'. Shape requirements of a water area are similar to those for dinghy sailing. Minimum water depth 0·92 m. Water must be weed free.

Cruising

Estuaries and inland waters

3.20 Cruisers require moorings as a basic minimum. Also needed, to a greater or lesser extent, are: boat storage, repair facilities (with lifting equipment), fuel supply, chemical wc disposal points.
Possible additional facilities: changing accommodation, lavatories, shops, restaurants, bars and car parking.

Moorings

3.21 Because of great demand—particularly in south-east England—moorings are scarce and expensive.
As traditional swinging moorings take up too much space, more compact methods must be used: either mooring alongside a jetty two abreast or mooring stern-on to a jetty with bows onto piles **5**. (These are the types provided by modern marinas.)

Marinas

3.22 Originally a US term, in Britain 'marina' means an artificial yacht harbour **4**, **5**. It is essentially an inward looking place facing the water activities. Though completely different in character from traditional yacht harbours, marinas provide the same facilities. Sites may be: estuaries—locked harbour basin or tidal basin (with tidal pontoons); estuaries and inland—'haul out marina' (this is cheaper, with boats stacked in boat parks on land and launched by ramp, trailer or crane); inland—non-tidal marina (on inland waters or canals).
Owing to the short season, marinas in Britain risk financial difficulties unless they provide 'pleasureland' facilities to attract vast numbers all the year. (The furore caused by the

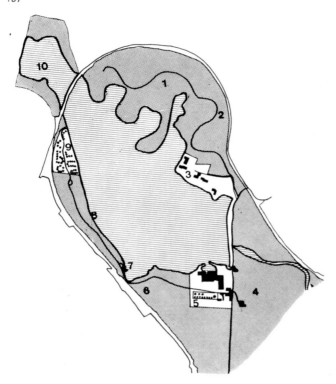

3 *Chasewater recreation area, Cannock, Staffordshire: nucleus is former canal reservoir among reclaimed waste land*

Key:

1 Parkland area
2 Forest Park
3 Boating and sailing centre
4 Golf course
5 South shore pleasure precinct
6 Pitch and putt golf course
7 Power boat club
8 West lakeside
9 Chalet group
10 North pool
Note: dot tone indicates woods and parkland

4

5

Brighton marina proposals is not over the harbour but the developments and access roads necessary.)

In addition to sport facilities the following may also be needed (see references 2, 8 and 9): water, electricity and telephones to each mooring; fire precautions; harbour-master's office; sleeping accommodation; provision for children.

Bird clubs

3.23 Location (dictated by bird habits) is usually by 'natural' waters but some examples are by reservoirs. Specialised requirements: 'hides', and freedom from disturbance, there-fore bird clubs are compatible only with angling and possibly sailing.

Slimbridge Wildfowl Trust runs 'pop' versions, more like zoos, in Gloucestershire and Northamptonshire.

Angling

3.24 Angling is about the most popular water sport. Its varied facets allow it to be practised almost anywhere, but zoning is important. It is best restricted to banks on one side only, leaving large free areas for fish. Water disturbance by violent sports may drive fish into the free zones.

Swimming

Pools

For detailed design criteria of indoor pools, see AJ design guides.[21], [22] The following notes will cover only those basic to *outdoor* pools.

4 *A large marina with full facilities for cruising boats and ample car parking.* **5** *shows a similar scene at eye level, with floating pontoons, locating piles, mooring bollards and over-head services. Installations on this scale need sensitive and strong handling if they are to be integrated with the landscape*

6 *The Wey at Godalming has the informal intimacy of the old river navigation system*

Outdoor pools
3.25 *Large pools:* Local authorities build few outdoor pools, though there are instances of recreational centres having both indoor and outdoor pools.
Small pools can be considered for caravan and camp sites, rural recreational areas, small recreational centres, schools, gardens.

Siting and design
3.26 Pools are best integrated with buildings or other hard elements. They can then be designed as part of the hard landscape. If freestanding, exceptional care is needed in siting and design. A would-be naturalistic pool will look alien in soft landscape, particularly for at least six months of the year, when it is not used.
Locate for maximum sunlight and privacy, screened from north and east winds and away from heavy shade trees and those with large roots (leaf-fall makes the water dirty). Check for soil bearing capacity. 'Cut and fill' should roughly balance, but use excess as banking for wind protection, or provide bleachers for spectators and sunbathers. Access is needed for bathers and cleaning equipment.

Construction and finishes
3.27 Construction and finishes may be of concrete block (maximum depth 1·14 m), brick, reinforced concrete and sprayed concrete construction, usually rendered and painted annually with cement paint or chlorinated rubber paint but marble chippings can be added to rendering to obviate painting. Other finishes: mosaic, tile or cement glaze.
Other materials: sprayed concrete, grp in one unit up to about 10·7 m × 4·25 m × 1·07 m to 2·3 m deep; flexible liner (usually vinyl) on framing—or as liner to concrete pool. (Flexible liner has a five-year life but is cheap to replace.) Keep surrounds clear, with non-slip paving at least 1 m wide

(3 m for public use), draining away from the pool. Surrounds may be stone, precast concrete slabs, bricks, mosaic, terrazzo or granolithic with carborundum finish. Asphalt, tiles and smooth cement are not recommended. A white lining to the pool gives the water a blue colour through reflection from the sky; cream is said to give a warmer and less chilly blue, while a darker colour makes the water warmer.

Planting
3.28 Planting near the pool softens glare. An adjacent pool for growing water plants can be incorporated. Planting, which must be at least 1 m back from the water, can be in raised beds, especially if it is of herbaceous or bedding types. Preferably use plants which drop no leaves during the bathing season—or evergreens which do not drop leaves so thickly.

Covers
3.29 Removable roofs are helpful in this climate. There are three types: blow-up structures, tents, and sliding transparent covers.

Filtration
3.30 Filtration is now much cheaper and more compact because of the use of diatomite filters. This is preferable to periodic emptying of pools or provision of complete water change after six hours. (Check that an outlet to sewers or ditch etc is available.)

Heating
3.31 Heating is either by conventional fuels (gas, oil or offpeak electricity) or solar heating batteries. It is usual to design for pool temperature to rise by about 4 deg °C from 10°C. Heating by poolside radiant heaters—overhead or embedded in paving—supplemented by wind screening extends the length of comfort season by the pool.

Furniture and equipment
3.32 Check for safety of equipment such as diving boards, especially in relation to pool depth. Access steps are necessary. Bridges, platforms for sitting in or over the water can make small pools more interesting. Locate seating (fixed or movable) around the pool. Sunbathing areas require shelter from prevailing winds. Though grass is obviously the best surface, in intensive situations pea shingle or hard surfaces can be covered with coir matting.

Size and cost of pools
3.33 For price guide to large public pools for general public, clubs and championship use, see AJ guides to indoor pools[21]. Private pools can be any size, depending on budget. Price for supply and construction complete with filtration plant but not surrounding buildings, range from about £150 for a 5 m × 2·7 m × 900 mm deep timber framed, vinyl lined, surface installation, through about £1500 for a pool 9·75 m × 5 m × 1 m to 2 m deep (minimum necessary to dive from 760 mm above pool).
For larger open air pools, see costs in MHLG *Design bulletin* 9 (1965) eg £8000 for a pool 25 m × 12·5 m × 1 m to 3·8 m deep.

Inland water
3.34 Suitability for swimming depends on pollution, obstructions and other uses to which the water is put. Where necessary, lakes etc can be treated to make them bacteriologically safe, eg by chlorination as at the Serpentine lido.

Services—connections and easements
Regulations—building lines, covenants on heights etc
Contiguous neighbours
Outlook—views out, introverted, enclosing elements
Soil—acid/alkaline (including drainage) plus existing vege-
tation
Garden and house character

3.02 Climate

Sun

Sunlight is important, not only to people, but also in the
way it highlights garden elements such as screens, plants,
water and trees. South or south-west aspect would suit most
people's free times. Note local elements such as urban haze
and topography causing mists and frost pockets **2**.

South walls reflect the sun, and should be covered in summer
with deciduous climbers or wall shrubs. Paved areas absorb
and re-radiate heat, increasing surface temperature.

Wind

Wind inhibits outdoor living in this country. If wind is
controlled, the microclimate of any location will improve
to the equivalent of 7° latitude southwards. Examine effects
on existing site, eg leaning trees, absence of plant material.
Wind cools people and desiccates and stunts plants. (Kata-
batic winds in early spring are very dangerous to newly
opening leaves.) Permeable screens, eg bamboo, open timber
or even netting are best against strong wind to avoid wind
eddies **3**. High (3 m) screens should be used on north faces,
and low screens on south faces. Houses themselves provide
the biggest screens.

Temperature

Experiments have shown that highly enclosed patio gardens,
with solid walls on all sides to retain heat and provide wind
shelter, maintain a consistently higher temperature than
that of surrounding areas. It should be possible to grow
more exotic types of plant in these gardens (compare old
kitchen gardens with high walls which often provide enough
shelter to cultivate peaches on them).

3.03 Access and circulation

Check pedestrian and vehicular access points. Analyse
circulation and 'desire lines' to give logical route network.

3.04 Topography

It is essential to conserve and intensify any changes of level
in the garden, as they add interest and scope for children's
play. But all new contours and changes of level should be
broad and sweeping, rather than 'pimples' on the surface **4**.

3.05 Services—overhead and underground

Check points for connections and easements. Check levels
to ensure that earthmoving operations will not expose them.

3.06 Regulations

Check for building lines, covenants or other regulations on
heights, types of walls, and other external elements. Check
also for road sight lines; also check building regulations for
position and construction of outdoor elements.

3.07 Neighbours

Consider neighbouring artefacts especially in terms of noise,
smells and pollution, and plant material such as overhanging
trees or voracious roots. Check whether views are liable to
be blocked by new artefacts or growing plants.

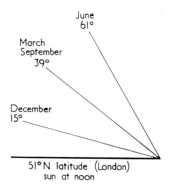

2 *Diagram showing angle of the sun at noon*

3 *Screens for wind shelter can also support climbing plants*

4 *Natural contours of this garden have been exaggerated and
enhanced*

5

6

5, 6 *Two gardens of totally differing character, one in undulating countryside, the other in a town.*

3.08 Outlook
Outward views can be borrowed and brought into the garden, as in the Japanese art of shakkei. Conversely, it can be shut out and the scheme introverted.

3.09 Soil
Check for depth, pH value and consistency. Check also for good drainage or otherwise. This will determine planting types and their location (ie uncorrected bad drainage would lead to raised planting beds). With some topsoil costing £3/m³ it is essential to conserve what there is on the site and to stop builders removing or burying it.

3.10 Vegetation
Existing natural vegetation can be an excellent soil indicator (see information sheet LANDSCAPE 10) while larger units (trees, shrubs) should be carefully surveyed for their

potential. Trees, especially if they are to be the main features of the site, should be checked carefully regarding their potential health. Far too many developments have been ruined by these centrepieces failing due to lowering of water tables, root truncation or soil level changes (see Arboricultural Association advisory leaflet no 3). As trees take so long to grow it is essential to take all steps to protect and preserve them during and after construction.

3.11 Garden character
This is somewhat nebulous, that which used to be called *genius loci*—or the extension and cultivation of potential. It is related to the ecology of the area either in terms of the natural soil base, or in the degree of urbanisation and pollution present **5, 6**. For detailed discussion of gardens and their relationships see information sheet LANDSCAPE 23.

3.12 Planting notes
For fuller information see information sheets LANDSCAPE 5 to 10 and 41.
Trees: check medium and small trees for most garden situations. Deciduous give summer shade but let in light in winter. Specials, such as the Victorian monkey-puzzle, can give character (see information sheet LANDSCAPE 6).
Shrubs: help to form basic background. They can be either fast-growing (eg broom, buddleia), or slow-growing (eg *laurustinus*).
Hedges: will need artificial screening to begin with. Hardiness is all important as some (eg *macrocarpa* cypress and *lonicera nitida*) can be patchy. There is a choice of slow-growing, easily manageable plants (eg yew), or fast-growing rampant plants (eg privet), which will need cutting frequently and which may be greedy and thus inhibit nearby plants from growing.
Climbers: These are invaluable in small spaces. There are two types: self-clinging (eg ivy, virginia creeper, climbing hydrangea) and non-clinging ramblers and twiners which require support (eg the clematises, honeysuckles). These require support from wires, trellises, or pergolas. Some shrubs can be used as 'wall shrubs' (eg *ceanothus*, roses, firethorn). Check catalogues for aspects.
Ground covers: are expensive but are most attractive low maintenance cover.
Herbaceous, alpine, herbs, annuals, bulbs: The client can exercise individuality with these against the basic background of other material.
Grass: needs careful control in tight plans but excellent for large sweeps.
Vegetables: some excellent foliage plants in this group, (eg asparagus).

Section 9 **Housing estates**

Information sheet
Landscape 25

Housing:
External space types

The basic premise of this information sheet is that the design of external spaces needs a disciplining of functions as taut as that relating to the internal planning of the dwelling. The objective of the external space type classification system given in this sheet is to create a tool that can be used at every stage in the design process from briefing, layout design, and resource planning, to detailed design, costing and management. Above all, it is intended as a method of comparing the performance and standards of the many different modern solutions, as well as traditional ones and those applicable to rehabilitation work.

The aim at this stage is to create a methodology that can grow, adapt and be added to—a sort of 'do-it-yourself' kit for architects. To exemplify the method, some model situations are illustrated and evaluated on the basis of this system.

NOTE: *This sheet should read with information sheets 26, 28, 29, 30, 31, which employ the same space analysis.*

The author, MICHAEL BROWN, *wishes to thank A. E. J. Morris and Richard Evans, Judith Allan (who has also assisted in extensive revisions) and Terry Nunns for their help, and particularly to acknowledge the valuable constructive enthusiasm, comment and help from very many other architects and landscape architects.*

Contents

Objectives and scope
Method of analysis of spaces, and application.
Design determinants (for checklist, legend and key to symbols and diagrams see pages 160-161
Key diagram showing space types covered in this information sheet
Assemblage of space types—application of the system where groups of spaces are identified in part of a housing layout.
EXAMPLES
Definitions
Design determinants—notes.
1 Terrace house types
2 Georgian streets and squares
3 Town house types
4 Suburban street types
5 Dwellings grouped round vehicle spaces—Pedestrian and vehicular spaces
6 Controlled aspect types
7 Courtyard house types
8 Deck access types
9 Grahame Park, Hendon
10 Beavers Farm—Hounslow
11 Dwelling group courtyards—Pedestrian and vehicular spaces
12 Car parking and garage spaces
13 Open car parking bays

General objectives
To identify the distinctive functions of the external spaces of which housing layouts consist in order to develop a critical method that may be used at any stage in the design process, from briefing, resource planning, layout design to costing, detail design and management.

Specific objectives
The system sets out to achieve the following specific objectives:

1 A method of assessing and subsequently comparing specific solutions with a view to identifying the factors that are relevant to performance and environmental quality. These could be carried out in respect of many different solutions whether contemporary or traditional and including those applicable to rehabilitation (see information sheet 31).

2 Cost guide lines which can be applied to external space types as readily as those already used for cost feasibility studies in building.

3 A simple, speedy method of quickly testing the feasibility of a design without developing it to a stage of refinement involving more effort and work than is justified at the initial stage of design. This would involve the application of knowledge from a vocabulary of comparative solutions or models with sufficient factors in common with the situations being examined.

1 Scope

1.01 The complexity of housing is such that the principal factors (eg density, access etc) cannot be considered in isolation from each other. A method of analysing and evaluating the landscape of housing is needed, which can inter-relate these problems in an integrated way, and at the same time enable the designer to examine the question 'what are the spaces for?' Unless every square metre of outside space is put to use as effectively as the space within the dwelling, land and resources may be wasted or misapplied.

1.02 This sheet is closely linked with information sheets LANDSCAPE 26, 29, 30 and 31 which deal respectively with car and service spaces and access, with detailed design, and with resource planning and costs and rehabilitation. The contents of the latter information sheets have been structured to fit into this space classification system so that these sheets can be used together.

1.03 The analysis is based on four main functional characteristics of external spaces. Definitions of these in the legend on pages 159-160.
They are:

DOMAIN	private space
	communal space
	private + communal space
CIRCULATION *for*	pedestrians
	vehicles
	pedestrians + vehicles
distinguishing	route space
	local access space
	non-route *not symbolised
EDGE CONDITIONS	non aspect
	controlled aspect
	open aspect, no privacy strip
	open aspect, with enclosed garden
	space under block
	garage/service space
	+ adjacent space *not symbolised
ACCESS *to dwelling*	linear
	single
	multiple
	end/linked
	deck

2 Application

2.01 The application of this system is illustrated by examples **1** to **12**.

2.02 The first diagram is a key to external space type classification, showing the four facets of domain, circulation edge condition and access to dwelling, and indicating the symbols which will be used to represent them in all the following figures.
The second diagram is an assemblage of space types, a plan which identifies, by the use of pictographs embodying the symbols referred to, the element spaces which are grouped to form part of an actual housing layout.

2.03 Various situations (indicated on the key page) reflecting particular combinations of circulation function, access type, and edge condition, are then illustrated in **1** to **12**. Most of these schemes are models—some drawn from one or more existing situations—and each represents a fairly typical, common situation in existing housing.
Since most housing layouts embody a number of edge conditions, grouped in a multitude of ways, it has been thought most valuable to study first the smaller element spaces where only one or two edge conditions are significant. Comments on the general characteristics of each of these model situations are shown by means of annotation; and the space types identified by pictographs as in the example assemblage, page 162.
The small key diagram in the upper right-hand corner of each sheet symbolises the circulation and ownership characteristics of the situation illustrated. It identifies the domain, ie whether private or communal and the type of access provided, ie whether for pedestrians, vehicles, route, non-route, etc.

3 Design determinants

3.01 These functional characteristics are accompanied by a check list of the principal determinants that vitally affect the treatment and character of the landscape of housing. The check list and determinants of these appear on page 160.

General
3.02 There is a need to clarify priorities in order best to resolve inevitable conflicts; these are most marked for high densities. Particular objectives will influence these eg required housing mix, privacy, access type, car provision and parking arrangements, management policies etc. Low densities pose particular problems also: more space may leave residual little used or neglected areas with problems of care, thus worsening the capital versus maintenance costs relationship. Although lower cost investment per unit area is possible, this may be offset by increased area of common land, or at least by attenuated and therefore less useful spaces along road and boundary edges. If it is not, private gardens may be bigger than necessary and loss of privacy may result from cheap boundary treatment due to excessive perimeter lengths. Fiddling densities by adjusting garden sizes is a common habit. What size is needed should be the question with first priority here.

Density
3.03 Density has an important although not exclusive effect on building form and grouping, which may themselves vary considerably within any one range of densities. High and low densities both produce their characteristic problems. It does not however follow that only high density schemes have to provide for areas of intense use: these will occur on many lower density schemes also.
Greatest conflicts with other determinants in high density schemes make it necessary to establish clear priorities and relate them to specific objectives ie housing mix, maintenance arrangements.
High densities pose particular problems of proximity, car provision, privacy.
Fuller provision of adjacent facilities can offer opportunities denied to lower density schemes.
Low density: ensure effective use of residual spaces, arrangements for maintenance which may need to provide for larger or at least more attenuated spaces.
Though lower cost investment may be possible per unit area, this may often be offset by increased area of common land and maintenance costs. Capital versus maintenance costs need this to be taken into account.

Ground coverage
3.04 This is a more relevant form of analysis for landscape external use, for it is a more appropriate measure of the effect of density on layout, and can be expressed in simple terms.
Careful interpretation of functional analysis can be vital, and usefully identifies disposition of resources. See information sheet 30.

Adjacent facilities
3.04 Greatest resources for common facilities are often more readily available at high densities. Lack of these may aggravate and attenuate vehicle access roads arrangements or cause social deprivation (new town blues) if facilities are not provided or are beyond walking distance.
Where these facilities do exist close to housing areas, reduced provision within the scheme may be possible: leading to economies in cost and land—eg adjacent public

open space or school fields that can be used for kickabout out of school hours.

Local intensity of use

3.05 Heavy use is a product of movement and routes and may occur at low densities as well as high ones. It will require appropriate materials and detailing.

Play spaces

3.06 Designation of specific areas for play is always somewhat arbitrary since short of establishing child or adult ghettoes the whole housing area must be regarded as common adult + child territory.

Site arrangement, size and density in relation to adjacent facilities can help significantly in resolving incompatibility between them, though children's play areas inevitably are intensively used.

Most play will occur informally. According to age group, children will make particular use of paths and paved areas for wheeled play at greater or lesser distances from the dwelling. The possibility of such areas being related so as to provide play circuits will make them especially attractive. These should be arranged to provide a safe counter-magnet to vehicle spaces. Steps, walls, changes of level, railings, are inevitably attractive to children for informal play. Adequate grass areas are desirable also but problems of erosion must be considered where heavy use is likely.

Sitting spaces

3.07 Distinguish between those spaces best related to routes—preferably in eddies adjacent to them—and those set a little away, eg on the edge of or within suitable spaces. Consider orientation and other conditions relevant to comfort, such as sense of enclosure, outlook. Take conflicts of privacy into account.

Access is important, especially where siting may risk undue erosion at corner of grass, planted areas. Walls, railings, changes of level, should be used to eliminate short cutting. Some sitting space should be sited close to areas suitable for younger children's play.

Access system and links

3.08 Check interrelationships and hierarchy of spaces and links to general movement pattern for vehicles and pedestrians. Consider convenience of access routes: are they on desired lines?

Check vehicle/pedestrian conflicts. Design principles and details should reinforce objective selected eg whether mixed or segregated layout and place in hierarchy of privacy and community.

Where mixed vehicle/pedestrian system is adopted, establish character intended: is pedestrian or vehicle to be dominant? Establish general principles for methods to be used for reinforcing routes to avoid short cutting. Consistent symbolism of limited range of details assists comprehension—see also identity.

Relate road widths, sight lines, turning radii, loading and other criteria to design objectives—see services, utilities and information sheet 26.

Relate important links to schools, play areas, shops, open space, vehicle stopping and storage points and other magnets. Check that spaces related to routes are well situated to provide dwelling access without privacy conflicts and that situation will reinforce intended use.

Car storage

3.09 There is a close relation between building form, density and the desirable degree of vehicle penetration. Decisions involved are fundamental to layout and have a vital effect

on the use of resources (see information sheet 30). Method of use, convenience, flexibility should be considered, with the need to avoid the customary sterile atmosphere of car courtyards. The advantages of segregated versus mixed access should be balanced. The advantages of segregated access (convenience, safety, economy) should be balanced against those of mixed access (economy, complete car accessibility to dwelling).

Provision of open, covered or enclosed storage, and long or short term use should be related to varying requirements.

Services and utilities

3.10 Requirements of various types of service or emergency access should be distinguished. Cases where special requirements (loading, space limitations) exist should be identified and it should be ascertained whether they are compatible with other uses such as pedestrian routes, paved amenity spaces, grassed areas.

Compare implications (running costs etc) of customary space consuming techniques with alternative methods utilising more flexible technologies (eg paper/plastic sack methods are less demanding in their requirements than 12T refuse collection lorries, refuse containers on clumsy paladins). Existing access requirements for fire vehicles can often be modified after discussion with fire officer. Possible adjustments in internal planning (doors, window positions) can be usefully considered with these. See access and links, and information sheet 26.

4 Site

4.01 Careful use of site and relation to building can reinforce sense of place. Consider orientation, views etc. Identify site constraints: eg avoid areas of poor drainage unless necessary steps can be taken and money is available to deal with consequences.

Regard existing assets as resources the replacement cost of which would diminish budget available. Take careful account of site assets. Survey condition, position and levels at base of trees; identify trees requiring remedial work or removal.

Fixing levels of buildings, roads etc should be fully integrated with existing contours. Utilise natural falls where possible. Take advantage of natural variation in slope and general topography where possible. Where major grading is required, soil conditions and type will affect settlement characteristics; it is frequently more economic to site buildings in cut than on filled material.

Use of careful grading plans with existing and new contours showing finished levels and falls can avoid risk of drainage problems and contractual misunderstandings, and enable accurate estimate of cut and fill prior to abortive contract work.

Conserve and protect existing topsoil for re-use, scrape aside BEFORE start of all other work. Consider soil improvement where necessary—this can be started whilst still in spoil heaps (eg legume planting, liming to improve organic content and soil structure).

Microclimate

4.02 Consider thermal properties, sun/shade, light/shadow, rain, noise, wind pollution and select appropriate landscape elements such as covered ways.

Arrange buildings to provide enclosure and shelter, but ensure provision for cold air drainage where, as in valleys, cold air flows are likely to cause fog or frost pockets which may therefore trap cold and moist air.

On flat exposed or windswept sites juxtaposed building heights and alignments, and a serrated skyline help to reduce wind flows without excessive turbulence. Complex broken plan layouts are better adapted to alleviate this problem than long or large blocks which canalise and speed up wind and cause turbulence, especially where vertical or horizontal slots occur in unfavourable wind situations.

Meteorological Office information is seldom of relevance and may be very misleading. Their observations are frequently taken at a level suitable for observing general climate conditions rather than local microclimate, which may be greatly altered by buildings not yet erected.

Specialist advice may be needed to interpret information or to apply observations from comparative situations elsewhere.

Where screen and shelter belts are required, provide adequate space at planning stage.

Consider internal planning in relation to exposure and orientation, also waterproofing of windows, eaves, and other details, where high winds and turbulence may tend to cause lateral or upward rain movement. Consider advantages of providing generous covered ways, eg from car parking areas to front door. Where possible exploit the possibility of putting covered spaces (garage areas under raised decks) to double up use for covered play. Site sitting play spaces, to take best advantage of orientation and shelter.

Privacy

4.03 Building arrangement or grouping of dwellings needs to accord with intended balance between degree of privacy and community to be achieved.

The treatment and position of the edge of the privacy zone to dwelling establishes mode and degree of privacy to be achieved. The possibility of choice by the resident is important. The edge condition should be regarded as the interface at which the privacy/community relationship starts: the relationship is inherent in internal planning and house type, and needs to relate well to layout in order to avoid incompatibility and conflicts. Where these occur, methods of dealing with them should be fully integrated with the layout of the dwelling and adjacent external spaces. Position of front door is critical.

Alternative degrees of privacy can be achieved for any one house type by juxtaposition of adjacent dwellings, garage/store blocks, stepped terraces, blind patios with or without upper storeys, balconies, roof terraces. Consider extent of choice and action to be left to resident by wall, fence, single aspect, raising building, lowering path—or just net curtains!

How much should be provided for them?

Where territorial boundary is to be visually indicated rather than created by a barrier near or above eye level, a range of alternatives exist, knee rails, may be used or plant beds, hedges, trees; there is a choice of surface treatment. Insert strip or studs let into ground surface may delineate extent of ownership and maintenance responsibility. Consider boundary of territory indicated in relation to arrangements for management, desire for outlook, and identify conflicts.

Identity

4.04 There are three major aspects:
1 Social identification/individual personalisation.
2 Awareness of visual physical grouping—this can help to make form comprehensible.
3 Sense of place—an intangible amalgam of 1 and 2 on a particular size with its characteristic existing or created landscape.

Planning may reinforce social contact and give or deny opportunities for personal involvement. Size of spaces and groups is important. Consider desirable degree to which

building and/or external spaces should be left partially incomplete within or even beyond realm of private domain. Balance is required between opportunities for personal change and effort and visual chaos. The strong framework of a unified design may best be able to accommodate this without creating disorder.

Proximity of particular dwelling types important, and therefore the housing mix.

Outlook

4.05 Pleasant interesting views should be provided. Where natural advantages cannot be exploited, variety and interest must be provided by changes of level, planting, additional spaces and so on.

Conflict may occur in relation to privacy requirements. Consider exploiting changes of level ie raised living room as traditional Georgian house, lowered path etc, or use of upper storey in patio type dwelling, or slots in terraces or enclosing walls or fences to courtyards.

Management and ownership

4.06 Who owns what? Who is responsible for what? What are the boundaries of responsibility? Clear answers are required. Problems can arise where edges of differing responsibility meet, or where overlaps occur: eg privately owned spaces may be visually public. Who pays for maintenance—there are advantages in residents being financially involved. Consider an annual contribution or declared allocation of rent for care of landscape. Arrangements must be made for security protection. Where residents are involved and contribute to upkeep, they can help in policy. Experience has shown that lively play leadership schemes with skilled play leaders help reduce occurrence and extent of vandalism.

Group ownership schemes or housing associations are now posing new possibilities, through leasehold agreements local authorities may be able to consider delegating responsibility to residents' groups.

Maintenance

4.07 Consider capital and maintenace costs. In relation to likely viable life span some materials, eg grass, are much more expensive than high quality hard landscape.

Likely standard of maintenance will have a vital effect on design decisions and should be reflected in the investment necessary for appropriate materials.

The vulnerability of all soft landscape is such that annual budget provision *must* be made for replacements by housing management. Failure to match design with maintenance can lead to neglect, vandalism and waste of money.

Balance and a sound value judgement are required in recognising where higher maintenance costs are justified and necessary: compare with normally accepted cost of street sweeping, floor carpet cleaning, building painting costs. Plant beds frequently need symbolic protection—knee rails, raising or lowering level of beds. Choice of plants—thorny plants are seldom effective until fully established—it is preferable to overplant for speedy establishment at initial stages.

Consider access for window cleaning eg stepping stones in plant beds. Provide for water supply and drainage for extreme rain or drought. Artificial irrigation may be needed where planting is justified under cover or on decks: much of SE England lies in area of annual drought.

Particular problems of maintenance occur immediately on completion of new housing schemes, especially where premature handovers and partially incomplete landscape may cause division of responsibility for damage: adequate replacement guarantees must be provided for. Maintenance

1 Terrace house types

KEY DIAGRAM

CIRCULATION & OWNERSHIP

A symbolic identification of the situation illustrated: shows circulation, access and relationship of private to communal space

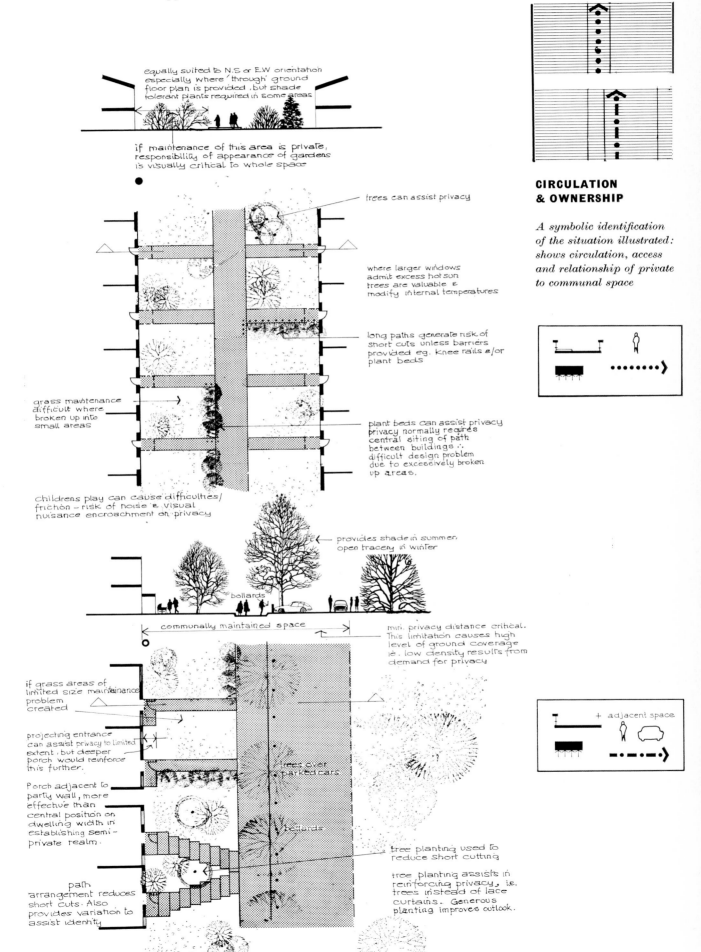

equally suited to N.S or E.W orientation especially where 'through' ground floor plan is provided, but shade tolerant plants required in some areas

if maintenance of this area is private, responsibility of appearance of gardens is visually critical to whole space

trees can assist privacy

where larger windows admit excess hot sun trees are valuable & modify internal temperatures

long paths generate risk of short cuts unless barriers provided eg. knee rails &/or plant beds

grass maintenance difficult where broken up into small areas

plant beds can assist privacy. privacy normally requires central siting of path between buildings ∴ difficult design problem due to excessively broken up areas.

childrens play can cause difficulties/friction - risk of noise & visual nuisance encroachment on privacy

provides shade in summer, open tracery in winter

bollards

communally maintained space

min. privacy distance critical. This limitation causes high level of ground coverage ie. low density results from demand for privacy

if grass areas of limited size maintainance problem created

projecting entrance can assist privacy to limited extent, but deeper porch would reinforce this further.

Porch adjacent to party wall, more effective than central position on dwelling width in establishing semi-private realm.

trees over parked cars

bollards

tree planting used to reduce short cutting

tree planting assists in reinforcing privacy, ie. trees instead of lace curtains. Generous planting improves outlook.

path arrangement reduces short cuts. Also provides variation to assist identity

+ adjacent space

2 Georgian streets and squares

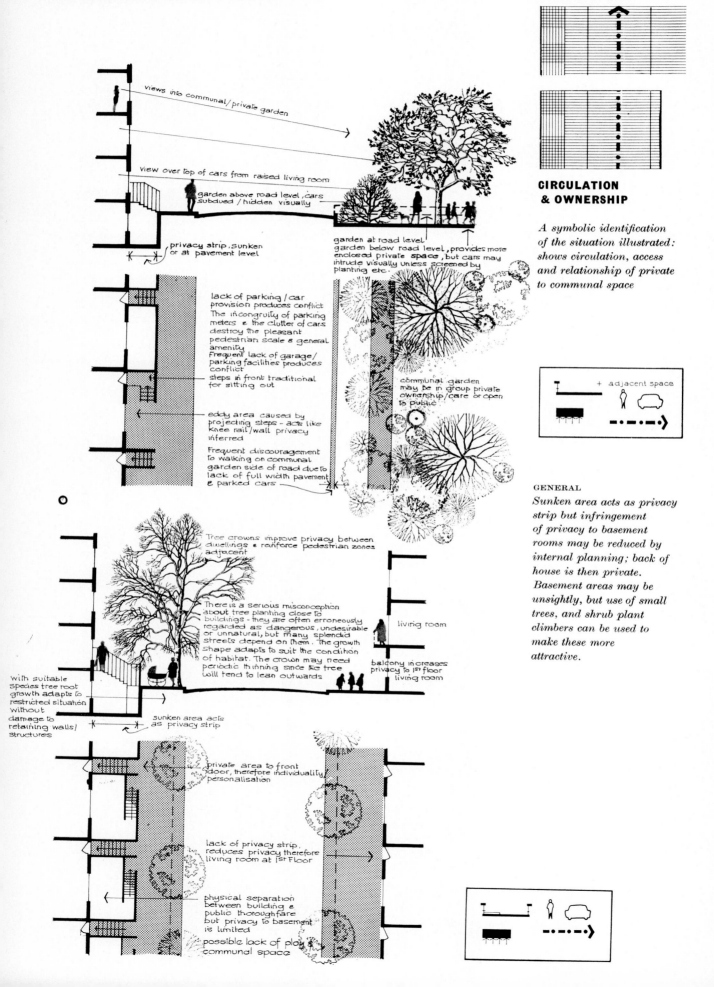

views into communal/private garden

view over top of cars from raised living room

garden above road level, cars subdued/hidden visually

privacy strip, sunken or at pavement level

garden at road level
garden below road level, provides more enclosed private space, but cars may intrude visually unless screened by planting etc.

lack of parking/car provision produces conflict
The incongruity of parking meters & the clutter of cars destroy the pleasant pedestrian scale & general amenity
Frequent lack of garage/parking facilities produces conflict
steps in front traditional for sitting out

eddy area caused by projecting steps - acts like knee rail/wall privacy inferred

Frequent discouragement to walking on communal garden side of road due to lack of full width pavement & parked cars

communal garden may be in group private ownership/care or open to public

Tree crowns improve privacy between dwellings & reinforce pedestrian zones adjacent

There is a serious misconception about tree planting close to buildings - they are often erroneously regarded as dangerous, undesirable or unnatural, but many splendid streets depend on them. The growth shape adapts to suit the condition of habitat. The crown may need periodic thinning since the tree will tend to lean outwards

living room

balcony increases privacy to 1st floor living room

With suitable species tree root growth adapts to restricted situation without damage to retaining walls/structures

sunken area acts as privacy strip

private area to front door, therefore individuality personalisation

lack of privacy strip, reduces privacy therefore living room at 1st floor

physical separation between building & public thoroughfare but privacy to basement is limited

possible lack of play & communal space

KEY DIAGRAM

CIRCULATION & OWNERSHIP

A symbolic identification of the situation illustrated: shows circulation, access and relationship of private to communal space

+ adjacent space

GENERAL
Sunken area acts as privacy strip but infringement of privacy to basement rooms may be reduced by internal planning; back of house is then private. Basement areas may be unsightly, but use of small trees, and shrub plant climbers can be used to make these more attractive.

3 Town house types

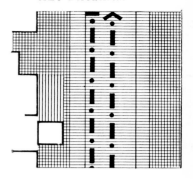

*A symbolic identification
of the situation illustrated:
shows circulation, access
and relationship of private
to communal space*

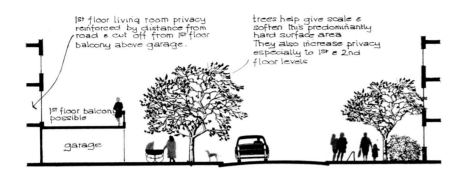

1st floor living room privacy
reinforced by distance from
road & cut off from 1st floor
balcony above garage.

trees help give scale &
soften this predominantly
hard surface area
They also increase privacy
especially to 1st & 2nd
floor levels

1st floor balcony
possible

garage

Generally:
The high intensity of use in this type of development and the very high proportion of ground
level area devoted to car provision necessitates the use of hard materials & leads to very
restricted areas for and dependent on tree planting & soft landscaping. In such areas, soft
landscaping is particularly vulnerable to damage & must be very carefully protected
& maintained. It is vital to use carefully selected, high quality materials, well
designed in places where intense use is to be expected; this results in a high
capital cost.
Effect of large numbers of closely spaced garage doors requires generous
planting to counteract sterility
Possible lack of communal/play spaces.

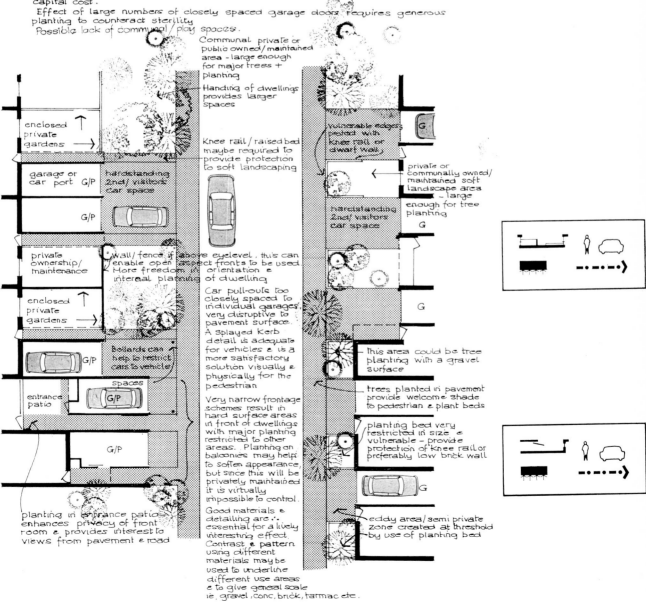

enclosed
private
gardens

garage or
car port G/P

G/P

private
ownership/
maintenance

enclosed
private
gardens

entrance
patio

spaces

G/P

G/P

Communal private or
public owned/maintained
area - large enough
for major trees +
planting
Handing of dwellings
provides larger
spaces

Knee rail/raised bed
maybe required to
provide protection
to soft landscaping

wall/fence if above eyelevel, this can
enable open aspect fronts to be used
More freedom in orientation &
internal planning of dwelling

Car pull-outs too
closely spaced to
individual garages,
very disruptive to
pavement surface.
A splayed kerb
detail is adequate
for vehicles & is a
more satisfactory
solution visually &
physically for the
pedestrian

Very narrow frontage
schemes result in
hard surface areas
in front of dwellings
with major planting
restricted to other
areas. Planting on
balconies may help
to soften appearance,
but since this will be
privately maintained
it is virtually
impossible to control.

Good materials &
detailing are ∴
essential for a lively
interesting effect.
Contrast & pattern
using different
materials may be
used to underline
different use areas
& to give general scale
ie. gravel, conc, brick, tarmac etc.

Bollards can
help to restrict
cars to vehicle
spaces

planting in entrance patio
enhances privacy of front
room & provides interest to
views from pavement & road

vulnerable edges
protected with
knee rail or
dwarf wall

private or
communally owned/
maintained soft
landscape area -
large
enough for tree
planting

hardstanding
2nd/visitors
car space

G

G

G

this area could be tree
planting with a gravel
surface

trees planted in pavement
provide welcome shade
to pedestrian & plant beds

planting bed very
restricted in size &
vulnerable - provide
protection of knee rail or
preferably low brick wall

G

eddy area/semi private
zone created at threshold
by use of planting bed

hardstanding
2nd/visitors
car space

4 Suburban street types

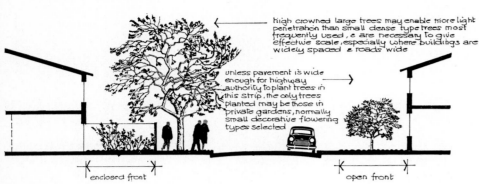

high crowned large trees may enable more light penetration than small dense type trees most frequently used, e are necessary to give effective scale, especially where buildings are widely spaced e roads wide

unless pavement is wide enough for highway authority to plant trees in this strip, the only trees planted may be those in private gardens, normally small decorative flowering types selected

enclosed front

open front

CIRCULATION & OWNERSHIP

A symbolic identification of the situation illustrated: shows circulation, access and relationship of private to communal space

General

Except where typical suburban semi detached dwellings occur in 'local access' rather than 'route' spaces there is a safety conflict due to temptation for children to use road for ball games, wheeled play etc. Down grading road by introducing bollards, gates or narrowing roads etc can help resolve this or by roughening road surfaces

Absence of safe traffic free areas for childrens play
No communal space for general amenity
Avoids need for residents /group/ communal responsibility for maintenance
Private gardens occupy all residual space resulting from byelaw, spacing e density restrictions

provision of strip between footpath e road enables large trees to be planted. Assists in separation of vehicle e pedestrians. This can be reinforced by planting e/or grass banks where sufficient extra available space e/or adequate maintenance can be carried out. Where flat gravel surface more practical than grass. Also admits air/water to the roots. Narrow grass **verges** readily damaged by short cutting e uneconomic to maintain

with widely spaced housing there is opportunity for personalisation of private domain, but visual chaos results without strongly unifying feature eg. trees, garden walls + consistent use of unified design details + materials etc.

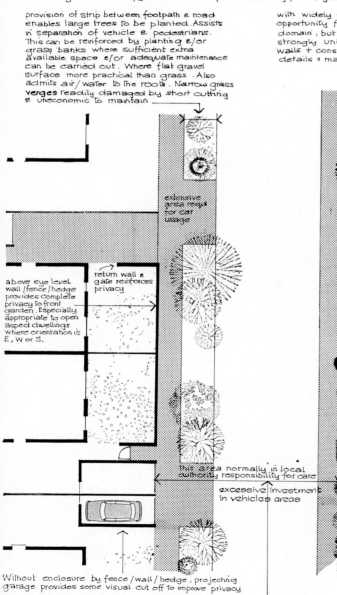

above eye level wall /fence/hedge provides complete privacy to front garden. Especially appropriate to open aspect dwellings where orientation is E, W or S.

return wall e gate reinforces privacy

extensive area reqd for car usage

this area normally in local authority responsibility for care

excessive investment in vehicles areas

Without enclosure by fence /wall / hedge, projecting garage provides some visual cut off to improve privacy

Responsibility for care + discretion for detail design normally rests with local highways dept. Frequent unquestioning adoption of normal practice + procedures for standards of highway design in suburban streets eg. road widths, kerbs, sight lines, lighting, tree care. But potential of these as major unifying elements can be sacrificed through uncritical compliance with standard practice

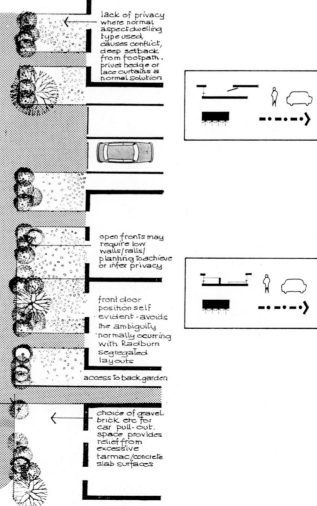

lack of privacy where normal aspect dwelling type used, causes conflict, deep setback from footpath. privet hedge or lace curtains a normal solution

open fronts may require low walls/rails/ planting to achieve or infer privacy

front door position self evident - avoids the ambiguity normally occurring with Radburn segregated layouts

access to back garden

choice of gravel, brick etc for car pull-out. space provides relief from excessive tarmac/concrete slab surfaces

On street parking or car standings in open fronts reqd where spaces between blocks are insufficient for garages.

Information sheet Landscape 28

Section 9: **Housing Estates**

Housing: Industrial building

In this information sheet MICHAEL BROWN *and* TERRY NUNN *discuss landscaping in connection with industrialised building. Heavy concrete systems pose particular problems, and these are illustrated with examples. Lightweight small component industrialised systems are covered in information sheets* LANDSCAPE 25 *to* 27

1 General

1.01 The use of heavy industrialised systems for housing poses certain design problems which are difficult to reconcile with good landscaping. Most problems arise because industrialised systems can justify themselves economically only by maximum standardisation of house type, layout, finish and elevation. This leads to excessive rigidity of plan and lack of identity of spaces between blocks. Also, systems with large slab components requiring cranes have innate inflexibility in coping with small-scale changes at ground level **1**. 'Cellular' systems, such as that of Yorkshire Development Group, **2**, **3**, **4**, have shorter component elements which can be joined in a variety of ways resulting in less conflict at ground level. Ideally, industrialisation should be on this component scale. Low-rise patio-type housing, such as Clarkhill, Harlow, and Albertslund, Denmark, is far more readily adaptable to industrialised systems. These problems are discussed in detail, with reference to examples, in para 2.

2 Appraisal of four industrialised schemes

2.01 The following list summarises certain problems of industrialised construction and their consequent effect on the landscape with reference to examples. Numbers preceding the text refer to those on relevant parts of all four plans **1** to **4**.

1 *Slab block housing layout based on the Laing-Jesperson system. Blocks are four storeys high, and longest block is approximately 0·4 km in length. Spaces between are dictated by minimum working transit distance of cranes. Contours on all plans at 250 mm vertical intervals*

2 *Enclosed linked five to seven-storey housing layout based on Yorkshire Development Group system (Leeds). This has more flexible crane system than **1**, leading to more interesting layout*

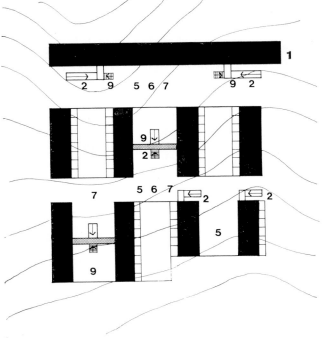

1

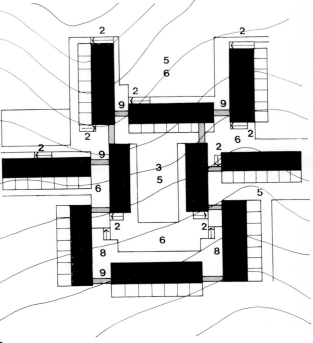

2

Key to plans

Para numbers refer to numbers on plans.

1 Long, simple blocks on plan; any variations in ground level must be taken up by stepping within the building, usually at the base. Lack of economy in long blocks running at right angles to contours, due to excess 'cut and fill'.

2 Ramps, steps and foundations have to be designed and built as 'one-off' jobs. This can be expensive and time consuming on contracts which are specifically geared to not using the traditional methods that can readily cope with them.

3 Crane runs make it difficult to leave existing topography. Phasing of craning to co-ordinate planting needs to be very carefully worked out.

4 Where blocks are stepped down the contours, retaining walls at garden junctions are needed, and there may also be damp-proofing problems at gable ends.

5 Cranes can be economically justified only by maximum use; this encourages high-rise blocks, excessively long blocks, four- or five-storey deck access blocks, all of which make microclimate problems, such as wind turbulence at ground level.

6 Long crane runs make it difficult to create small intimate spaces. Repetition of regimented blocks leads to lack of identification between spaces. There is thus especial need for the landscaping to provide identification and individuality.

7 Economies of erection, design and crane runs can lead to excessive rigidity of plan.

8 Heavy industrialised systems tend to use concrete cladding units, often with minimal variety. As in 6, this creates lack of identification between spaces and the plain surfaces invite vandalism. The potentialities of adapting traditional materials for industrialised use (eg brick veneer set into concrete slab) could be considered.

9 In the case of linked blocks, the link itself could be adapted to accommodate small differences in level, thus saving expensive substructure work. Links are often erected quickly to provide access for trades, before landscape work commences. This can lead to problems of access for cranes, large trees and machinery for landscaping.

10 Where roads run up or down rather than across the slope, serious anomalies can occur where rate of slope of road does not tie in with rate of stepping of block. An interlocked system of courtyards as in plan **2**, with little vehicle penetration of the centre, reduces this conflict.

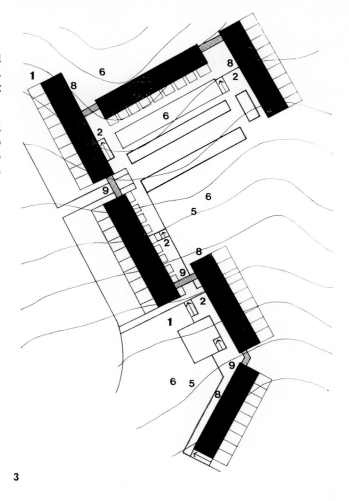

3

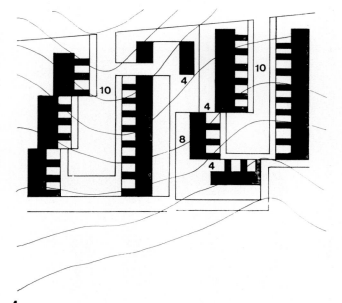

4

3 *Linear linked six-storey housing layout based on Yorkshire Development Group system (Hull). Greater vehicle penetration than* **2** *may cause problems in heights of links over roads*
4 *Low rise two-storey housing layout based on Midland Consortium system. Blocks which can be staggered have more inbuilt flexibility than long slab blocks*

Information sheet
Landscape 29

Housing: Detailed design

In this information sheet MICHAEL BROWN *comments on a miscellany of examples of external housing spaces, drawing attention to the advantages and disadvantag esof particular types, and evaluating the specific examples shown. This sheet should be read in conjunction with information sheet* LANDSCAPE 25, *which explains terms such as 'open aspect', 'controlled aspect', and so on*

1   2

5

3

4

6

1 *Open aspect situation. Tree planting close to dwellings (in spite of narrow pavements) contributes to character, and reinforces privacy. Simple traditional doorstep detail; attractive contrast in textures*
2 *Where grass edges are vulnerable, protection is essential*
3 *Open car parking area. Shows value of providing pedestrian forecourts for sitting/playing adjacent to car park. Bold tree planting reduces visual effect of parked cars*
4 *Town house type with controlled aspect front. Planting in left-over spaces difficult, and made feasible only by using protecting rails. These spaces would have been more useful*

if big enough for tree planting
5 *Grass banked open space provides enclosure for sunken sitting area. Generous young tree planting for quick effect; simple steel knee rail provides essential protection. Brick paving used for sitting area provides rich texture*
6 *Open aspect, pedestrian local-access space. Minimal separation in spacing of Victorian houses produces privacy conflict but achieves a sense of intimacy and identification. Grouping round tiny space on exposed sloping site is effective microclimate solution. This example would not be allowed today*

7

8

9

10

11

12

7 *Siting of back gardens above route reinforces privacy—
very important as only low open fence is provided. Ground
cover may be difficult to establish in early years*
8 *Front patio garden for pedestrian route. Sense of
enclosure and privacy, combined with good outlook*
9 *Vehicle/pedestrian local access route. Provision of
minimum-width, common drive contradicts myth that turning
radii and sight lines are correlative with safety.
Contrasting paving materials establish hierarchy of traffic use*
10 *Open aspect front of vehicle/pedestrian route space where
foot-path passes dwelling. Tree planting reinforces privacy*
11 *Single aspect types forming intimate pedestrian housing
group. Illustrates pedestrian route space which frequently
occurs with this type*
12 *Varied character of alleyways, made possible by bridging
over sections, helps modulate space*

13

14

13 *Use of covered way to give sheltered access*
14 *Narrow covered alleyway; note crisp detailing of screens, and use of setts to edges of alley for drainage*
15 *Linear access deck can produce sterile monotonous character. Varied width of setbacks could help solve problem*
16 *Formidable character of concrete balustrade and elevational treatment, unrelieved by tree planting, is a missed opportunity. Bridges provide space modulation.*

17 *Deck schemes provide excellent opportunity for high density and complete segregation. But below-deck garages can be bleak, cavernous and vandalised. Many people are reluctant to use them due to isolation and fear of molestation*
18 *Above deck. Important to create interest, variety, intimate spaces. Limited scope for planting produces problems; provision of set-backs to accommodate tall trees, planted in ground below, is one possible solution*

15

17

16

18

19

20

22

19 *Covered carports give cheaper shelter than garages; can be widened to act as covered ways for pedestrians*
20 *Attached projecting garages reinforce privacy and provide mixed pedestrian/vehicle area. Simple yet adequate knee rail*
21 *Illustrates symbolic use of different surface treatments to identify and reinforce hierarchy of paths; use of ground cover (heather) to provide unified sweep of soft carpeting without clutter; use of setts to take up irregular edges*
22 *Exploiting change of level to provide amenity/playspace*
23 *Varied arrangements of garages; contrasting textures avoid stretches of sterile asphalt*
24 *Single aspect dwellings on sloping site allow pedestrian and vehicle routes to be arranged at different levels. Good detailing of low rail and stepped ramp. Use of setts enables junctions to be well handled*

23

21

24

25

26

25 *Mixed pedestrian/vehicle courts where narrow roads are used also by pedestrians. Low investment cost creates maintenance difficulties—note erosion at corners. Use of soft landscape to form enclosure can create problems of establishment in early years*

26 *Stepped alleyways between single aspect blocks on sloping ground frequently provide opportunity for creating interesting and exciting townscapes.*

27 *Good space enclosure making use of garages to exploit situation. Concrete block walls need to be humanised by trees*

28 *Informal paths; generous planting; use of rough banks to screen car parking*

29 *Domestic entrance courtyard given over to storing car and bicycles. Plenty of climbers can make such multiple-use spaces attractive in spite of the vehicles.*

30 *Use of small groups of attached garages to create garden spaces. Unusual door shape, and alternating pattern of garage and garden walls, is welcome improvement on usual bleak garage situation*

27

29

28

30

31

32

33

34

35

31 *Adequate tree planting is particularly important with industrialised building*
32 *Exposed vulnerable areas of grass or planting require protection, especially during early years*
33 *Gravel is an economic, practical surface material, but requires great care in siting and detailing. Should preferably not be used on routes and should be at lower level than pedestrian paving*
34, **35** *Contrasting use of horizontal and vertical timber fencing. In each case fencing must accommodate changes of ground level. This is easier with vertical types*
36 *Reed or rush fencing—an unusual solution*

36

Information sheet
Landscape 30

Housing: Resource planning and costs

This information sheet by MICHAEL BROWN *and* BRIAN PUGH *is an attempt to point the way towards a methodology which will enable architects to allocate available resources more strictly in accordance with need, when planning housing schemes*

1 Need for analysis and comparison

Current approach

1.01 The cost of spaces between buildings has not hitherto been the subject of as much analysis and consideration as the buildings themselves. In most cost analyses, the element 'external works' covers a multiplicity of situations and solutions, and gives little information on function, cost and quality.

In the public housing sector, in particular, cost planning has often concentrated on constraining the design of externals within the 'external works' portion of the yardstick.

Future approach

1.02 If the spaces between buildings are to be used to their best advantage it is essential that methods of analysis and comparison be evolved which will enable the designer to analyse the functions and uses of external spaces very rigorously, and then allocate available money in relation to *need*. The major objective should always be to solve conflicts of usage, ensure privacy, and concentrate expenditure on areas of highest intensity of use.

Methodology

1.03 Such a methodology does not exist yet; but the following cost analyses of a selection of housing estates, and the accompanying notes, will give an indication of the kind of thought which needs to be devoted to the costs of external spaces. Even if it is too early to provide a method, designers can begin to develop the correct approach.

Intention of notes

1.04 The notes on the various examples are intended to be read only as an illustration of this analytical approach, and should not be taken as hard and fast judgements on the schemes under discussion; for the latter purpose more detailed information would be required than that contained in these bar charts. One would need to know more about the detailed circumstances which underlie the particular cost distribution of each; about the exact definitions used for calculating the costs; and above all the percentages given for each scheme would have to be related to the *total* cost in each instance, if comparisons between various schemes are to be reliable. Nevertheless, the percentage breakdowns

shown do give an indication of the priorities of investment within each scheme; and will serve as examples of different patterns of resource allocation **1**. To avoid misunderstanding, it should be noted that the element 'buildings and private gardens' is included in the upper part of the bar chart (area) in each case, but excluded from the lower part (cost).

2 Examples

2.01 *Beaver's Farm, Hounslow* The two schemes analysed give an indication of the consequences of different levels of car parking provision. The most interesting point is that a large increase in car provision has resulted in a relatively small increase in investment. The most likely explanation for this apparent anomaly is that the bulk of the money is spent on an infrastructure which has to be provided regardless of whether car parking provision is 63 per cent or 98 per cent; once this has been provided, additional car parking is comparatively inexpensive.

2.02 *Grahame Park, Hendon* Has similar density, but slightly lower car parking provision than the 98 per cent car parking Beaver's Farm scheme, and therefore makes an interesting comparison. The relatively low cost of the Grahame Park car areas is partly explained by the fact that some of the roads in this case also serve adjacent areas, as part of a comprehensive development, and the cost is shared; whereas in the case of Beaver's Farm the total cost is borne by that estate. A larger proportion of total investment has therefore been devoted to hard and soft landscaping, and pedestrian routes, in Grahame Park.

2.03 *Livingstone Road, Battersea* A high-density medium-rise scheme; the intensity of ground usage associated with this type of estate requires comparatively large areas of hard landscaping which can stand up to hard use, and smaller areas of soft areas, adequately protected by knee-rails, banking etc. Cost of both hard and soft landscaping is therefore abnormally high for this scheme, and have been shown to be justified. Investment in motor car provision could be kept low because the estate is in a fairly low-income, low car-ownership area. Again, this has been shown to be justified; even though the estate is several years old, car parking provision still seems adequate.

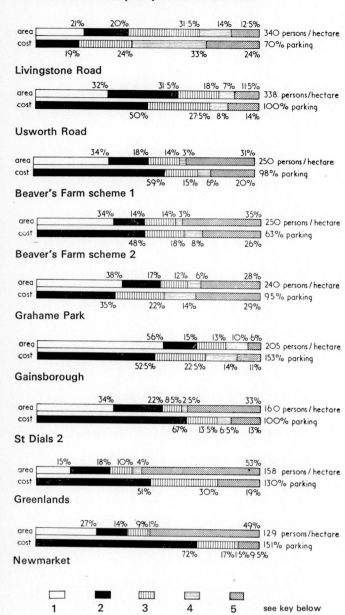

area   21%   20%   31·5%   14% 12·5%   340 persons/hectare
cost   19%   24%   33%   24%   70% parking

Livingstone Road

area   32%   31·5%   18% 7% 11·5%   338 persons/hectare
cost   50%   27·5% 8%   14%   100% parking

Usworth Road

area   34%   18%   14% 3%   31%   250 persons/hectare
cost   59%   15% 6%   20%   98% parking

Beaver's Farm scheme 1

area   34% 14% 14% 3%   35%   250 persons/hectare
cost   48%   18% 8%   26%   63% parking

Beaver's Farm scheme 2

area   38%   17% 12% 6%   28%   240 persons/hectare
cost   35%   22% 14%   29%   95% parking

Grahame Park

area   56%   15% 13% 10% 6%   205 persons/hectare
cost   52·5%   22·5% 14% 11%   153% parking

Gainsborough

area   34%   22% 8·5% 2·5%   33%   160 persons/hectare
cost   67%   13·5% 6·5% 13%   100% parking

St Dials 2

area   15% 18% 10% 4%   53%   158 persons/hectare
cost   51%   30%   19%   130% parking

Greenlands

area   27% 14% 9% 1%   49%   129 persons/hectare
cost   72%   17% 1·5% 9·5%   151% parking

Newmarket

```
□        ■        ▥        ▤        ▦
1        2        3        4        5      see key below
```

1 *Analysis of land use and cost on a selection of housing estates. Percentages are approximate and do not always add up to 100 per cent:*
1 *'Building and private gardens' includes area of all buildings except car storage, and entirely private gardens only*
2 *'Car access and storage' includes internal roads (not peripheral roads); car parking areas (open or covered); garages and service access areas*
3 *'Major pedestrian routes' include all major footpaths*
4 *'Other hard areas' include playgrounds; incidental (ie non-essential) walkways; sitting and other paved areas*
5 *'Soft landscape areas' includes all non-constructed landscaping (eg banking, planting and grassing); and all public or semi-public garden areas*

2.04 *Usworth Road, Washington* Comparing this scheme with Livingstone Road, several interesting points emerge: densities are much the same, but because this is a comparatively low-rise scheme, a larger proportion of site area has been devoted to buildings and private gardens. Car parking provision is 100 per cent as compared with 70 per cent for Livingstone Road, consequently there is a much higher investment in car access and storage, both in terms of area and cost. This leaves only a small area for hard and soft landscaping.

2.05 *Gainsborough, Corby* One is struck by the large area devoted to dwellings and private gardens, and the low area of soft landscaping. The explanation is that private gardens are both larger and more numerous than in the foregoing schemes; and that there is usable open space adjacent to the estate, so that there was less need for soft areas to be provided. The high ratio of private to public areas is therefore justified in this particular case. The surprisingly low area of car parking space (only 15 per cent for 153 per cent car parking provision) is explained by the fact that garages are situated underneath dwellings.

2.06 *St Dials 2, Cwmbran* What stands out is the abnormally high investment in car parking. Area devoted to car parking is, however, fairly average; it would be instructive to discover the reason for the discrepancy. Ratio of private to public spaces is more representative than in the case of Gainsborough.

2.07 *Greenlands, Redditch* Scheme is situated on a hilly site, and had to incorporate a lot of open space, which explains the high proportion of soft landscaped areas. But, even though area is large, investment is fairly average. In comparison with St Dials which is of equivalent density, a much higher provision for car parking has been achieved for a lower proportion of total cost outlay. The comparatively high cost of hard areas and pedestrian routes in the case of Greenlands can probably be explained by the hilly site (steps, retaining walls and so on).

2.08 *Newmarket* This scheme incorporates attributes such as low-density cluster layout, combined with high car-parking provision, which are currently very fashionable. The apparently enormous expenditure on car parking therefore requires careful investigation; if this were typical of such schemes, it would point to a very distorted investment of money. The comparatively low investment in the very large proportion of soft landscaped area adds to this impression of distorted investment.

References

1 BROWN, M. Landscape and housing *Official Architecture and Planning*, 1967, June, p791–799 [06:8]
2 BROWN, M. Landscape and housing *Housing Review*, 1968, May–June, p95–103 [06:8]

Information sheet
Landscape 31

Housing: Rehabilitation

1 General notes

Character

1.01 Areas needing rehabilitation are usually closely-built, two-storey terraces with a small rear yard and back alley. Front gardens are rare and entrance to dwelling is direct on to pavement or road. Roads are long, monotonous, and usually treeless. (Where complex patterns of streets exist there is opportunity for a more enriched pattern of rehabilitation, illustrations **7** to **18**.)

Public open space

1.02 These areas lack communal open space and density and proximity of dwellings often restricts size of new communal spaces. But many small areas are useful especially if sited on pedestrian routes.

Noise from children's play may disturb residents where size of communal spaces is restricted. Lack of ball game areas leads to bouncing balls on house walls etc.

Infill development

1.03 Social and physical character of rehabilitation areas can be enriched by introducing infill building **1, 2**. Infill at street ends may close it off to form a cul-de-sac. Through traffic is stopped, and the number of dangerous minor crossroads can be reduced. Visually infill across a road becomes a barrier, giving each street identity, and it could be a useful amenity such as social centre, nursery school, or housing for old people. (As no vehicular access is necessary, space in front of infill could be soft surface such as grass with trees and benches.)

Variety in building, space and landscape (often lacking due to repetitive form), can also be introduced by replacing some older terrace properties by blocks of garages and play areas. New infill should be set back to vary the skyline and townscape, allow tree planting, benches etc.

Different levels can be exploited to assist enclosure and privacy, and to add interest and variation.

Vehicle problems

1.04 Improvement of external space must take place within whole areas, so that vehicle and pedestrian flow can be considered as a whole. By-law streets are characterised by lack of provision for car, whether parked or in transit (except in areas such as Islington where small as well as large houses frequently front on to wide streets). On-street parking is usually inevitable but setbacks and closing of streets can provide open or closed car storage.

Planting

1.05 Generous tree planting should be provided either in communal areas (eg pedestrian sections of streets, bays, paved areas, between parking bays etc) or in residents' gardens (incentives should be provided to residents to plant trees). The latter can add variety to streets where open spaces are too restricted for tree planting or where they adjoin communal areas.

This information sheet by MICHAEL BROWN *and* JUDITH ALLAN *considers the opportunities for improving spaces commonly found in rehabilitation areas and gives some examples of the variety of ways in which they can be improved. Housing in rehabilitation areas was discussed in detail in* AJ *10.6.70 and 1.7.70*

1

1, 2 *Infill development in a rehabilitation area at Lambeth includes a health centre and day nursery*

2

Existing trees should be surveyed, and arrangments made for tree care and surgery. Trees should be graded as to quality and tree preservation orders imposed where appropriate.

Edge protection is usually necessary for plant beds, and arrangements for responsibility and maintenance should be made. Highly used areas pose particular problems, and residents' society or equivalent should assume responsibility for maintenance.

Lack of rear access to gardens causes problems of refuse collection. Privacy strips at dwelling fronts can sometimes include a small refuse store.

References

1 Housing Act 1969 Chapter 33. 1969, HMSO [81 (Ajk)]

2 MINISTRY OF HOUSING AND LOCAL GOVERNMENT Circular 64/69 (Welsh Office Circular 63/69) House improvement and repair. 1969, HMSO [81 (Ajk)]

3 MINISTRY OF HOUSING AND LOCAL GOVERNMENT Circular 65/69 (Welsh Office Circular 64/69) Area improvement. 1969, HMSO [81 (Ajk)]

2 Examples of rehabilitation

2.01 The following points are located on plan 5. This is not a comprehensive rehabilitation scheme, but an assemblage of different situations indicating the ways in which external spaces can be improved.

1 Alley with pleasant intimate urban scale where vehicle access has been eliminated. Distances between dwellings are less than for present daylighting requirements. Only very restricted space for planting or trees but opportunities for residents initiative (eg window boxes and tubs of flowers) to confer privacy and identity to windows.

2 Width of street is sufficient for parking and use is restricted to residents. Several small parking bays may be planned on one side only, interspersed with areas for trees and planting. Where necessary, maintenance arrangements can be made.

3 Wide carriageway with use restricted to local access provides many opportunities for redesigning the space between the buildings and for providing alternating car parking, tree planting and bays.

4 Mews town houses inserted at rear end of long gardens. Requirements for car movement restrict space for trees so there is particular dependence on choice of materials, texture and colour and on residents initiative (eg window boxes).

5 Restricted outlook can be improved by climbers on non-aspect walls.

6 Flats with linear deck access gallery over garage block inserted at end of long gardens. Requirements for car movement restricts space for trees so particular dependence on choice of materials, textures and colour.

7 Paved and planted area with stair up to access gallery contrasts with sterility of garage court.

8 Long linear pedestrian route space can vary by widening in places, with planting, trees, and climbers to improve communal outlook. Small areas for sitting and play may be achieved by shortening gardens but these will then need a high fence for privacy. Where these spaces are overlooked by open aspect dwellings they are ideal protected areas for younger children's play.

9 Very small main garden adjoining main pedestrian thoroughfare requires high fence for privacy.

10 Where open garden occurs on pedestrian through route there is particular need to indicate the private/public boundary by use of short wall or knee rail. Renewal of fences is frequently required to improve character of space.

11 By restricting parking and service access to end of cul-de-sac a communal pedestrian open space may be formed with greatly improved outlook to the dwellings.

12 Where open aspect dwellings overlook new communal pedestrian spaces a privacy strip may be necessary. This can be achieved by use of knee rail or fence, by projecting line of party wall, by new building extension (eg ground floor bathroom). Where there is no rear access to gardens there is frequently refuse storage and collection problem. A new refuse store in front of dwelling could also act as a privacy strip.

13 Where road width permits, parking may suitably be provided adjacent to non-aspect gable ends.

14 Where road width (ie dimensions between houses) permits, a new block of garages (with a flat over) would close off the road and provide an enclosed courtyard.

15 Setting back infill block to provide main garden in front gives more privacy and varies street and pedestrian way character.

16 Consider possibility of donating trees or providing them at cost to residents for planting in back gardens. Of particular value where these back onto pedestrian ways and where they will add variety to streets with spaces too restricted for tree planting. These trees may require the protection of a tree preservation order.

17 By closing off street to vehicles a pedestrian area is achieved between gable ends of existing blocks. A wall would reinforce enclosure and value for play. The positions of the wall should take orientation into account. Problem with noise from bouncing balls.

18 Gardens facing onto a play space should have high walls (2 m) to provide enclosure and privacy. This also provides a hard vertical surface for ball games.

19 Closed off sections of road and junctions and removal of end houses of terrace blocks, provide linked communal spaces within existing alleyways. Construction of small garage blocks enables pedestrian space to be set back from road but related to pedestrian route. Gable ends and garage walls provide enclosure for play space.

20 Gate at junction of communal area and pedestrian route space could reinforce residents group maintained realm.

21 Infill housing or garages, set back (in alignment with existing terraces) gives variety of space suitable for tree planting and sitting.

22 At road junctions gardens are often stopped off by gable end of adjacent terrace blocks, if the garden is long enough, this is an ideal space for off-street parking.

23 Where road width is excessive and use is restricted (ie in cul-de-sac) widen pavement, plant trees and provide benches.

24 Low wall at end of parking bay to screen windows from car head lamps.

25 Garage roofs could be used as raised play deck but enclosure important for safety and privacy (eg overlooking of gardens and open aspect dwelling). More intensive use of land may be achieved by exploiting opportunities for multi-level use (ie play space or balcony over garage which may also assist privacy and reinforce pedestrian/vehicular separation).

26 Garage blocks inconspicuously sited in closed-off road junctions or spaces formed by demolition of some housing.

3

3, 4 *Portland Grove, Lambeth, before and after rehabilitation. New communal space is paved, but surface treatment changes near houses to provide privacy*

4

2 Characteristics of bulk materials

Generally

2.01 To create stable conditions for establishing and maintaining vegetation cover of slopes, the nature of existing geology and desirability of bringing in new material; eg topsoil, should be studied.

Behaviour of slopes

2.02 Resistance of fragmented material to movement is due, in part, to its cohesion, and in part to friction. Friction is reduced by the weight of overlying material and is therefore related to angle of slope. Cohesion is reduced by increase in water content. In some clays this movement can be induced by a moisture content as low as 10 per cent.

Non-cohesive soils
Sands and gravel: shear strength arises entirely from friction. Failure of these slopes is a surface phenomenon producing saltation, with dry particles rolling down slopes. Flow slide is a condition of this failure occurring when saturated fine sand is disturbed; eg by vibration.

Cohesive soils
Clays: friction and the cohesive qualities of colloids serve to stabilize the slope of such soils. Slope failure occurs at angles greater than 20°, and as in all materials, slope angle decreases with height. Table II approximates general limits for angle of repose for various soils.

Table II Approximate limits for angle of response in soils

Soil type	
Non cohesive soils and chalk	35°–40°
Rock waste	45°
Very wet clay and silt	15°
Wet clay and silt	25°
Dry sand and gravel	50°
Dry clay	35°
Moist sand	40°

Table III Safe angles of repose in rock

Rock type	tonnes/ cu m of solid material	Safe slopes cuttings angles refer to horizontal	Angles of repose embankments
Hard massive sandstone	2·40–2·72	70°–90°	38°–42°
Soft sandstone	2·08–2·40	50°–70°	33°–37°
Shale	2·40–2·56	45°–60°	34°–38°
Marl	1·92–2·24	55°–77°	33°–36°
Limestone (hard eg carboniferous)	2·64–2·80	70°–90°	38°–42°
Limestone (soft eg Portland beds)	2·24–2·48	70°–90°	38°–42°
Chalk	1·92–2·80	45°–80°	33°–36°
Igneous rocks	2·56–2·96	80°–90°	37°–42°
Metamorphic rocks	2·56–2·88	60°–90°	34°–48°

Table VI Slope distances from situations or activities

Situation or activity		Min level area required
Rural roads		0·6 m to 1·2 m
Main roads		3 m
Buildings for:	construction operations foundation inspections service, fire and private access building maintenance landscape maintenance	1 m to 3 m depending on activity
Boundaries for:	maintenance of fences walls and hedges	1 m

Failures
Watch points for failures: examination of material at bottoms of cuttings can reveal possibility of failure. Thin rock beds weather rapidly and to a greater extent than thick rock beds. Water along bedding planes causes rock slips by chemical disintegration and leaching of cementing properties. Weight increase due to the presence of water is taken up by the soil causing stress and pressure in face of slope, which is relieved in the form of vertical cracks which will lead to failure **1**. There is considerable settlement in peat as it shrinks after drainage. Table III shows safe angles of repose in rock.

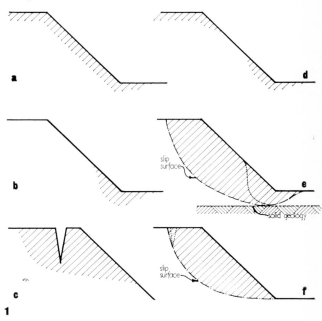

1

1 *Illustrates critical zones in slopes. Resistance of fragmented material to movement is due in part to its cohesion and in part to its friction. Friction is reduced according to the weight of over-lying material. Cohesion is reduced by an increase in water content. The interaction of these two conditions can result in slope failures:*
a *Surface softening due to loss of cohesion after increase of water content*
b *Softening at toe of slope due to loss of cohesion after increase in water content caused by bad drainage.*
c *Shrinkage due to loss of cohesion and deep seated softening due to water penetration at cracks*
d *Shaded areas indicate danger zones to be protected by suitable drainage facilities*
e *Deep seated slip resulting in cohesive soils over solid geology following surface and two softening*
f *Deep seated slip resulting in cohesive soils following shrinkage cracking and deep seated softening*

Rainwater run-off volume

2.03 Factors affecting run-off volume:
1 Rainfall duration.
2 Type of precipitations: snow will give a much more sudden release of water than rainfall.
3 Precipitation intensity.
4 Topography—ie catchment shape: an elongated catchment is less likely to flood than a broader shape. Slope angle and orientation, both to solar radiation and prevailing winds.
5 Type of vegetation.
6 Percolation and infiltration: rate of percolation and infiltration is affected by:
a Physical characteristics of soil.
b Soil moisture content.

c Surface cover: vegetation and snow increases infiltration.
d Gradient of slope.
e Rainfall characteristics.
f Organic content: high organic content promotes drainage.
g Inorganic content: gravel (particle size 20 mm to 60 mm) freely draining; sand (particle size 0·06 mm to 2·00 mm) freely drained with very little shrinkage or swelling; silt (particle size 0·002 mm to 0·060 mm) particles have similar characteristics to those of sand, but are less well drained; clay (particle size less than 0·002 mm) has very restricted drainage and holds more water than other soil types, thus restricting the amount available for plant growth.

Types of movement

2.04 Following are various types of soil movement:
1 Soil creep: slow process not exceeding 2 m per year and occurring particularly in stiff fissured clays. Usually only upper layers are affected, but occurs on slopes to 1 in 5½.
2 Fragmental slides: these occur in non-cohesive materials; eg sands and gravels, and exhibit slip if near their angle of repose. Embankments of these materials are not desirable.
3 Detritus slides: these occur where there are shallow layers of cohesive materials, or in fine grained materials, which take up water and slide under the influence of gravity.
4 Rock slides.
5 Rotational shear slips: where earthwork slopes are being constructed through clay formations it is desirable to create only moderately high embankments and cuttings as rotational sheer slips are deep seated and common in clays, though they do not occur in non-cohesive soils.

3 Design limits

Maintenance

3.01 The following factors should be considered as design limitations imposed by maintenance machinery:
1 Minimum turning circles of machinery.
2 Manoeuvrability of machines: slopes curved on plan fit more easily into the sequence of operation of machines than straight slopes. When straight slopes meet at an angle the problem is acute.
3 Operability of machines on steep slopes: steep slopes should be avoided; angulation usually upsets lubrication and fuel feed before the angle defined by the machine's centre of gravity is reached. Though gang mowers can accommodate any reasonable slope on undulating ground, cross slopes of more than 1 in 30 are liable to be 'skimmed-off' by the cutter bar leaving bare patches in the grass.
4 Slopes should be rounded at their tops and bottoms.
5 See table v for recommended gradients for mowing.

Affecting variation to slope limits

3.02 Soil materials are not stable if constructed with steeper slopes than their natural angle of repose unless reinforced.

Topsoiling
On inclines steeper than 1 : 1½ it is necessary to hold top soil in place with wooden frames, longitudinal boards or wire mesh staked in place.

Ground preparation
Organic matter is spread over the surface and worked in to improve top soil structure and water retention. To do this at low cost, any immediately available type of organic matter can be used; eg grass cuttings, leaf litter, sawdust, threshed soya bean plants.

Inert resins and emulsions
These have been used successfully on many areas as they can be sprayed cheaply, ready mixed with seed and fertilisers, from machines. They have the same retention properties as mulches.

Matting
Mats of brushwood can be pegged or embedded on slopes to retain water and prevent erosion, and through which the plants are established. Cheap jute matting is used for extensive areas, but for long lasting continuous support of steep slopes, polypropylene netting should be used.

Seeding
Compounds, paving, bricks, tiles, setts, cobbles and timber. These hard surfaces will also increase slope limits above natural angles of repose.

Costs; effects of construction equipment and techniques

3.03 Following factors should be considered as design limitations imposed by costs, construction equipment and techniques:
1 Balance of cut and fill is economically desirable, but an average of 25 per cent more cut than fill should be allowed for because of compaction
2 Minimum turning circles of equipment often establishes minimum curvatures of ground modelling in design or are a deciding factor in selection of machinery for use on sites with limited movement
3 Haul distances between points of cut and fill become important as scale of design increases
4 Availability of machinery
5 Desire to use only one machine
6 Nature of material to be excavated
7 Time for completion
8 Season and weather conditions
9 Water table and other site conditions
10 Whether topsoil and subsoil operations are separated
11 High mounds and deep depressions become costly on sites over a hectacre

Cost reducing factors

3.04 No precise statement for cost design differences is possible, but in general:
1 Circumferential deposition of earth is usually the most economical technique
2 Cut and fill operations within a single site is advisable
3 Profits and overheads on contracts for small sites are relatively greater than for larger sites
4 Hill and valley designs are less expensive than terracing designs and are relatively more visually effective for amount of earth moved
5 Variations in designs do not result in large cost variations, for sites less than 2 hectacres.
6 High rises and deep depressions become very expensive on sites greater than 1 hectacre

4 Three dimensional design

Surrounding topography

4.01 Landform of sites are enriched by designs which take into account the surrounding topography. In an urban setting, topography surrounding sites will also include buildings which must also be considered in the design solution. Surrounding topography can be ignored to an extent when sites are enclosed by mounds or embankments to reduce noise levels or improve microclimates.

Abstract and geometric forms

4.02 Choice of abstract or geometric landforms is a matter for the designer to decide, but following points could be considered:

1 Continuity between one form and another
2 Interlocking and overlapping forms
3 Spiral, wave and cellular forms in nature
4 Symmetry, assymmetry and rhythm
5 Expression of mathematical formulae as with sand dunes which express relationship between frictional resistance of sand grains and wind.

Building forms and land forms

4.03 Land adjacent to buildings can be developed to relate the buildings to surrounding landscape. Some designers often design buildings to grow out of sites **2**, or emphasised buildings as artefacts in landscapes by placing them on landform platforms **3**. Another approach is to use the landform to emphasise the form of the building. Attention should also be paid to approaches to buildings, considering them as part of the landform design **4**.

Microclimate and landform

4.04 Effects of wind funnelling and frost pockets occur in large and small landform situations. But, although knowledge now available on these effects in building complexes is relevant, much research has still to be carried out as regards to landforms.

Warm places within a site can be achieved with landform design when orientation and shelter are considered along with time of day and year when area will be used.

Land uses and landform

4.05 Many activities and buildings require level surfaces. The inherent lack of interest in flat surfaces can be countered by arranging spaces at different levels to each other. As the several processes of an industrial plant need not be at the same level, by varying them, not only can sites be more economically prepared in terms of cut and fill, but the landform design can make the industry more visually acceptable.

Existing undulating landform need not always be greatly altered as some activities such as parks and play areas benefit from variety in landforms and sites capable of subdivision into small units, as in housing, can also be located without substantial change to topography.

5 Drainage

Slope erosion

5.01 Stabilisation of slopes is an essential part of ground modelling, especially on slopes which have no vegetation, or on slopes where vegetation has not fully established itself. There are two types of slopes: cut and fill. Erosion on either is unsightly and potentially dangerous, and, on the latter type, liable to be unnoticed for some time, requiring extensive repairs when discovered. Though erosion can be by

2 *Wright's Herbert Jacobs house, an extreme example of a building designed to grow out of a site*
3 *Mias' Farnsworth house is emphasised as an artefact in the landscape by placing it on a landform platform*
4 *Approach to house integrates landform and building*

2

4

3

several agents, water is the most common one in an urban setting.

Cut slopes

5.02 The usual method for reducing amount of run-off on cut slopes is by positioning an intercepting ditch at tops of slopes. Soil loss is then only caused by water falling directly on the face. Such ditches lose their value if not kept clean.

High cuttings

5.03 Low cuttings are not subject to rapid soil loss, and it is an advantage to be able to terrace a high cutting into a series of low ones. Terraces should be designed to intercept run-off water and to lead it to one side for dispersal to the bottom of the cutting via a paved ditch or pipe.

Vegetation

5.04 Vegetation naturally and attractively controls erosion. Roots mechanically reinforce soil, decaying organic matter improves soil structure and foliage, alive or dead, protects surface against rain or wind.

Slope failure

5.05 Most failures occur during the first winter after installation of the slope, before vegetation has been completely established. Immediate attention to failed areas can forestall serious repairs until vegetation matures.

Most frequent failures are caused by surface slippage. Failure in top third of slope indicates possibility of water seeping or percolating from above into a porous layer of subsoil. Failure by slippage in bottom two-thirds of slope is usually caused by saturation of soil caused by inadequate compaction before rains start.

Repairing erosion to cuttings

5.06 In most cases only gulleys will need attention. They should be backfilled, fertilised, seeded and mulched. Old slopes which have never received a stabilisation treatment and are eroded badly require a light cultivation of the compacted soil to smooth out gulleys and rills, break up channels and make a more favourable seed bed.

Repairing erosion to fill slopes

5.07 Repair work to deeply eroded fill slopes is a long term proposition. Large gulleys or slip-outs require careful and quick attention to protect the surface adequately. There are ways to quickly control fill erosion:

1 A logs and coarse brush crib is constructed at the toe of the fill failure. Loose brush is then placed in the gulleys and covered with a thick layer of backfill material. Additional brush is spread over the surface and covered with soil. In this way further layers are provided until the fill contour is restored.

2 A logs and coarse brush crib is constructed at the toe of the fill failure. Backfill material is furnished from the top of the slope and a bulldozer is used to spread, compact and shape the material to the original fill contour. Brush layers are installed at suitable intervals as the fill is built up.

3 A further method is to use metal cribbing into which the backfilling can be dumped. This, possibly, is the most efficient and long lasting method.

Provision for flash floods

5.08 Usually drains are only sufficient to cope with the normal rainfalls for an area. Provision should be made for flash floods where there is a history of their occurrence, by increasing drain sizes and numbers.

Cuts below water table

5.09 When landscape designs are likely to disturb the local or regional water table, the various characteristics of subsoil water should be ascertained at the earliest possible stage—ie during site survey. Where possible designers should avoid unneccesary cutting below the water table. If it is unavoidable, as in the case of pipe laying etc, the depth, extent and direction of flow of ground water should be accurately determined. This can be done in three ways:

1 By extensive test boring
2 From geology and hydrology maps
3 From previous excavations and local knowledge. Characteristics of the material above the water table should also be considered to determine the effects of, say, heavy rainfall on the excavated site

Dewatering

5.11 One way to overcome this problem is to eliminate it. This can be done with a system of wells and pumps, but it is costly and mainly applicable to sands and gravels. However, most excavations allow for the removal of ground water from the site floor as the cutting proceeds with ditches and sumps. Ditches are positioned normal to the direction of flow and sumps are placed as near as possible to the main source of flow. Sumps can then be pumped or gravity fed through the ditches for disposal.

Ignorance of the existence of ground water can lead to gross miscalculations of excavation costs.

6 Calculations

Level of accuracy

6.01 Size of sites will control, to an extent, the degree of detailing. Designs for small sites usually drawn to large scales will often be prepared with considerable detailing, but as they are likely to require only one earth moving machine, they do not need sophisticated calculations. Large sites, however, may have many machines involved and large volumes of earth work. In such cases the degree of accuracy in the design will depend greatly on the accuracies possible with the machinery and the scale at which the drawings can be produced. An inaccuracy of 1 mm on a drawing at 1 : 200 represents an inaccuracy of 200 mm on site. Table VI lists acceptable deviations from planned contours.

Calculation of volumes

6.02 There are several methods depending on the degree of

5 *Sites for a 'ranch house' development in Los Angeles. Combination of effects due to cohesive soils, flash flooding and local seismic problems has resulted in several slope failures on developments such as this*

Information sheet
Landscape 35

Trim and change of level

This information sheet by SHIRLEY ANDREW *describes methods and detailing for separating areas of paving and other surfaces and for steps, ramps and ramped steps*

1 Trim

Purpose of trim

1.01 Trim used with paving generally has one or more of the following purposes:

1 To protect the edges of the paving and/or to prevent lateral spread of the base **1**.

2 To mark boundaries between paving and other surfaces— grass, water, roads.

3 To define areas of paving.

4 To form construction joints.

5 To collect surface water.

6 To control traffic.

7 To mark changes of level.

Choice of material, method of construction and detailing of trim depends on its intended purpose, required appearance, cost, durability and permanence.

Appearance

1.02 The appearance of an area of paving can be enhanced or spoilt by the treatment of its trim. Special care should be taken to choose materials which are in character with the paving and its surroundings.

Cost, durability and permanence

1.03 These factors usually have to be considered together as they are interrelated. Initial cost tends to rise with choice of the more durable materials. However, if initial cost is balanced with subsequent maintenance costs, choice of more expensive materials is often justified.

Permanence

1.04 The permanence of trim as distinct from durability must be decided. Sometimes it is appropriate for paths to use a trim material with greater permanence than that of the path paving (eg granite setts used as edge treatment to a gravel path), but generally the permanence of the trim materials should be same as that of the paving.

2 Materials

Precast concrete

2.01 Precast concrete kerbs are either hydraulically pressed or cast in moulds; the former are said to be more durable. They are cheaper than natural or reconstructed stone. Standard dimensions and profiles are illustrated in **2**.

Precast reconstructed stone

2.02 Some manufacturers produce reconstructed granite kerbs. They are made of hydraulically-pressed precast concrete using ordinary granite aggregate and conform with the British Standard[2].

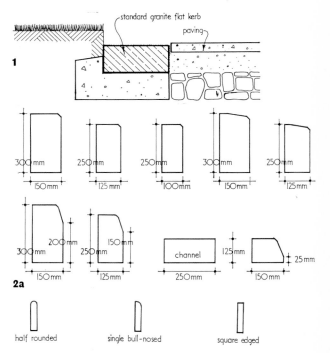

1 *Use of kerb, set flush with paving, to prevent spread of the base*

2 *Standard profiles and dimensions to* BS 340[1]

a *Precast concrete kerbs and channels;* **b** *Precast concrete path edgings. Available sections: 915 mm × 760 mm, 810 mm, or 860 mm.*

Natural stone

2.03 Natural stone kerbs are usually of granite or whinstone. They are extremely durable but cost considerably more than precast concrete. BS 435[3] specifies standard dimensions, profiles and finish.

Brick

2.04 Requirements for brick used as trim or edging to paving are basically as for brick paving itself. See information sheet LANDSCAPE 34.

Granite and whinstone setts

2.05 Requirements for granite and whinstone setts used as trim or edging are basically as for paving. See information sheet LANDSCAPE 34.

Timber

2.06 Suitable hardwoods are elm, larch and oak. Softwoods should be pressure-creosoted.

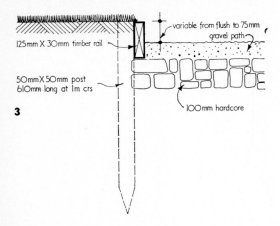

125mm X 30mm timber rail

variable from flush to 75mm
gravel path

50mm X 50mm post
610mm long at 1m crs

100mm hardcore

3

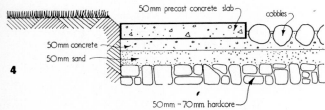

50mm precast concrete slab

cobbles

50mm concrete

50mm sand

50mm – 70mm hardcore

4

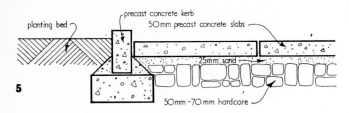

planting bed

precast concrete kerb

50mm precast concrete slabs

25mm sand

50mm – 70mm hardcore

5

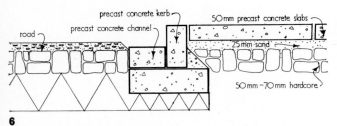

precast concrete kerb

road

precast concrete channel

50mm precast concrete slabs

25mm sand

50mm – 70mm hardcore

6

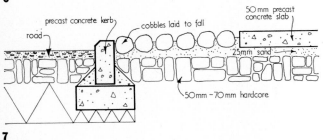

precast concrete kerb

cobbles laid to fall

50mm precast concrete slab

road

25mm sand

50mm – 70mm hardcore

7

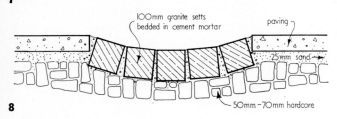

100mm granite setts
bedded in cement mortar

paving

25mm sand

50mm – 70mm hardcore

8

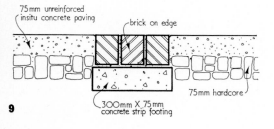

75mm unreinforced
insitu concrete paving

brick on edge

75mm hardcore

300mm X 75mm
concrete strip footing

9

3 *Junction of gravel path and rough grass using continuous timber rail kerb*
4 *Junction of cobble paving and grass using precast concrete slab as mowing border*
5 *Junction of precast concrete paving and planting using standard precast concrete kerb (see BS 340[1])*
6 *Junction of precast concrete paving and road using standard precast concrete kerb and channel (see BS 340[1])*
7 *Junction of precast concrete paving and road using standard precast concrete kerb and separating border of cobbles laid to fall to road*
8 *Granite setts used as surface water collecting channel in paving*
9 *Brick on edge used to form joint between bays of in situ concrete paving*
10 *Precast concrete or natural stone treads and brick or granite sett risers on a concrete base. Treads should be 50 mm thick*
11 *In situ concrete steps. A non-slip finish can be provided by brushing with a stiff broom before hardening, by hand tamping, by the addition of carborundum to the top surface or by inserting strips of non-slip material*
12 *Steps formed with timber risers on long inclines not steeper than 1 in 12. Risers should not exceed 100 mm if they are to be negotiated by prams*

3 Change of level

Steps

3.01 Rise should be between 80 mm and 150 mm and a going should be not less than 300 mm. Projection of treads over risers should never exceed 15 mm otherwise there is a danger of people tripping. Satisfactory gradients are between 1:2 and 1:7. Various constructions and details are illustrated in **10** and **11**.
Eleven steps is a comfortable length for a series of flights with landings 1 m to 2 m wide. Flights should not exceed 19 steps.

Ramps

3.02 For short distances a pedestrian ramp may be as steep as 1 in 6·5. For wheelchairs and prams the gradient must not exceed 1:10 (1:12 is more desirable). Surfaces should always be non-slip and surface water should be shed across the width of the ramp.

Ramped steps

3.03 On long ascents, ramped steps should be considered. Inclines should not be steeper than 1 in 12 and risers should be only about 100 mm if perambulators are to use the steps **12**. If only for pedestrian traffic, three or four steps can be introduced between ramp sections. Steps can be formed in the same way as illustrated in **10** and **11**. Nosings must be clearly defined to ensure that users see the steps.

4 References

BRITISH STANDARDS INSTITUTION
1 BS 340:1963 Specification for precast concrete kerbs, channels, edgings and quadrants [(90·22)Ff]
2 BS 1217:1945 Cast stone [Yf3]
3 BS 435:1931 Granite and whinstone kerbs, channels, quadrants and setts [(90·22)Fe1]

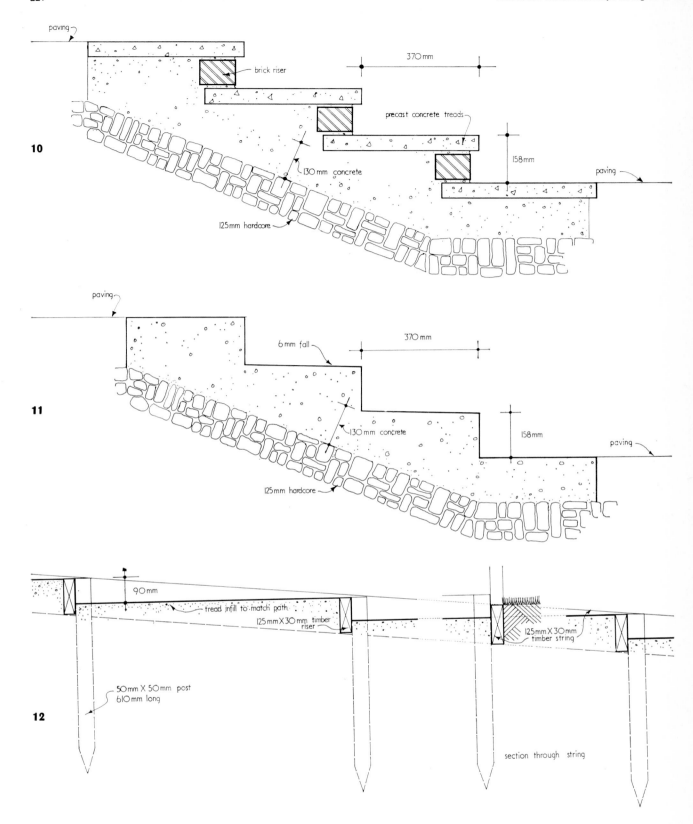

paving

brick riser

370 mm

precast concrete treads

10

130 mm concrete

158mm

paving

125mm hardcore

paving

6 mm fall

370 mm

11

130 mm concrete

158mm

paving

125mm hardcore

90mm

tread infill to match path

125 mm X 30 mm timber riser

125mm X 30 mm timber string

50mm X 50mm post 610 mm long

section through string

12

Information sheet
Landscape 36

Enclosures and barriers

This information sheet by SHIRLEY ANDREW *is a guide to the choice, design and construction of walls and fences, and also refers to other forms of enclosure and barriers such as ground formation.*

1 Forms of enclosure

1.01 This information sheet covers:
walls, including screen walls and retaining walls
fences
ground formation, including earth banks and depressions.
Other forms of enclosure are dealt with in the following information sheets:
trees—information sheet LANDSCAPE 6
hedges—information sheet LANDSCAPE 8
water—information sheet LANDSCAPE 33
paving—information sheet LANDSCAPE 34
bollards—information sheet LANDSCAPE 39.

2 Functions

2.01 Enclosures or barriers may fulfil the following functions: to form a *physical* barrier; to form a *visual* barrier; to form a *noise* barrier; to form a wind break; or to define space.

Physical and visual barriers
2.02 Unless both physical and visual barriers are needed (ie for both security and privacy) physical barriers need not block the view **1**. The precise function of physical barriers must be established. For example are they required to keep people in or out, or animals in or out, or both? If animals are the only objective and it is undesirable to block the view then a cattle grid may serve the purpose adequately.

Sound
2.03 Motorways in urban areas have emphasised the unpleasant effects of excessive noise where people live, work or play. Traffic noise[1] recommends that sound barriers should be of 'imperforate construction with a surface density of not less than 8 kg/m²'. To be most effective the barrier should be as close as possible to the noise source or in some cases to the recipient. A barrier midway between the two is least effective. The barrier should be at least three times as long as the distance between it and the recipient. A technique involving the use of protractors for establishing noise reduction due to screening and distance is described in the same bulletin.

Wind
2.04 Where a site is exposed and requires a wind break, it should first be established whether the barrier must fulfil other functions such as security. Where the only function is that of wind break, trees forming a shelter belt would be suitable. See information sheet LANDSCAPE 8.

Space definition
2.05 Where spaces must be defined, ie for different uses or to control traffic flow or to mark boundaries, choice of form of enclosure will again depend on whether other functions must also be performed.

Screen walls
2.06 The need often arises for enclosure for security, or the defining of space without presenting a complete visual barrier. This is where the *screen wall* should be used, as its surface perforations can provide interesting large scale texture.

3 Choice of enclosure

3.01 Choice of the most suitable form of enclosure is governed by some of the following considerations:

Function
3.02 Table I relates forms of enclosure with function.

Permanence
3.03 There may be design reasons for using a cheaper and less permanent material (eg post and wire fence is simpler and quicker to erect and take down than a cast in-situ concrete wall.)

Durability
3.04 Durability must be considered in relation to resistance to wear and vandalism, to weathering, and to required life of the enclosure. There is no point choosing a material which will last 100 years when it need only last five.

Relationship with other landscape elements
3.05 In choosing material and form of an enclosure attention should be paid to related elements of landscape and to local character.

Local techniques
3.06 Many parts of the country still use construction techniques passed down from generations (eg Pembrokeshire stone hedging, para 4.32). Local techniques use readily available materials and are more likely to blend with the character of the area. But choice should also relate to function, cost, permanence etc.

Availability of materials
3.07 Check local availability of materials, particularly where time and cost are important.

15 *Continuous bar fencing*

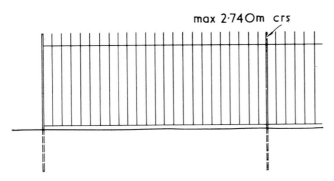

16 *Vertical bar fencing (unclimbable)*

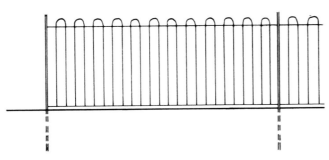

17 *Vertical bar fencing with hairpin tops for use in children's playgrounds*

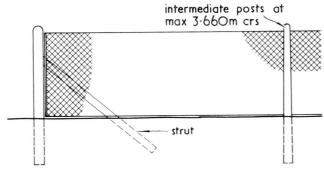

18 *Chain link (diagonal mesh) fencing*

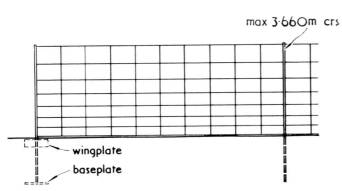

19 *Woven wire fencing*

Construction

5.06 Holes for posts should be as small as possible and filled with well-rammed excavated soil. Where the soil is not suitable for consolidation, posts should be set in concrete for half the depth of the excavation and the rest filled with well-rammed excavated soil.

Precast concrete

5.07 Precast concrete for fencing is usually used with other materials (eg strained wire fencing and close-boarded fencing, where the boards are timber and the posts and rails concrete). BS 1722 parts 1 to 6 and 10[18] covers types of fence incorporating concrete posts.

Metal

5.08 Ornamental wrought iron fences were popular in the late 18th and early 19th centuries. Wrought iron design then flourished not only in one-off examples but also in mass-produced castings from foundries **24**.

5.09 Most metal fences today are mild steel. BS 1722 : part 8:1966[18] and BS 1722: part 9:1963[18] specify recommended construction and erection. Tables II to V taken from these British Standards list relevant dimensions.

Protection

5.10 Mild steel rusts easily and should therefore be properly protected and subsequently maintained. BS 1722 describes standard ex-works finishes and recommended protective treatments on erection and subsequently.

Continuous bar fencing

5.11 This form of fence **15**, often used as a barrier to farm stock, is also suitable for separating parkland from driveways. Horizontal members are available in round and flat bar sections. See table II for recommended sizes. Standards may be flat, T or I section. Continuous bar fencing is factory-made and gates to match are also available.

5.12 Slight falls can be taken up by fencing but the manufacturer should be consulted. Fencing usually runs parallel with the ground. Slight curves on plan can be taken up but bars can be bent in the works to suit specific situations.

Table II *Dimensions of continuous bar fences*

Purpose	Height of fence mm	Standards		Number of horizontals	Length of pillar mm
		Depth in ground mm	Distance apart mm		
Sheep	1000	300 to 450	900	4	1500
General	1200	350 to 530	900	5	1750
Extra strong	1400	350 to 610	900	6	2000

Vertical bar fencing

5.13 This form of fence **16** is often referred to as unclimbable. For playgrounds the type with hairpin tops **17** should be used as the other type can be dangerous if children attempt to climb them. Vertical bars are available in circular or square section and may terminate in spikes, blunt tops or wrought iron spear heads. The standards are generally mild steel like the railings but precast concrete posts are also used. Raken panels of fencing can be specially manufactured to take up site falls. Spaces between verticals should not be less than 100 mm and not more than 120 mm. See BS 1722[18] part 9 for dimensions.

Chain link fencing

5.14 This form of fence **18** is commonly used as a barrier to farm stock. Materials, dimensions and construction are specified in BS 1722: part 1: 1963[18] from which table III is taken. Straining and intermediate posts may be of timber, precast concrete or mild steel.

Woven wire fencing

5.15 As with chain link, this form of fence **19** is most generally used for farm or estate work. Materials, dimensions and construction are specified in BS 1722: part 2: 1963[18] and table IV is taken from this. Straining posts, struts and intermediate posts may be of timber, precast concrete or mild steel.

Strained wire fencing

5.16 As above, this fence is commonly used for farm work. Materials, dimensions and workmanship for three types of strained wire fence (general pattern, dropper pattern and Scottish pattern) are specified in BS 1722: part 3: 1963,[18] table V is taken from this. Posts may be of timber, precast concrete or mild steel **20**.

Table III Chain link fences

Applicability	Height of top of fence at posts (mm)
House garden fronts and divisions	1000
Children's playgrounds	1200
General agricultural	1200
House gardens, playing fields and recreation grounds	1500
Highways and railways	1500
Commercial property	1800
Industrial security fencing	2100

Table IV Woven wire fences

Applicability	Height of top of fencing at posts (mm)	Number of horizontal wires
Light general purposes	760 to 800	5 to 8
Sheep	900	6
Cattle and sheep	1100	8

Table V Strained wire fencing

Height at top of wires (mm)	Number of horizontal wires
830	3
1000	5 or 6
1200	6
1400	7 or 8

Other materials
Plastics

5.17 Proprietary systems of post and rail fences are available using unplasticised polyvinyl chloride rails fixed to timber or pc or plastic coated posts. Plastic-coated chain link fencing is also available.

Gates

5.18 'A gate must appear as the way through a fence or wall. It is part of its function to state visually that there is a possible entrance **14, 21, 24**. If the gate looks stronger than the fence that flanks it, it will, in aesthetic terms, contradict its function. Many gates, sensible enough in themselves, look ridiculous because they ignore this principle.

Guard rails

5.19 Very small forms of enclosure are used to discourage movement off a given circulation area ie to protect flower beds, lawns or other areas of planting, or to preserve privacy. These should not form visual barriers and need not be particularly robust, though they should be strong enough

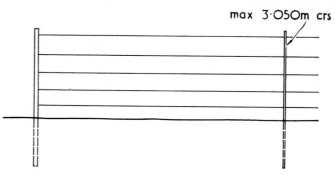

20 *Strained wire fencing*

21 *Tubular steel farm gates up to 4·25 m wide by 1·2 high*

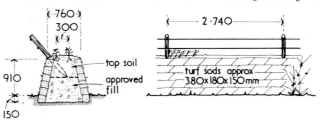

22 *Section and elevation of hedge bank*

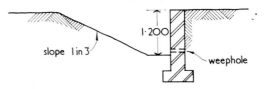

23 *Section through traditional ha-ha*

24 *Ornamental iron work at Beaminster Church*

to remain in position and undamaged when sat on or when children climb on them.

6 Ground formation

6.01 Where the function of a barrier is visual only or is a wind break, enclosure can be created simply by reshaping the contours into slopes and hollows or forming earth banks.

Hedge bank
6.02 This traditional technique is basically an earth bank. Turf sods roughly 150 mm thick × 380 mm × 180 mm are cut as parallelograms and laid on one of the long sides. The base of the new bank is stripped of turf to a depth of 150 mm and prepared to slopes. Turfs are built up in bonded courses and the centre filled with well-rammed soil as work proceeds. The height of a bank is about equal to its width at the base and the fences of the bank are battered. High banks are rarely built and it is more usual to provide a fence along the top and to one side. Rough posts about 75 mm diameter and 1·4 m long are driven into the top of the bank at an angle at 2·75 m intervals and two strands of no 8 galvanised wire fixed to them **23**.

Ha-ha
6.03 The ha-ha is a ditch which provides a physical barrier without obstructing the view. Although much used by the 18th-century landscape architect in this country it is supposed to have been devised by the French. A traditional ha-ha is usually one about 1·2 m deep with retaining wall on the garden side and with the other side sloping up from its base at about 1 in 3 in order to allow maintenance **24**.

7 Hedges

7.01 The use of hedges for enclosure is dealt with in information sheet LANDSCAPE 8.

8 Trees

8.01 Trees form an effective shelter belt against the wind. See information sheet LANDSCAPE 6.

9 Bollards

9.01 Bollards are a traditional method of forming an enclosure to prevent vehicles encroaching on pedestrian areas while maintaining the flow of pedestrian traffic. See information sheet LANDSCAPE 39.

25 *Water can prevent access without spoiling views*

10 Water

10.01 Water can be an effective physical barrier while, like the ha-ha, not interrupting the view **25**. See information sheet **33**.

11 References

1 GREATER LONDON COUNCIL Urban design bulletin. Traffic noise. London, 1970. The council [MS]
2 BEAZLEY, ELISABETH Design and detail of the space between buildings. London, 1960 (3rd impression 1968), Architectural Press (68:90) *Price £2·10*
3 WEDDLE, A. E. (editor) Techniques of landscape architecture. London, 1967, Heinemann Ltd. [08] *Price £4·50*
4 BUILDING RESEARCH STATION Digests 65 and 66 (second series): The selection of clay building bricks 1 and 2: 1965 and 1966, HMSO [Fg 2]
MINISTRY OF AGRICULTURE, FISHERIES AND FOOD
5 Fixed equipment of the farm leaflet 6: Permanent farm fences, 1969, HMSO [260(90–21)]
6 Fixed equipment of the farm leaflet 7: Cattle grids for private farm and estate roads, 1962, HMSO [260]
7 Fixed equipment of the farm leaflet 8: Farm gates, 1964, HMSO [260(90–3)]
8 Fixed equipment of the farm leaflet 17: Preservation of timber and metal, 1968, HMSO [260]
9 MINISTRY OF TECHNOLOGY Forest Products Research Laboratory leaflet 11: The hot-and-cold open tank process of impregnating timber, revised February 1964, HMSO [Yi]
BRITISH STANDARDS INSTITUTION
10 BS 12:1958 Portland cement (ordinary and rapid hardening) [Yq2]
11 BS 146:1968 Portland blast furnace cement [Yq2]
12 BS 187:1967 Calcium silicate (sandlime and flintline) bricks [Ff1]
13 BS 882:1201:1965 Aggregates from natural sources for concrete (including granolithic) [Yp1]
14 BS 890:1966 Building lines [Yq1] *Price £1·0*
15 BS 915:1947 High alumina cement [Yq2]
16 BS 1180:1944 Concrete bricks and fixing bricks [Ff2]
17 BS 1198–1200:1955 Building sands from natural sources [Yp3]
18 BS 1722: part 1: 1963 Chain link fences, part 2: 1963 Woven wire fences, part 3: 1963 Strained wire fences, part 4: 1963 Cleft chestnut pale fences, part 5: 1963 Close-boarded fences including oak pale fences, part 6: 1963 Wooden palisade fences, part 7: 1963 Wooden posts and rail fences, part 8: 1966 Mild steel or wrought iron continuous bar fences, part 9: 1963 Mild steel or wrought iron unclimbable fences with round or square verticles and flat studs and horizontals, part 10: 1963 Anti-intruder chain link fences, part 11: 1965 Woven wood fences [(90·21)Yy]
19 BS 3921: 1965 Bricks and blocks of fired brickearth, clay or shale [Fg2]
20 BS 2028: 1964 Precast concrete blocks [Ff]

12 Sources of information

Brick Development Association, 3 Bedford Row, London WC1 (01-242 1836)
British Precast Concrete Federation, 9 Catherine Place, London SW1 (01-828 8746)
Cement and Concrete Association, 52 Grosvenor Gardens, London SW1 (01-235 6661)
Timber Research and Development Association, Hughenden Valley, High Wycombe, Buckinghamshire (Naphill 3091) *or* 26 Store Street, London WC1 (01-636 8761)
Building Centre, 26 Store Street, London WC1 (01-636 5400)

Information sheet
Landscape 37

Services

This information sheet by SHIRLEY ANDREW *describes usual practice for laying public utility services underground and their effect on design of paved areas.*

1 Recommendations

Location of public service

1.01 In 1946 a joint committee set up by the Institution of Civil Engineers and the Institution of Municipal Engineers prepared a report[1] recommending standard practice for location of public utility services under paved areas. This information sheet is based on the latest edition of this report.

Co-ordination

1.02 The report of the joint committee recommends that the work of the various statutory undertakings be co-ordinated by the engineer of the appropriate highway authority. In minor and private housing schemes architects can fill this role satisfactorily if the problems of the undertakings concerned are understood.

Ascertaining requirements

1.03 Their various requirements should be established before any planning. Each undertaking will want to plan its work programme in advance and to order materials, delivery of which may take a considerable time.

Preliminary drawings

1.04 Copies of preliminary drawings should be forwarded to the undertakings for them to show their requirements more precisely. This is the time to raise any queries, as alternative positions for mains may be equally satisfactory.

Departure from recommendations

1.05 In order to ensure that mains are under footways, one may depart from recommendations of the joint committee and delay laying mains until kerbs have been laid in case there are any changes in the scheme.

2 Services

Electricity

2.01 Cables are laid directly into the ground, except in particularly busy streets and across carriageways where they are drawn through 100 mm diam earthware ducts (older 75 mm ducts are still in use).

Low voltage

Low voltage cable should be at a minimum depth of 450 mm below paved surface. Runs are usually restricted to 122 m lengths as long runs are wasteful in area.

High voltage

High voltage cables of 22kV and over are subject to agreement with the highway authority. Underground link disconnecting boxes are required at intervals on the low voltage system, usually at street intersections, with a pavement cover 760 mm × 610 mm. High voltage cables are of armoured cable with file covers.

Gas

2.02 Access is rarely required to gas service pipes and then, only to valves or to pumping pipes to remove condensate. Covers are usually 230 mm × 230 mm.

Mains

Mains are usually cast iron or steel, 100 mm minimum diameter. They should be laid 610 mm to 760 mm deep.

Service pipes

Service pipes are usually steel, 25 mm minimum diameter. They should be laid 460 mm to 610 mm deep.

Water

2.03 Cover required for water service is given in **1**. Access is indeterminate and is required for repair and fixing new branches. Easily removable paving is desirable over water mains and at least 1·2 in diameter clear space should be left around stopcocks above ground.

Mains

Mains are mostly of spun or vertically cast iron and steel, sometimes asbestos. They range in size between 50 mm and 3·35 m diameter but are commonly between 75 mm and 300 mm; about half of all mains being 100 mm.

Communication pipes

Communication pipes are lead or polythene between 12 mm and 50 mm diameter.

Telephones

2.04 Polythene cables are laid in ducts or straight in the ground. Earthenware duct in units of one, two, three, four, six and nine ways, all with 90 mm bore is the most popular. Asbestos cement ducts with 50 mm and 80 mm bore and 50 mm pvc ducts are used on housing estates. Polythene cables of up to 100 pairs are often used without ducts. Distance between jointing chambers should not exceed 155 m. When beneath a footway minimum depth for protected cable is 230 mm; for steel ducts 350 mm; and for

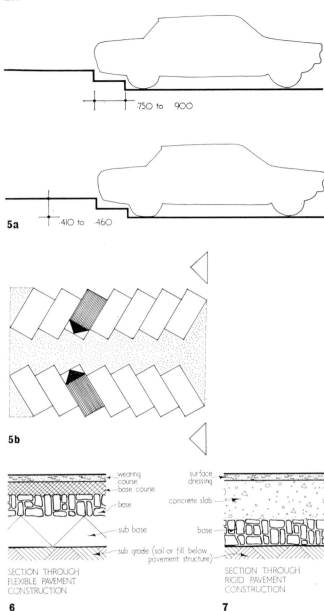

1 *Parking parallel to traffic flow*
2 *Parking at 45° to traffic flow*
3 *Parking at 60° to traffic flow*
4 *Parking at 90° to traffic flow*
5a *When raised pedestrian areas are provided, remember that a car projects beyond wheelbase. Difference in level should be too great to prevent bumper riding over higher area*
5b *Tinted area shows possible raised pedestrian path*
6 *Flexible pavement construction*
7 *Rigid pavement construction*

4.02 In urban situations and particularly in congested areas where large car parks are usually required, planting may be affected by atmospheric pollution in several ways.

4.03 Information sheets LANDSCAPE 6 and 7 contain lists of trees and shrubs with an indication of those suitable for situations where they will be exposed to town smoke and industrial fumes. Such species are suitable for car parking areas, but it should be noted that deciduous trees with large

leaves may cause problems in autumn; intermittent maintenance is needed to keep drainage clear. Some trees should not be used. (See list 1)

List 1 Trees that should not be used in car parks because they drop gums or berries or heavy leaves.
Lime varieties—*Italia platyphyllos*
Tilia tubra
Tilia euchluva
Maiden hair— *Ginto biloba*
Horse chestnuts—*Acer aesculus*
hyppocastorum

5 Construction

Bases and sub-bases
5.01 For other than the lightest traffic a suitable foundation must be provided, onto which the surface treatment of the parking area is applied. For flexible surface treatments (gravel, cold asphalt and coated tarmacadam) the component parts of the foundation are illustrated in **6**. For unit pavings (bricks, setts and cobbles) the foundation is basically the same. For a rigid pavement (eg concrete slab) the component parts of the foundation are illustrated in **7**.

Flexible pavements
5.02 For guidance on construction of parking areas surfaced with flexible pavements see information sheet 1423 (AJ 9.11.66).

Unit pavings
5.03 Where bricks, setts or cobbles are used to pave the surface of a parking area the construction of the base and sub-base is as for flexible pavements. See information sheet 1423 (AJ 9.11.66).

Rigid pavements
5.04 For guidance on the construction of parking areas surfaced with in situ concrete see information sheet 1424 (AJ 9.11.66).

Surface treatment
5.05 Choice of surface treatment is governed by the intended life of the parking area, the intensity, nature and intermittency of use, site conditions and of course cost (capital and maintenance). The following common methods of surface treatment are set out in roughly ascending order of permanence, durability and construction cost.

Grass
5.06 Grass is suitable for parking on if use is intermittent or not intense, but the area must be well drained. Ideally the grass should be coarse and kept mown or scythed. Long grass is more sparse and weak and much more easily damaged.

Stabilised grass
5.07 To give a more durable surface grass can be stabilised with bitumen. Newly planted grass seed is spread with sand to a depth of about 30 mm and sprayed with bituminous emulsion. The emulsion should be a non-toxic water based type and used at the rate of $0 \cdot 75$ litres/m². After the grass has appeared a further topping of about 6 mm stabilised gravel or sand should be given. The grass grows through this and forms a dense sward.

Stabilised gravel
5.08 Gravel surfaces can be stabilised by sealing with bituminous emulsion and rolling fine gravel into the surface.

This provides a surface more impervious to weeds and not subject to displacement by traffic like loose gravel. Bituminous emulsion to BS 434:1960[2] is sprayed on at rate of 1·5 litres/m² and blinded with coarse dry sand. After a few days a second layer is sprayed at the rate of 1 litre/m² and blinded with fine pea gravel (approx 6 mm diam; 1 m³ spread over 160 to 190 m²) and rolled with a 300 to 500 kg. roller.

Firepath pots
5.09 Firepath pots are precast concrete paving units, usually hexagonal or circular in shape, 100 mm thick with a hole in the middle. This hole and the spaces between pots are filled with soil and grass is grown. The result is an unobtrusive paved surface suitable for light traffic **8**. For notes on construction see information sheet LANDSCAPE 34 table VII.

Gravel
5.10 Gravel may be used as a surface treatment either sealed or unsealed. For notes and construction details see information sheet LANDSCAPE 34 para 1.42 and table VII.

Tarmacadam
5.11 Standard specifications for traffic areas using a tarmacadam surface treatment are given in *Specification for road and bridge works*[3]. General guidance is also given in information sheet 1423 table III (AJ 9.11.66).

Asphalt
5.12 Hot rolled asphalt is commonly used for areas of heavy

traffic and is a two-course surface treatment (ie a base course and a wearing course). General guidance is given in information sheet 1423 table III (AJ 9.11.66), standard specifications in *Specification for road and bridge works*[3].

Unit pavings
5.13 Unit pavings such as bricks, precast concrete or granite setts and cobbles are suitable surface treatments for parking areas. They are unlikely to be economical for other than small areas, and must be laid on a suitable sub-base and base. For a description of materials and laying techniques see information sheet LANDSCAPE 34.

Concrete pavements
5.14 Concrete (rigid) pavements are dealt with in information sheet 1424 (AJ 9.11.66).

Surface water drainage
5.15 Surface water drainage for paved surfaces is dealt with in information sheet LANDSCAPE 34 paras 3.15 to 3.37.

Trim
5.16 See information sheet LANDSCAPE 35.

References

1 MHLG Design Bulletin 12. Cars in housing 2, HMSO, 1967.
2 BSI BS 434:1960. Bitumen road emulsion (anionic). The Institution.
3 MOT. Specification of road and bridge works. HMSO, 1963.

8 *Firepath pots give fairly unobtrusive paved area. Grass can be grown in holes in pots. Suitable for light traffic*

Information sheet
Landscape 39

Street furniture

This information sheet by SHIRLEY ANDREW *is a guide to the design, choice and layout of street furniture in the urban landscape*

1 Design principles

General
1.01 Although the term *street furniture* covers a wide variety of items, from litter bins to lighting standards, most of them have the common characteristics that they are relatively small in scale in the urban environment and tend to be present in large numbers—for example, parking meters.
It is mainly because of these characteristics that street furniture so often emerges as a disruptive element in the landscape. But there are of course other reasons, such as lack of design sensitivity, and the fact that several different authorities are often responsible for the various items.

1.02 Poor design, and the difficulty of locating the better designs, have also had an effect. However, the situation is steadily improving, largely as the result of the efforts of bodies such as COID which not only actively encourages good design but publishes a guide to aid selection[1].

1.03 The following notes cover the general principles to be observed in choosing and siting street furniture.

Function
1.04 The first rule should be to establish that an item of street furniture is really necessary in the situation under consideration.

Siting and layout
1.05 Successful results are easier to achieve when the landscape designer is responsible for the several items of street furniture which may be required, because in this way it is often possible to group them coherently.

Form and appearance
1.06 When the landscape designer is responsible for all street furniture it should not be difficult to ensure that there

is design continuity, or at least design sympathy, between the design of individual items. Even when other authorities are involved in the provision of street furniture, for example letter boxes and bus shelters, it is highly desirable that consultation should take place and that the landscape designer should co-ordinate the work.

1.07 The apparent size of an item of street furniture in relation to its surroundings is what constitutes scale. While actual size is governed by function and sometimes also by statutory requirements, it is important to select individual items that combine to provide the right scale in any given situation.

1.08 Practical considerations influence the choice of materials (see para 3 below), and colour is often dictated by the nature of the material.

1.09 As a general guide colours should be as neutral as possible unless the function of the street furniture demands otherwise.

1.10 Design does not finish with the selection of the appropriate items of furniture, and their layout. Most items either stand on the ground or are fixed to walls, and the detailing of these junctions is highly important. Where the base of a fitting is on (or comes through) paving, for example, it is essential that the paving be properly finished around it, and relaid if necessary. Street furniture should look as if it has always belonged with the street rather than having been thrust upon it **1**.

1 *It is not enough for street furniture to be well designed and correctly laid out; equally important is the problem of incorporating fittings into surrounding surfaces so that they 'belong', and do not obtrude. This successful example is part of Lecture Halls at Cambridge, by Casson, Condor & Partners*

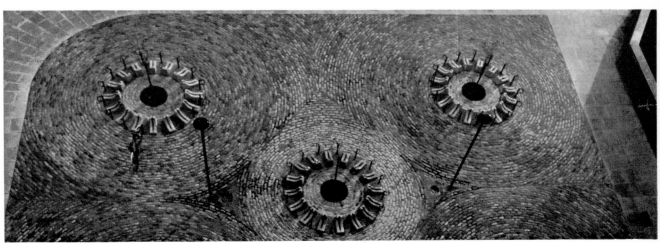

1

2 Choice

2.01 Table I is a checklist of the factors to be taken into account in the choice of suitable street furniture.

Table I: Checklist for choice of street furniture

Function	List functions to be served by each item of street furniture and note the conditions required to enable these functions to be carried out effectively. See para 3
Durability	Check climatic and exposure conditions for effects on materials and construction. Check likelihood of vandalism and other exceptional conditions
Permanence	Related to durability. Requirements for street furniture at fairs and exhibitions may differ from those of more permanent situations
Intensity of use	Consider in relation to durability and permanence
Cost	Consider first cost in relation to maintenance
Local character	Check limitations on choice of materials imposed by local character

3 Street furniture types

Seating

3.01 Sitting areas should be located in sheltered positions and where they are not too close to traffic.
On the other hand when people are sitting down they often like to be able to watch nearby activity such as traffic, shopping or children's play areas.

3.02 The form of seating is influenced by the nature of the material used: a hardwood bench should differ in form from a precast concrete seat. But ergonomic considerations should always be the basis of good design **2**.

Materials

3.03 Usual materials are hardwood (Burma teak, iroko, oak, afrormosia. African mahogany, African walnut, utile, afzelia, agba and keruing), precast concrete, and metal (aluminium, mild steel, cast iron). Cast iron is not much used these days because of cost. Softwood is suitable provided it is adequately protected with a paint system and subsequently repainted regularly. A fairly new development is the use of polyvinyl chloric in plank form. Most seating design uses a combination of at least two of the above materials **3**.

Plant containers

3.04 Plant containers are useful in defining spaces and forming enclosure. They can also define changes of level. As a general rule they should not be used where plants will grow naturally in the ground. In locating plant containers care must be taken to ensure that the conditions will be favourable for the plants. The main consideration is adequate light (sites under balconies for example are not generally desirable). It is advisable to avoid traffic fumes and wind.

3.05 The general principles of plant container design are illustrated in **4**.

Materials

3.06 Plant containers can be constructed in bricks, precast concrete blocks, setts, or formed of in situ concrete, provided suitable arrangements for drainage are made in the detailing. See AJ information sheet LANDSCAPE 36 for notes on types of brick and construction principles.

3.07 Proprietary plant containers are available in precast

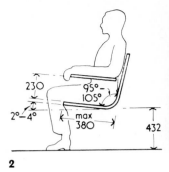

2

3

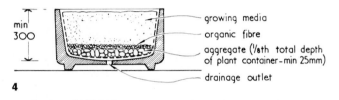

growing media
organic fibre
aggregate ($^1/_8$th total depth of plant container-min 25mm)
drainage outlet

min 300

4

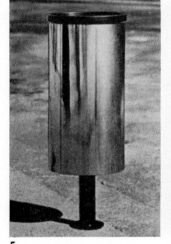

5

6

7

8

Segregation of function

3.03 Various functions of streets and open spaces can be separated, and enhanced at night by appropriate lighting without conflict of requirements:

1 Provision of walkways and shops at a higher level than the carriageway, and with bridges or subways for crossing the highway.

2 Off-street parking.

3 Provision of pedestrian-only shopping precincts with separated parking and service access.

4 Provision of a 'stoa'—ie with buildings overhanging the footway and supported on columns which visually screen the footway and shops from the carriageway.

5 Separation of pedestrian and vehicle routes in residential areas.

Lighting special features

3.04 Ideally attention should be drawn naturally to important features:

1 Drivers should be able to find their way easily, picking out traffic signals and signs and discerning other road users without being distracted by commercial lighting.

2 Shoppers should be able to find the shops they need quickly.

3 Fine buildings should be well shown or incorporated in surprise views, with less worthy buildings left inconspicuous.

4 Gardens and fountains should display their beauty without distorting the colour of surrounding foliage.

5 Monotonous areas can be enlivened by lighting a few attractive foci—turning them into landmarks.

Floodlighting features

3.05 Floodlit buildings **2** can be striking when seen from unexpected viewpoints or through openings—a floodlit church on a slight rise can appear to float over the whole town, and some engineering works (eg cooling towers, elevated roads and bridges) can be beautiful when appropriately lit at night. Lighting should not be indiscriminate. Each feature should have a dark surround (see para 10).

Commercial lighting

3.06 Commercial lighting is comprised of lighted displays in windows, and luminous advertising signs, each trying to outdo competitors **3**. Traders sometimes mutually agree on restraint, and local authorities may restrain displays on sites away from recognised commercial areas, but usually the desired effect of displays and signs is completely lost. Though signs at right angles to facades of buildings are individually more conspicuous from a road than those on the building face; in the mass they hide and conflict with one another; so a sign on the facade may be as effective without unnecessarily interfering with the scene.

Commercial signs must never confuse or conflict with traffic signs or signals; local authorities and the DOE have powers to have offending signs extinguished.

Traffic signs

3.07 Design, siting and illumination of all traffic signs is officially prescribed and little latitude is permitted.

1 *Confusion of signs, street lighting and traffic directions in a crowded shopping street on a wet night*
2 *Floodlit building giving punctuation and coherence to scene*
3 *Overcrowded advertisement signs mutually interfere*
4 *In Trafalgar Square, illuminated fountains and floodlit building providing visual foci*

1

2

3

4

However, siting them blindly according to regulations can result in absurdities or confusion.

Overall plan
3.08 It is important when drawing up a coherent lighting scheme to study the complete scene as perceived from key positions. When drivers' needs are considered, it is essential to include all features important to them, such as traffic signs and their backgrounds, so that their effectiveness can be appraised.

Though such planning can be seen in some cities rebuilt after the War, and in concerted action by a group of neighbouring authorities, it is generally rare. Valuable results may be possible however, by individual efforts on a smaller scale.

4 Lighting of city centres

4.01 Special lighting is required in the central areas of cities, for instance: civic centres with the principal municipal buildings and monuments; centres of night life and amusement, or of transport and traffic; shopping and commercial centres; or places of natural resort such as seaside promenades. Smaller towns and suburbs may not possess a large centre, but most have main streets or special vistas, which are natural centres by which the town is remembered.

British standard code
4.02 The Code[2] part 9 discusses lighting of areas of importance, including pedestrian precincts, public car parks, pedestrian subways, and, briefly, floodlighting and decorative lighting. Part 1 gives guidance on the daylight appearance of lighting installations.

Lighting level
4.03 Civic centres should be brighter than surrounding areas. The Code recognises this and provides for two grades of civic centres, specifying lighting levels on the horizontal surface for each. The level of illumination on vertical surfaces and shop windows is more important to the overall impression than the gross amount of light.

Visual foci
4.04 Monuments and fountains often afford natural foci for civic centres and can be most effective when appropriately lit **4**.

Parks and gardens
4.05 Light should not attempt to adorn gardens by way of visible lamps, but to serve it by revealing selected trees and plants, using white light to display their natural colours.

Festive lighting
4.06 Festive lighting may be needed. Provision of appropriate circuits can be made with outlets at public lighting standards and elsewhere. Though temporary, the lighting must be well engineered and capable of resisting rain and wind without failing or offering hazards to the public—this is specially important at seaside resorts.

Lighting equipment as street furniture
4.07 Lighting equipment should look as good by day as by night, and be sited so as not to interfere with day or night views. Guidance on these matters is given in the Code[2] parts 1 and 9. Scale of equipment, especially if column-mounted, must suit that of adjacent buildings. Important vistas must not be cluttered with too many columns; it is often better to use fewer and more powerful units on higher columns where the scale of the surroundings permits. In narrow streets it may be desirable to mount lighting

equipment on facades of buildings, though this involves difficulties of wayleaves, maintenance and siting (see para 5.05).

5 Lighting of traffic routes

British standard code
5.01 Technical provisions for lighting traffic routes are controlled by BS CP 1004 : 1963[2] and are outlined in para 7.01.

Architectural aspects
5.02 For lighting equipment a degree of choice is possible; different types and finishes of columns and lanterns are available, and lamps and the colour of the light may be chosen to suit the urban scene; though this is largely governed by technical and economic factors.

Daylight appearance
5.03 Daylight appearance of lighting installations and their relation to their surroundings is discussed in the Code[2] part 1 clause 1.205. Lighting furniture can contribute to more formal situations, but the Code points out that inconspicuousness is generally best and that where safety permits, heights of columns should relate to heights of adjacent buildings. The Code also considers sizes and types of lantern; types of bracket, lantern and standard; and materials and finishes used. The array of lanterns—(whether they are seen against sky or buildings) is also important. Lanterns are usually best not sited directly in front of significant buildings or monuments, nor allowed to interfere with important views. The Council of Industrial Design publishes approved designs of standards, lanterns and brackets[6].

'One-off' equipment
5.04 Situations occasionally arise to justify designing special equipment. This is an expensive solution which should not be lightly undertaken. Where it is necessary to comply with the Code requirements for light distribution, considerable development work must be done and complexities involved in maintenance and stocking of spares should be appreciated.

Siting and fixing
5.05 Incongruous siting of fixtures is more likely to result from failure to consider architectural implications than from technical difficulties. Columns in narrow streets are particularly awkward though attaching lanterns to buildings for an uncluttered effect **5** often presents difficulties too: except in Scotland (where special powers exist), each fixing must be negotiated separately and the results can be aesthetically and technically untidy. It is often impossible to find sufficiently strong fixings on old buildings and wide footpaths limit the use of maintenance equipment. For technical reasons special siting rules apply at junctions and turns, lanterns must not form misleading patterns in perspective.

Street lighting for new buildings
5.06 It is occasionally possible to incorporate street lighting in new buildings. The relevant authority must be contacted to ensure that it forms part of the complete installation. Questions of ownership, access to the equipment, maintenance, electrical supply etc must be resolved.

Where buildings overhang footways to form a 'stoa', footways can be lit independently of the street lighting: the lighting should also be independent of shop windows. Lighting of a colour different from that of the street lighting may be considered; and there may be aesthetic advantage in lighting the footways strongly to silhouette columns of the 'stoa' against a brightly lit background. Questions of ownership, electrical supply, maintenance, access etc will have to be negotiated here also.

Lanterns parallel with street axis

5.07 Lanterns may be used parallel with the street axis, mounted on building faces. This has special advantages in very narrow streets; and in all cases, lanterns are almost invisible by day and inconspicuous at night. Such systems demand very short spacings and high power compared with a conventional system, and the problems noted in para 5.05 also apply. A system of this type uses lanterns similar to linear floodlights and mounted high on buildings, using either linear tungsten halogen lamps or a special mercury-iodide lamp. This system is best suited to streets of uniformly high buildings.

6 Lighting residential streets

British standard code

6.01 Technical provisions for lighting lightly trafficked streets and footways are controlled (part 3 of the Code[2] outlined in para 7.01). They allow more latitude when siting lanterns and for distribution of light (especially in the case of footways) than requirements for traffic routes.

Minor streets and footways

6.02 The highway authority determines whether streets are to be categorised Group B1, 'lightly trafficked streets' or B2 'footways'. Lighting of the former is the responsibility of the highway authority, whereas footway installations are under the control of lighting authorities who are not highway authorities. Requirements for Group B1 are based on the requirements of vehicular traffic, but footways (B2) make no allowance for vehicles.

Lightly trafficked streets

6.03 Group B1 lighting should reveal the carriageway, footways and junctions, and avoid glare. In addition, heavy shadows as from trees must be avoided, and gardens should be lit to reassure pedestrians and assist police.
Lighting should suit amenities of the district—eg lower mounting height as tall columns are incongruous in streets with low houses. Lower mounting height can be an invitation to malicious damage in some areas. Anti-vandal enclosures of very tough plastic are available and reduce damage.

5 *Lanterns attached to buildings (high-pressure sodium lamps)*
6 *Symmetrical diffusing post-top lantern in residential area*

Where there are good gardens and trees, smaller fluorescent tubes or high pressure mercury fluorescent lamps are to be preferred to low pressure sodium lamps, light from which is devoid of colour rendering.

Footways

6.04 Requirements for footways are aesthetic rather than technical. Installations should be harmonious with surroundings; glare (often the result of long spacings between low mounted units) should be avoided, and there should be no badly lit patches to reassure those using the footway that no one is lurking in the dark. Lamps should be provided with anti-vandal enclosures.

Radburn and other layouts

6.05 The Code[1] does not cover lighting for residential areas not arranged on conventional streets, such as housing on Radburn and similar plans, high-rise blocks or blocks with footways and roads separated. In these areas lighting should primarily be of footways. Diffusing lanterns are often used with a symmetrical distribution of light **6**, and lanterns with canopies to reduce light reaching bedroom windows. Smaller paths, especially between houses, must be well lit for their whole length; small wall-mounted bulkhead fittings may be sufficient. Lighting should facilitate finding addresses.
Where there are carriageways for cars and trade vehicles, they should be lit as for group B1. Where vehicles and pedestrians are segregated, lighting can clearly differentiate the two, eg by using a white light for pedestrian ways and low pressure sodium for vehicular ways. Where there are high rise flats in areas subject to malicious damage, lighting can be by downward directed floodlights fixed to parapets and maintained from the roof by swinging them inboard on hinged brackets. The effect is not unlike moonlight, but lacks the intimacy of lower mounted lanterns and may create areas of dense shadow under overhanging parts.

Means

7 Lighting of streets

British standard code

7.01 The BS CP 1004: 1963[2] is issued in nine parts and indicates sound practice in the lighting of various features of streets, as follows:
Part 1: General principles ⎫
Part 2: Lighting for traffic routes ⎬ issued together.
Part 3: Lighting for lightly trafficked roads and footways (group B).

5

6

Part 4: Lighting for single-level road junctions and round-abouts.

Part 5: Lighting for multi-level interchanges (to be issued).

Part 6: Lighting for bridges and elevated roads.

Part 7: Lighting for tunnels and underpasses (to be issued).

Part 8: Lighting for roads with special requirements (ie roads in the vicinity of aerodromes, railways, docks or navigable waterways).

Part 9: Lighting for town and city centres and areas of civic importance (including pedestrian precincts, public car parks, pedestrian subways and stairways, and briefly floodlighting and decorative lighting).

British standard specifications

7.02 British standard specification for street lanterns[9] is a construction and performance specification for lanterns suitable for use in conjunction with the Code[2]. BS cover concrete[10], steel[11] and aluminium[12] columns, giving dimensions and performance. They do not specify particular designs.

Lighting of streets: principles

7.03 Technical basis for lighting streets is set out in the Code[2] part 1. Aims of the lighting are to reveal to drivers the run of the road ahead, and the presence and movements of other users of the road. This is best achieved with lighting from discrete sources of light suspended at a significant height above the surface of the carriageway, preferably in positions near the lines of the kerbs. Other considerations, especially reduction of glare, cost and aesthetics, lead to a spacing between lanterns of up to three or four times the mounting height.

The relationship between the geometry of the installation and the light distribution is complex. In general, the less the ratio of the spacing to the mounting height, the less critical is the requirement for light distribution. Therefore, results are better as the mounting height increases and the spacing reduces. However, there are aesthetic and practical disadvantages in short spacings, and the tendency has been to increase mounting heights to reduce the ratio.

Lighting traffic routes

7.04 The usual mounting height for lighting traffic routes is 10 m, though occasionally lower heights are called for (mainly in streets of architectural importance where higher units would be incongruous), or greater heights (usually in very wide or important streets). In multilevel intersections much higher mountings are often used (see para 8.03). Spacing is usually of the order of 20 m to 45 m, and lanterns should emit approximately 12 000 lumens in directions below the horizontal.

Cutoff and semi-cutoff

7.05 Cutoff and semi-cutoff are the alternative techniques for lighting carriageways. In the former, light distribution diminishes sharply to nearly zero above about 75° to the downward vertical; in the latter the diminution is less severe and emits light to higher angles. The respective geometries are linked to the distributions; for cutoff systems, spacings should not exceed 3·2 times the mounting height, but for semi-cutoff systems they may be up to 4·4 times the mounting height. Cutoff systems produce less glare and less light is directed at buildings, but at the expense of shorter spacings. They work best on rougher road surfaces. Semi-cutoff systems are less costly, as spacings are greater; buildings are better lit; advantage can be taken of less rough surfaces; but they tend to be more glaring.

Tables in the Code indicate the maximum spacing for various mounting heights and carriageway widths, with (in the latest amendment) preferred values indicated, for the two systems and for various arrangements of lanterns and widths of carriageway.

City centres

7.06 Part 9 of the Code permits lighting of city centres by large diffusing lanterns of higher power than usual and often at greater mounting height than in normal streets. In these cases requirements for light distribution are relaxed.

Siting lanterns

7.07 Part 2 of the Code provides for siting lanterns in various patterns:

1 Road of normal width—staggered arrangement.

2 Wider roads—opposite arrangement.

3 Dual carriageways—combinations of opposite and central or twin central. Trees may necessitate central lighting on narrower roads.

Lightly trafficked roads

7.08 Lighting to group B1 roads is generally similar to that for traffic routes, but with a mounting height normally 5 m, or where special reasons apply, eg wide roads, 6 m. Corresponding spacings are 33 m and 40 m respectively, ± 10 per cent. Light distribution is not rigidly laid down but 3000 to 5000 lumens (not lower hemisphere) at 5 m high and 5000 to 8000 lumens at 6 m must be provided.

Footways

7.09 For group B2, footways, mounting height must not exceed 13ft (3·962 m) (this is included in the definition of motorways in the Act); spacing must not exceed 60 m and is normally much less. A light distribution ranging from 900 to 3000 lumens from a simple diffusing lantern is usual.

8 Lighting particular features

Bridges

8.01 Lighting of bridges is discussed in part 6 of the Code[2]. Distribution of light from lanterns on bridges often has to be specially designed; a cutoff distribution is imperative. Objects on bridges may have little or no background against which they can be seen; lanterns on a humped bridge may form a confusing pattern against which vehicle lights can be lost. Bridges crossing railways or navigable waterways must not show lights which could confuse with signals or beacons.

Appearance of lighting equipment on bridges is important. The Code[2] discusses the view both from points on the bridge and from the side. Best views are often skew, and columns, especially in staggered formation, can present an unpleasing array. The relationship of lighting equipment to bridge parapets is also important, and the best solution may be to keep equipment clear of the structure. Lighting from parapets seldom succeeds. See para 12.03.

Vehicular tunnels

8.02 Lighting vehicular tunnels presents many problems and specialist advice is essential at the early planning stage. Part 7 of the Code[1], dealing with tunnels, has not yet been published.

Lighting tunnel interiors

Lighting equipment is usually placed in the haunches of tunnels or, occasionally, on roofs. Lighting is usually with fluorescent lamps in continuous diffusing fittings providing about 150 to 200 lux by day, and reducing to about 50 lux by night. Fittings should be waterproof, sealed against ingress of dirt and corrosion resistant.

Short tunnels

Short tunnels, ie those through which daylight penetrates and where the exit can be seen from the entry, present no great problems to the entering driver and lighting as described above is usually sufficient.

Long tunnels

Long tunnels where the exit cannot be seen from the entry, or where daylight from the exit does not effectively penetrate through present problems at the entry. The great range of brightness in daylight prevents drivers entering the tunnel from seeing obstructions just inside until entering and too close to avoid a collision. (It is not, as often thought, a problem of the time taken by the eyes to adapt.)

To overcome this, entry zones must provide an intermediate level of brightness, such that when outside, drivers can just see into this zone, and when in it, they can just see into the tunnel. The luminance of the zone must be about 600 apostilb and its illumination about 1000 lux. Length of the zone is usually around 60 m. Lighting should not be graded along the length of the zone. There are several techniques for lighting the zones:

Fluorescent lamps: If these are used the zone will require 20 or more continuous rows of tubes according to the width, switched in sections to accommodate various weather conditions.

Lamps with high light output: Usually low-pressure sodium, placed at haunches and incorporated with continuous fluorescent tubes, which are used for night lighting. In tunnels with a curved entry zone they can be used to light the wall to form an effective background; careful location of this is essential.

Daylight can be used by providing an enclosure outside the tunnel with a louvred roof designed to exclude all sun and admit sufficient daylight to provide the necessary light. Capital cost is high, but operating cost, apart from cleaning and painting, is small. Artificial light is needed at night, and it is necessary to deal with snow which may fall through the louvre **7**. A shorter daylight louvre combined with an artificially lit zone within the tunnel proper may be used.

Tunnel surfaces

All tunnel lighting systems depend upon the provision and maintenance of light surfaces, which must permanently resist adverse atmospheric conditions including damp, diesel exhaust and frequent cleaning; and should not become electrically charged (as plastics do), which attracts dirt. Dark ceilings have no visual advantages, but may be necessitated when acoustic damping is provided on the roof. Carriageway surfaces should be dark outside the portal and light within the tunnel. All surfaces should be permanently maintained at the designed reflection factors.

Multi-level interchanges

8.03 The problem consistent with multi-level interchanges is that conventional lighting appears as a confusing constellation of lights. A method widely used is to provide lanterns on masts 25 to 35 m high and spaced 75 to 100 m apart. The result is to reduce the visual clutter **8**.

7

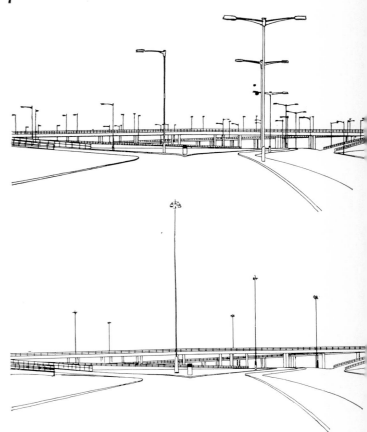

8

7 *Vehicular tunnel with louvred entry to use daylight to reinforce entry zone lighting*
8 *Multi-level interchange perspectives showing conventional lighting giving considerable clutter, and lighting by high masts showing orderly aspect*
9 *Night view of multi-level interchange using high masts*

9

A common arrangement is three to six 400 to 1000 W HP mercury fluorescent or HP sodium lamps to a mast (several units to a mast avoids trouble if a lamp fails). Such a system should provide illumination to 50 lux over the whole area. Slender high tensile steel masts are inconspicuous. Costs have been found comparable with those of conventional lighting if one mast can replace seven to 10 conventional lamp columns **8**, **9**.

9 Lighting for other features

Lighting of large areas
9.01 Method of lighting depends upon the use and shape of the area, nature of surrounding buildings etc. The Code[2] part 9 discusses methods and gives examples.

Areas bounded or traversed by streets may be sufficiently lit by the street lighting installation, upgraded if necessary.

Intersections of several streets may be lit by large diffusing lanterns each with three or four large discharge lamps (high-pressure mercury vapour fluorescent, high-pressure sodium or mercury iodide) mounted on columns higher than usual—12 to 15 m high.

Pedestrian areas are often lit by diffusing lanterns using high-pressure mercury vapour fluorescent lamps, or several tubular fluorescent lamps, on fairly low columns (4·5 to 6 m high) distributed throughout the area. Where there are balconies or side galleries with walkways below them, such lanterns can be set on parapets of the gallery which give good height for lighting areas below them[4]. Illumination below such galleries or similar canopies can also be by fluorescent lamps on soffits.
Pedestrian areas may be floodlit from adjacent buildings; but this should be done with caution as severe glare may result. See para 6.05 (high rise flats).

Car parks can be lit by floodlighting equipment mounted on columns located to light along principal tracks and to avoid dense shadows between cars. They must not be liable to be struck by cars. White light should always be used to enable car colours to be recognised; low pressure sodium should never be used.

Large areas can advantageously be lit by multiple units on high masts—25 to 30 m high. See para 8.03.

Gardens and parks
9.02 White light is best for illuminating gardens, as coloured light produces colour distortions.
Sodium lamps should be avoided for lighting adjacent gardens.
Lighting equipment in gardens must be proof against accidental disturbance and vandalism, and accessible to maintenance staff only. Accessible low-mounted equipment must be particularly well designed to avoid any possibility of shock even if damaged; sunk units must be thoroughly watertight and precautions taken to avoid overheating. Units at ground level should be sited so that people cannot walk over them, nor cast shadows on the lighted beds when walking past them.

Flower beds are often lighted by low 'mushroom' units set in the beds, screened so that they do not emit visible light directly. Floodlights can be directed across beds, and will also light taller shrubs than can be accommodated by

'mushroom' units. Small PAR reflector lamps (para 10) can be used bare in suitable holders.

Trees are best shown by light which reaches their foliage directly from concealed sources; either floodlights from a distance or by projectors placed below them, preferably well away from trunks and directed upwards through foliage, possibly placed in sunk waterproof glazed boxes.

Paths in gardens can be treated as footways.

Large grassed gardens may be lit by a high mast system.

Fountains and pools
9.03 Best lighting effects for fountains and cascades are produced by submerged equipment, though cascades may be effectively floodlit. Choice between elaborate changing water and light displays and very simple displays using white light only will depend on cost and occasion **4**. Colour changing and changing jets require a control room with programmers, electrically controlled valves etc. Colour changes are best effected by separate fittings with different colour screens; motor-driven colour wheels have been used, but they are elaborate and costly.

10 Floodlighting

IES Report
10.01 Techniques of floodlighting are discussed in IES technical report 6[6] which should be consulted.

Principles
10.02 Floodlighting is the technique of lighting exteriors of building **10** on monuments by projecting beams of light on them. To obtain satisfactory modelling with floodlighting, the principal direction of light should make an angle of approx 45° to 60° with the principal direction of view. This is to show changes in illumination of moulded surfaces and shadows cast by mouldings and projections, to enable the form of the building to be picked out. Views from the same direction as the projected light ('down light') look flat and featureless. It is preferable that light should reach the building coherently from one principal direction.

Location of floodlights
10.03 To produce coherent lighting source does not imply the use of only one projector or group of projectors; it is possible and usually convenient to use many, but the directions in which they project light should be co-ordinated. It is often desirable to provide some light in directions opposed to the principal modelling direction.
Best results are obtained by locating narrow beam projectors some distance from the building or monument. This is not always possible; in extreme cases equipment may be required on the façade—lighting from close offset. On such occasions lighting from underneath projections eg cornices, inverts natural daylight shadows, falsifies proportions and gives the façade a 'surprised look'.
Lighting must never be sited where it can cause glare to drivers of vehicles or to the public in important places, or throw shadows from moving objects.

Monuments
10.04 Floodlighting monuments and statuary from close off-set is usually disastrous especially with faces lit from below. Light should fall appropriately, eg it is ridiculous if figures marching forward with high purpose have light on the backs of their heads and their faces in darkness.

Colour
10.05 A single colour can be used (or two or more colours

10

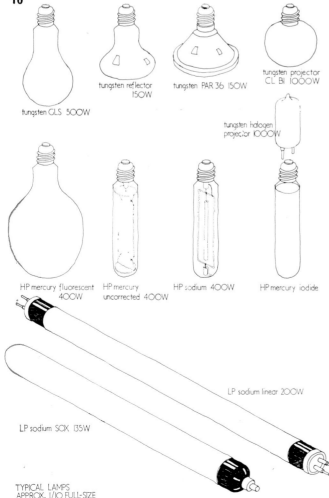

tungsten GLS 500W

tungsten reflector 150W

tungsten PAR 36 150W

tungsten projector CL BI 1000W

tungsten halogen projector 1000W

HP mercury fluorescent 400W

HP mercury uncorrected 400W

HP sodium 400W

HP mercury iodide

LP sodium linear 200W

LP sodium SOX 135W

TYPICAL LAMPS
APPROX. 1/10 FULL-SIZE

11

10 *Floodlit building: Direction of incidence is from directly in front; viewed from side. Better results would have been obtained by lighting from 45° to side, since principal viewpoint is from directly in front; with present lighting the effect is too flat*

11 *Comparison of lamps typical in urban lighting; approximately $\frac{1}{10}$ full size*

provided they are from different directions), but with great discretion if a building is not to appear tawdry: multi-colour effects are best suited to temporary displays. Single-colour floodlighting can be used to contrast with the colour of light used, say, for adjacent street lighting. It is pointless to floodlight coloured surfaces with light of a colour which they do not reflect well, eg to use light from mercury lamps (which is greenish) on red brick.

Amount of light

10.06 The amount of light needed for floodlighting a building depends upon:
1 Brightness of its surrounds.
2 Its surface finish.
3 Cleanness of surface.

IES technical report[6] tabulates recommended values for various surfaces. For fairly dirty surfaces the values should be multiplied by 3; however, the usual result of flood-lighting dirt is to reveal it, and it is better to have the surface cleaned.

Floodlighting equipment

10.07 Details of floodlight equipment and performance are given in manufacturers' catalogues. Floods are available giving symmetrical and asymmetrical beams of differing widths and intensities. Floodlights with stray light shields which project a beam with no spill light avoid lighting irrelevant nearer objects and disclosing positions of floodlights. One type projects an adjustable rectangular beam to fit the building.

Floodlights using linear tungsten halogen lamps and giving fan beams with different widths in perpendicular directions are specially useful for medium and close effects, and are, moreover, very small and easily concealed, though they run very hot. For short throws, sealed beam lamps of the PAR type are very useful. See para 11.

Installation and maintenance

10.08 Floodlights, though concealed from principal viewpoints and inaccessible to the public, must be accessible for maintenance. Back opening fittings often aids access. Some fittings have aiming stops that allow them to return accurately to the correct position following maintenance. Where there is no convenient fixing for floodlighting it is often legitimate to provide one on a column or pole.

11 Lamps

Principal types

11.01 The principal types of lamps used for outdoor lighting 11 are:

Tungsten filament lamps
There are four types:
1 General lighting service (as used for domestic lighting).
2 Reflector (blown and PAR sealed beam types); these have a bulb formed as a reflector and project a beam of light.
3 Projector with small filaments for use in projectors.

4 Tungsten halogen (projector and linear); linear type lamps are used in floodlights to give a fan-like beam. Tungsten halogen lamps are brighter than conventional tungsten filament lamps, and have longer life.

Low pressure fluorescent tubes
1 Standard type (as used in domestic fluorescent fittings).
2 Window type; lamp incorporates white reflector which leaves a window; has greater brightness than usual.

Low pressure sodium lamps
These lamps provide a yellow monochromatic light devoid of colour rendering:
1 SOX type; the most efficient of all lamp types, with U-tube.
2 Linear type; somewhat less efficient, but suits certain fittings.

High pressure lamps
1 High-pressure mercury (uncorrected type); has a short line source and gives a greenish light of poor colour rendering.
2 High-pressure mercury fluorescent, has a large bulb and provides a white light of good colour rendering.
3 High-pressure sodium; has a short line source, very efficient with a warm yellow light of good colour rendering.
4 Mercury iodide; a similar lamp but with a purplish-white light of good colour rendering.
All lamps except tungsten filament lamps require auxiliary apparatus to enable them to start and run. For details the manufacturers' catalogues should be consulted.

Lamp characteristics

11.02 Characteristics of lamps vary over a great range and the choice of the most appropriate for a given purpose often

Table 1 Comparison of lamp characteristics

Lamp type	Size and shape	Source luminance	Light package	Colour appearance	Colour rendering	Luminous efficiency	Life	Lamp price	Operating cost	Main uses outdoors
Tungsten general lighting service	Small	Very high	Long range	Good	Good	Low	Short	Low	High	Floods; signs
Tungsten reflector			Small	Good	Good	Low	Short	Low	High	Small floods
Tungsten halogen linear	Very thin and long	Very high	Long range	Good	Good	Low	Short	Medium	High	Floods
Low-pressure fluorescent tubes	Very long	Very low	Low	Very good	Very good	High	Short	Low	Low	Signs; some floods; tunnels
Low-pressure sodium	Very long	Low	Long range	Yellow	None	Very high	Long	Medium	Very low	Streets; tunnels; floods
High-pressure mercury uncorrected	Thin, long	High	Long range	Blue	Poor	High	Long	Medium	Fairly low	Floods
High-pressure mercury fluorescent	Large	Medium	Long range	Good	Good	High	Long	Medium	Low	Streets; floods
High-pressure sodium	Thin, long	High	Large	Yellow	Good	High	Fairly long	High	High	Streets; floods
Mercury-iodide	Thin, long	High	Large	Good	Good	High	Fairly long	High	High	Streets. floods
High-tension cold cathode	Very long	Low	Varies	Many	—	Fairly low	Very long	High	Medium	Signs

Information sheet Landscape 42

Section 10: **Elements of landscape construction**

Roof gardens

TONY SOUTHARD *discusses not only gardens on roofs but all gardens on artificial structures. He deals with all aspects of such gardens from design and environmental conditions to planting and costs*

1 Why roof gardens?

1.01 Roof gardens dealt with in this information sheet may be located at any level from a few feet below ground to several hundred feet above, but they are all separated from natural ground by a man-made structure.

1.02 Roof gardens are becoming more important for several reasons: full use of roofs in crowded city centres can create extra space for recreation and this is increasingly becoming commercially viable; increasing segregation of pedestrians and traffic in town planning schemes often results in pedestrian levels above ground which can be improved by gardens; roof gardens can enhance the appearance of the seas of flat roofs seen from high buildings, elevated transport systems and so on; they can also reduce isolation feelings of people in high buildings.

2 Contribution of roof gardens

Appearance
Shape
2.01 Roofs can be given interesting form by exploiting structural shapes: eg the many types of pitched roof.

Colour and texture
2.02 Many types of finish can be used singly or in patterned combinations to improve appearance **1, 2** (see para 7).

1 *Use of bold and varied textures and patterns to provide interest from high level*
2 *Willows, mounds of grass and paving to provide varied textures*

2

1

2.03 Living material can provide colour and texture. Initial cost is not high if soil depths are kept to a minimum but maintenance costs are increased. Grass is the obvious material but other low ground cover plants are suitable (see para 10.04).

Uses
Private
2.04 Private roof areas range from tiny paved balconies to extensive roof gardens attached to penthouse flats complete with paving, water, grass, low planting and trees. First requirements are adequate privacy and wind screening; the higher the situation, the more shelter becomes necessary to protect plants and people. If their orientation is correct, screened spaces can become quite hot in summer. They are used mostly for sitting, growing plants, eating outdoors and toddlers play. Lighting can extend the period of use.

Group
2.05 Group private spaces are those reserved for members of a company, school or other organisation. They are often on roofs of low blocks possibly with higher blocks adjoining. Insufficient privacy may result in spaces not being used, so screening is desirable. Plenty of sitting space is required on benches (preferably with backs and arms for comfort) and on the grass. People do not usually sit on stone, concrete or brick except on the hottest days of the year and then only when such materials have been warmed by the sun for an hour or so.

2.06 If outdoor eating is proposed it is wise to cover at least 50 per cent of tables with a roof of translucent sheeting against rain and glare. Occasionally ball or tennis courts are provided.

Public
2.07 Active uses of public roof spaces include circulation and recreation. Any form of recreation is possible that normally takes place on the ground provided it does not involve excessive loading. Roof areas are most logically used for organised games that require hard surfaces: tennis, roller skating and children's play. Fencing for ball games should be 1 to 3 m higher than at ground level. A netted 'roof' may be worth considering. Lighting will extend the period of use.

2.08 Passive spaces for people to sit, read, munch sandwiches and chat are needed. Grass is satisfactory for summer use, but seats considerably extend the season and are preferred by many even in summer sunshine. These spaces should be sheltered, open to the sun and free of downdrafts caused by taller buildings. They may be screened and tucked away or just slightly withdrawn from main pedestrian routes. Good views are appreciated. On one roof terrace, seats have been dragged out from specially constructed shelters to the exposed edge of the roof because users' prime motivation was the view **3 a, b**.

3 User requirements

3.01 User requirements are complex and often similar to requirements for the same activities at ground level. Outlined below are some special requirements.

Shelter
3.02 Wind protection makes physical conditions more pleasant for those using roof spaces and prevents tall or slender plants from being loosened or uprooted. Only the

3a

3b

3a *Seating designed under shelters*
3b *Seating dragged to edge of roof by users so that they can look at view*

toughest species will resist scorching from too much transpiration unless screening is provided. Some species are very wind resistant but even they grow faster and healthier if sheltered.

3.03 Shelter is best provided by perforated or slatted fencing which should be as high as possible. Perforations prevent eddying and work best with two-thirds solid and one-third void. Some sheltering effect is felt on the windward side and useful shelter on the leeward side will be felt for approximately 10 times the height of the screen **4**. Effectiveness falls off towards the end of a screen and when wind is not at right angles to it.

3.04 It may be worth considering similar screening in a horizontal position against the face of tall buildings to prevent downdrafts and beneath buildings on stilts to nullify the Venturi effect **5**.

3.05 Privacy from horizontal and vertical view is a similar problem as in open space at ground level, but often acute.

Safety
3.06 Normally by-law balustrade regulations apply but where active games are played or if children are encouraged to congregate without supervision, a higher enclosure is necessary.

Watering

9.03 Watering is best applied by pop-up sprinklers which may water circles or segments. Fixed free standing sprinklers are more trouble-free but unsightly unless situated within a carefully designed planted area. Care must be exercised when siting sprinklers that water does not spray passers by, or end up on neighbours' property.

9.04 Where low planting is envisaged it is best to sight sprinklers in adjacent grass or the sprinkled area may be reduced **14**. Where buildings overhang, soffit sprinklers may be used.

9.05 Rainwater may be piped from roofs to planted areas at lower levels and distributed through perforated underground pipes as in the Lillington Street balconies.

9.06 One system, which is now widespread in Israel but not yet used in this country, gives underground supply based on subterranean droppers (see AJ 18.9.68 p758). George Patton in the US has used perforated pipes below ground in gravel trenches **15**.

9.07 All irrigation systems should be operated by skilled men. Sprinklers are often turned on and forgotten; this can be overcome by supplying them from their own header tank, the capacity of which is just below the water required for a single watering session. The supply pipe to the header tank is restricted so that the tank fills very slowly. Sprinkler spray slowly sinks when the tank empties and enough water has been applied.

9.08 Sprinklers can be automatically controlled by a programme switch. Controls for time of day and period of watering can be built in or sensing devices are available which switch on the system when humidity at ground level drops too low.

9.09 The better the drainage and the shallower the soil, the more watering will be required. Very shallow soils may need watering twice a day in hot, dry situations.

9.10 The more water that passes through the soil profile, the more nutrients are leached out and the greater the need for replacement. Chemical fertilisers can be used but regular application of organic manures as a mulch is desirable to maintain soil fertility, especially when plants are fairly mature. Liquid fertilisers can be applied through the irrigation system by dosing a tank in the supply line.

9.11 Roots of plant material over underground garages in very cold climates tend to become frozen; in the case of evergreens this may prove disastrous. The phenomenon has been successfully overcome on some roofs in Cincinnati, US, by using electric heating cables in the plant beds.

10 Suitable species

10.01 When choosing grasses, plants and trees for roofs the following special considerations must be kept in mind:
1 Maintenance standard to be expected (determine possibility of regular watering in summer)
2 Depth of soil
3 Exposure to wind and draughts (this can be very severe on roofs)
4 Overshadowing or sheltering from rain by buildings
If in doubt, keep to dry soil species. Information sheets LANDSCAPE 6, 7 gives plant characteristics but some particularly suitable species are listed below. The same considerations apply to choosing grass mixtures as at ground level (see information sheet LANDSCAPE 7), except where watering cannot be relied upon. In the latter case dry soil types should be represented in the mixture.

10.02 Some suitable trees are:
Betula vars
Crataegus vars
Platanus acerifolia (needs large soil volume)
Robinia pseudacacia
Sorbus aria
Sorbus aucuparia
Tilia vars
Willows and Poplars might be good where water supply can be guaranteed ie water table system para 8.18.

10.03 Some shrubs which have proved to be specially suitable are:
Galluna vulgaris
Cotoneaster vars
Cytissus vars (short lived)
Erica vars
Euonymus vars
Medera vars
Juniperus vars
Rhus typhina
Sambucus nigra
Ulex vars (fire risk)

10.04 Suitable ground cover plants include:
Cotula squalida
Cotoneaster (low growing vars)
Hypenicum calycinum
Mentha rotundifolia
Thymus serphyllum (on poor shallow soil)
Vinca minor.

11 Costs

11.01 Intuitive estimates of costs of the roof gardens vary from 'practically nothing' to 'prohibitively expensive'. Most architects seem to be frightened of the financial implications, but comparisons are almost impossible to find. Clearly costs vary from one type of structure to another and depend to a large extent on the type of finish or planting on the roof.

11.02 Trying to clear away a little of the mist surrounding this subject the author briefed a structural engineer, Allan Hodgkinson of J. C. Bianco & Associates and a qs Peter Gray of James Nisbet & Partners to prepare comparative costs for various types of 'finish' placed upon two building types (table I).

11.03 For estimating, it was assumed that the whole of a roof would be covered in the same type of 'finish'. If an estimate is required for a combination of finishes, the figure for the highest additional structural costs should normally be used throughout unless the design relates so closely to the structural grid that special structural measures can be taken in selected places only to deal with heavier loads.

11.04 Allowance has been made for additional costs from increased loading imposed by finishes on the foundation, frame, cross-walls, roof slab and associated internal finishes, with balustrades and additional heights to edge kerbs.

11.05 Roof loadings which are reasonable under normal conditions have been assumed. Loadings must normally be agreed with the district surveyor or other authority responsible for applying building by-laws.

11.06 Even if a roof is likely to be used for viewing a procession in a street below, it is likely to be subject to crowd loading of only 10 700 kN/m² with about five persons deep at its edges and a 5350 kN/m² overall loading should easily cope with this. However, if a roof is to be used for public meetings and so on and not just casual public use, 10 700 kN/m² loading might have to be assumed overall.

11.07 To simplify calculations it has been assumed that letable floor space would not be lost by increasing column size but that increased loads would be dealt with by increased reinforcement.

11.08 Costs of retaining walls between the various thicknesses of finish have not been allowed for as the complexity of the design drastically affects the quantities and ground modelling might well take up the difference between the constructional thicknesses for trees, shrubs and grass **11** to **13**.

Notes on table 1

1 PRICE LEVEL is at early 1971.
2 NO ALLOWANCE has been made for preliminaries and contingencies.
3 BASIS OF CALCULATIONS.
Four-storey maisonettes Estimates based on one bay 9m wide × 5m span between loadbearing cross-walls.
Ten-storey offices Estimates based on one bay 12·5m wide × 5m span between cross-beams of a reinforced concrete framed structure.
Single-storey basement car parks Estimates based on one bay 7·6m × 7·6m between cross-beams of a reinforced concrete framed structure.
4 FINISHES.
Paving Costs allow for pc slab paving at £2·175 laid ie not the cheapest. Alternative finishes can be calculated on a pro rata basis. If paving is used in conjunction with thicker finishes allowance must be made for making up levels or retaining the soil adjacent to paving.
Water Costs allow for enclosing walls to pools average 40 m² in area. No allowance has been made for pumping or filtering plant, fish or plants.
Grass Costs allow for 300 mm topsoil, 75 mm peat, 25 mm glass fibre filter, and 100 mm graded aggregate and turf at £0·660 per m² laid. Cost of grass can vary between £0·150 per m² for seeding to £0·700 per m² for turf, depending on quality.
Shrubs Costs allow for 600 mm topsoil, 75 mm peat, 25 mm glass fibre and 100 mm graded aggregate, and shrubs at £4·720 per m². Costs of shrubs can vary between £1·500 per m² and £4·720 per m². The £4·720 figure should allow a wide choice of species and a proportion of larger plants grown in containers for quick effect.
Trees Costs allow for 1200 mm topsoil, 75 mm peat, 25 mm glass fibre and 100 mm graded aggregate and one tree at £32 per 14 m² but use of advanced nursery stock rather than semi-mature trees has been assumed (ie £32 rather than £70 to £80). With difficult access, these prices would be higher.
5 IRRIGATION.
Costs do not allow for provision of irrigation, which can vary from simple, manually operated systems (about £1 per m²) to sophisticated automatic humidity-detecting systems, or systems which inject fertilisers. Irrigation is normally by sprinklers, which works better on grass areas or narrow shrub areas than on more extensive shrub areas.

Table 1 *Additional costs of roof garden compared with normal asphalt covered concrete roof*

Finish		Paving	Water	Grass	Shrubs	Trees
		50 mm precast concrete paving £2·175 per m²	water 300 mm deep 50 mm gravel rejects enclosing walls	turf (£0·660 per m²) 300 mm top soil 75 mm peat 25 mm glass fibre 100 mm aggregate	shrubs (£4·720 per m²) 600 mm topsoil 75 mm peat 25 mm glass fibre 100 mm aggregate	trees (£2·360 per m²) one at £32 per 14 m² turf below trees (£0·660 per m²) 1200 mm topsoil 75 mm peat 25 mm glass fibre 100 mm aggregate
		Per m² roof area £	Per m² roof area £	Per m² roof area £	Per m² roof area £	Per m² roof area £
Four-storey maisonettes	additional structural costs	3·445	3·330	5·050	7·235	10·450
	finish	2·185	3·215	2·065	6·835	6·545
	total	5·630	6·545	7·115	14·070	16·995
Ten-storey offices	additional structural costs	3·960	3·905	7·405	11·885	17·165
	finish	2·185	3·215	2·065	6·835	6·545
	total	6·145	7·120	9·470	18·720	23·710
Ground level over single-storey basement car park	additional structural costs	—*	—*	3·445	5·510	11·425
	finish	2·185	3·215	2·065	6·835	6·545
	total	2·185	3·215	5·510	12·345	17·970

* It has been assumed for the purposes of this exercise that the design of the structure, which will already be designed to be accessible for fire appliances to adjacent tall buildings, will not attract additional costs to support 'Paving' or 'Water'.

Information sheet
Landscape 43

Section 10: **Elements of landscape construction**

Space requirements:
People and cars

This information sheet has been prepared by HAL MOGGRIDGE, *and is intended to be read in conjunction with information sheets* LANDSCAPE 26 *and* 38. *The table preceding the diagrams showing space requirements has been designed as a general checklist for most circulation conditions*

Table I Checklist of user requirements for external urban space

Use	Characteristics and/or factors	Specific provisions
General circulation on foot	Narrow spaces induce fast movement. (See information sheets LANDSCAPE 25 and 26)	Variety and interest. Safety. For surface treatments see information sheets LANDSCAPE 33, 34, 35
General circulation by invalids or prams	Slow but flexible	Flat ramps, absence of steps, low kerbs
General circulation by bicycle		Safety precautions for children
General circulation by vehicle	Space consuming see information sheets LANDSCAPE 26 and 28	Ample space required for turning and reversing
General circulation of maintenance equipment, barrows, cutters, etc	Needed everywhere out of doors. See information sheet LANDSCAPE 7	Modern mechanical road sweepers, gang mowers
Pedestrian access to entrances	See information sheet LANDSCAPE 26	
Access round buildings for fire equipment	Bearing capacity and distances from buildings (laid down by fire authorities) see LANDSCAPE 26	Ramped access from roadways for wide vehicles
Seating in selected positions		Shade, shelter from wind, view, intimacy, litter baskets
Leaning on railings	See information sheets LANDSCAPE 25 and 26	A view on the other side of the railing. Western aspect is particularly satisfying for evening use
Outdoor gatherings, debates, functions, in all weathers	Limited to centres of urban areas with easy public access; of little use in suburbs	Avoid narrow exits, which can cause crushing. Plenty of access points. Changes of level—platforms. Statutory very suitable
Outdoor gatherings, debates, functions in dry weather		Define space. Extensive open space all round for access
Collecting water against excessive run off	Low-lying areas into which hard paved areas drain. See information sheet LANDSCAPE 32	Avoid too heavy a soil
Improving temperature gradient of air	All vegetation tends to shade ground surface and produce cooler air at ground surface	
Car parking: occasional use	Suffices for weekend use. Rows may be indicated by trees, shrub belts on low parts. No marking of bays. See information sheet LANDSCAPE 38	
Car parking: continuous use	Space standards fully defined in AJ Metric Handbook section 10. See information sheet LANDSCAPE 26 and 28	
Play	Ball play, running, sandpits	Plenty of level space. Preferably walled. Minimum of special equipment
Open-air eating		Screening against wind, dust, insects. Alternative shelter under cover. Access to tables

1 *Pedestrian movement between walls or fences; all* **1b** *dimensions are sufficient for prams, wheelchairs and bicycles*

a *Requiring careful movement*
b *Allowing free movement*

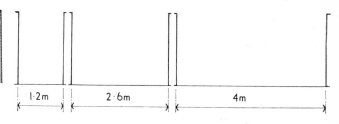

500	900	2·2m	3·2m		1·2m	2·6m	4m
twisting movement	single file	double file	three abreast				

1a   **1b**

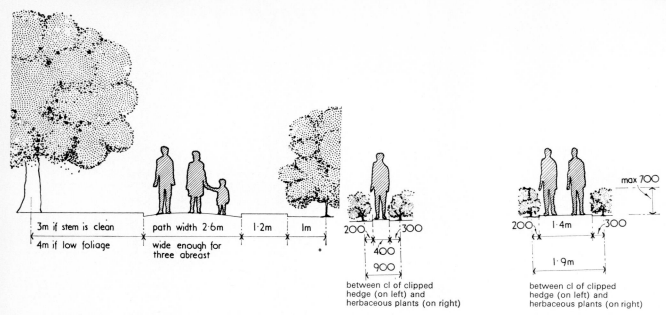

2 *Space requirements for narrow paths across open space*

3 *Minimum path widths between low planting (impassable by prams). Planting beds should be at least 400 mm and 600 mm wide for clipped hedges and herbaceous plants respectively*

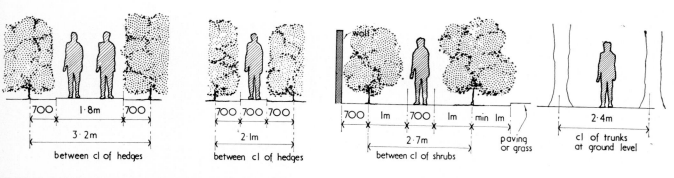

4 *Dimensions shown require careful movement when walking between clipped hedges. For free movement or for prams etc, path widths should be as for* **1b**

5 *For pedestrian access between free growing shrubs. Dimensions are minimum and where prams are to be used 3 m should be allowed between centre lines of planting*

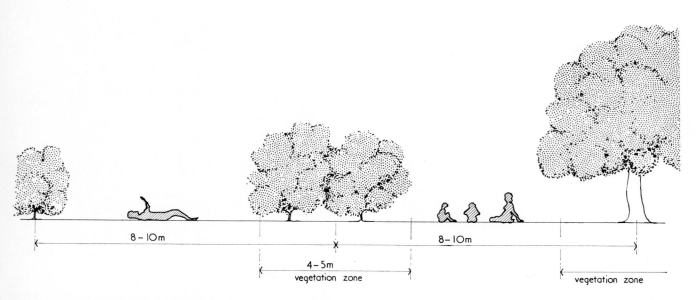

6 *Illustrates distance between individuals or groups in public spaces. Diagram applies to casual groupings in heavily used urban areas*

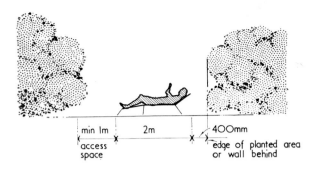

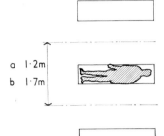

7 *Sets out minimum space requirements for couch type deckchairs. Dimension a is for an intimate relationship between chairs or for crowded areas, b for where more space is available*

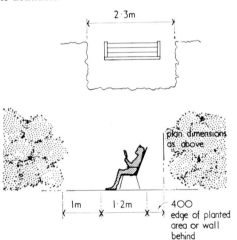

9 *Shows requirements for upright deckchairs and garden chairs; and for a recess for a bench to seat two or three people*

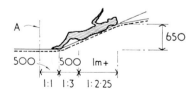

11 *Ground shape for reclining: level section at base is essential for comfort. Different angles must be finished in sweeping curve (shown in heavy broken line). Bottom may form a flat concave curve rising again for a similar bank opposite—in such case, lowest point should be beyond 'A'*

12 *Minimum widths for prams and wheelchairs*

a *Allows for a straight approach from both sides of an opening in wall. No manoeuvre can be attempted within 2·5 m of opening*

b *This is minimum opening width for any approach other than noted in **a**. Diagram also illustrates the greater width of paving required to allow for the manoeuvre*

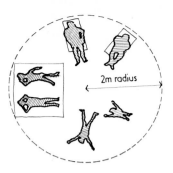

8 *Illustrates area required for family group of six on a lawn or terrace. This dimension excludes access and is also the minimum useful hard paved area for domestic use. For 10 people (the largest convenient single group), dimension should be increased to radius of 3 m; which is minimum useful lawn size for domestic use. Both these dimensions apply equally well to groups sitting in deck chairs on hard-paved surfaces, though if spaces are to allow people to lie out, the radius in both cases should be increased by 500 mm. Ground should be nearly level as slopes as low as 1:20 will cause rolling*

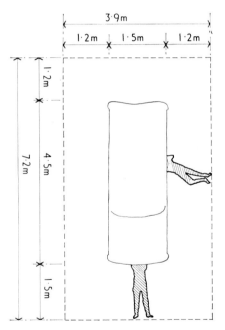

10 *Washing and maintaining cars: dimensions 4·5 m × 1·5 m are for normal family saloons; other cars may need a larger size, but there is no need to increase the space around*

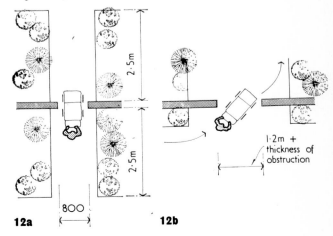

12a   **12b**

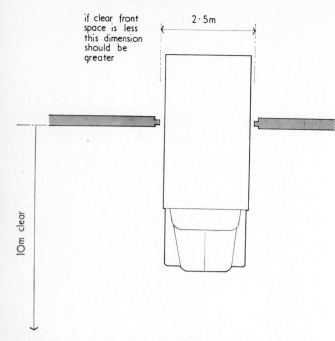

13 *Shows opening width required for lorries manoeuvring backwards. Openings of 2·3 m will allow for free passage of most cars*

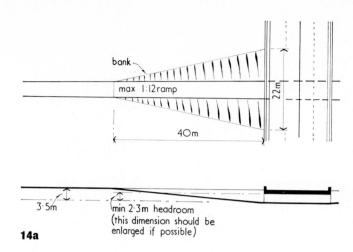

14a

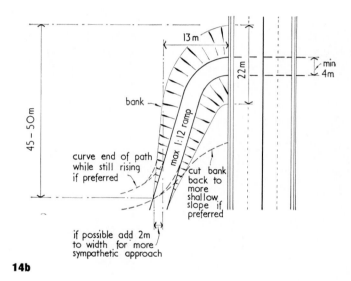

14b

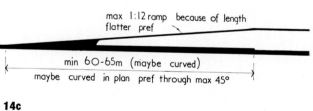

14c

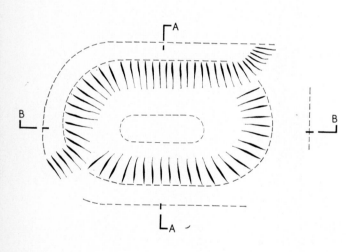

section A–A

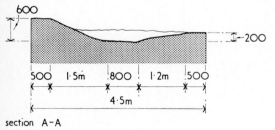

14 *Paths crossing roads: these are recommended minimums where ground is level. Tunnels should never be less than 4 m wide*
a *straight ramp under road*
b *bent ramp under road*
c *bridge and ramp over road*
15 *Play dell for up to four children; an incidental play area suited to any urban location. This diagram is capable of extensive variations. The following are limitations: section* BB *shows maximum length for gradient at 1:2·5, greater lengths should not exceed 1:4 for safety without supervision. Ground finish may be grass or hard. Bottom of dells should be drained and access should be from lower side*

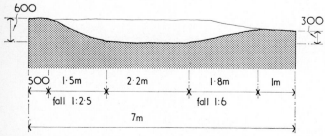

section B–B

15

Information sheet
Landscape 44

Maintenance

This information sheet outlines aspects of maintenance which should be considered at design stage, and lists principles of care of plant growth. Comprehensive recommendations for grounds maintenance are being prepared by BSI technical committees, and will be published in due course as a British Standard

1 General principles

1.01 The natural pattern of renewal and growth of plant life must be controlled by sympathetic maintenance. Landscape design will rarely reach maturity until several years after contract completion, and its realisation depends on correct maintenance.

1.02 Maintenance is usually required to be as low as possible. (An exception might be a keen gardener with plenty of time, who enjoys caring for plants.)

Ecology
1.03 Maintenance is minimal if the natural balance of plants and soils is maintained. Poor soil, such as heath, will readily support rhododendrons, azaleas and heathers, but *not* rosebeds or lawns; conversely chalk soils will produce good lawns if clover is accepted, but will *not* support rhododendrons or heather.

1.04 The water table is a significant factor in deciding choice of plants.

Balance and use
1.05 A wild or natural landscape would seem to be the answer to maintenance costs, but if the area is too small, use by people will upset natural balancing factors. Natural landscape is suitable only for large parkland areas **1**.

Cost
1.06 Areas of high use are usually associated with high initial cost and low maintenance—cost of hard paving for pedestrian ways is several times that of a simple grass landscape. But hard areas must be balanced with soft areas from design point of view (see information sheet LANDSCAPE 29).

2 Layout and maintenance

2.01 Maintenance will be reduced if layout design considers the following points.

Grassed areas
2.02 For more detailed information see information sheet LANDSCAPE 7 para 8.
1 Grass areas should be simple in shape and not broken up by plant beds or obstructions **2**.
2 Trees planted in grass areas should be wide enough apart to allow grass cutting machinery to pass through.
3 Allow for mowing margins against walls and beds **3**.
4 Manhole covers should be aligned with grass slope.
5 Consider pop-up sprinklers where expense is justified.

1 *In some cases natural landscape can be retained without maintenance, as in this rocky pine-covered landscape in Finland*

Planted areas
2.03 For more detailed information on maintenance of gardens, see information sheet LANDSCAPE 24 para 2.
1 Choose plants that do not need staking or pruning.
2 Suppress weeds by reducing the area of bare soil.
3 Plant beds should be simple in shape.
4 Allow space for trimming on both sides of hedges.
5 Where project allows initial heavy maintenance, followed by no maintenance, use ground cover.

Hard areas
2.04 For more detailed information, see information sheet LANDSCAPE 24 para 2 for hard areas in gardens, and infor-

2

3

2 *Paving between grassed areas and plant beds allows easy mowing. In comparison knee rails on grass edges* 3 *make mowing difficult and lead to neglect*

mation sheet LANDSCAPE 17 for hard sports areas.
1 In public areas allow for maintenance by mechanical sweepers (eg ramps).
2 Consider subsurface heating to melt snow and ice.

Water
2.05 For more detailed information on water see information sheet LANDSCAPE 9.
1 Ponds should be shallow for easy maintenance, or designed for proper biological balance.
2 Avoid overhanging trees as falling leaves must be cleared from the surface.
3 Circulate water wherever possible.

Edges
2.06 For more detailed information on materials see information sheet LANDSCAPE 35.
1 Edging materials include turf, timber, stone, brick, tiles, metal or plastic trim.
2 Should be clean cut line in vertical and horizontal plane.

3 Plant growth and maintenance

3.01 Detailed maintenance of plant types has been considered in the following information sheets:
Grass—information sheet LANDSCAPE 7 para 9 deals with mowing, aeration and rolling.
Ground cover and shrubs—information sheet LANDSCAPE 7 para 3 deals with pruning and maintenance programme.
Screens and hedges—information sheet LANDSCAPE 8 para 3 deals with fertilising and pruning.
Water plants and ponds—information sheet LANDSCAPE 9 para 3 deals with discoloured water and weed control.
Trees—information sheet LANDSCAPE 6 para 3 deals with annual inspection, pruning, tree surgery and vandalism.

3.02 Proper maintenance is essential to plant life, and should be considered under the following headings.

Watering and inspection
3.03 Ensure water supply is adequate for plants in containers.

Weed control
3.04 Weed control includes:
Hoeing—most traditional method.
Mechanical means—ie scything.
Chemical means—weed killers.
Mulching—ie laying on compost to suppress weeds.

Mulching and feeding
3.05 Soil round shrubs should be fed annually with a general fertiliser at the rate of 120 g/m.

Pruning
3.06 See para 307 for relative information sheets on pruning of shrubs, trees and hedges.

Protection
3.07 Lower branches of trees may be destroyed by cattle. Protect by stakes and ties.

4 Maintenance of hard areas

4.01 Though hard surfaces are usually chosen because they will require less maintenance, they should still be swept, cleaned and sealed periodically. They should also be inspected regularly for repairs. Cracks in paving slabs should be treated regularly with weed killer.

4.02 For maintenance of hard sports areas see information sheet LANDSCAPE 17.

References

1 MINISTRY OF HOUSING AND LOCAL GOVERNMENT. Design bulletin 5 Landscaping for flats. 1963, HMSO [(A3f)]
2 INSTITUTE OF LANDSCAPE ARCHITECTS Landscape maintenance, report of symposium held at the RIBA. 1963, The Institute [087 (W1)]
3 CONOVER, H. S. Grounds maintenance handbook. New York, 1958, F. W. Dodge Corporation, second edition [087 (W1)] £4·17
4 ANDREW, S. Grass. *Architectural Review*, 1967, March, p234 [Yx5]
5 MCMILLAN, R. C. Problems of maintenance. *ILA Journal*, 1962, April [087 (W1)]
6 HACKETT, B. Maintenance costs and landscape design. *Municipal Journal*, 1953 March 6 [087 (W1)]

Index to handbook

References show the type of section followed by its number.
For example, TS 4 *refers to technical study 4: Urban*
landscape review: Housing; INF 38 *to information*
sheet 38: Car parking
See also contents list on page 5